MILITANT
ANTI-FASCISM

MILITANT
ANTI-FASCISM

BY M. TESTA

AK PRESS
EDINBURGH · OAKLAND · BALTIMORE

Militant Anti-Fascism: A Hundred Years of Resistance
© 2015 M. Testa

This edition © 2015 AK Press (Oakland, Edinburgh, Baltimore).
ISBN: 978-1-84935-203-1 | eBook ISBN: 978-1-84935-204-8
Library of Congress Control Number: 2014940777

AK Press   AK Press
674-A 23rd Street   PO Box 12766
Oakland, CA 94612   Edinburgh EH8 9YE
USA   Scotland
www.akpress.org   www.akuk.com
akpress@akpress.org   ak@akedin.demon.co.uk

Visit our websites for the latest news as well as the complete catalogue of several thousand books, pamphlets, zines, audio and video products, and stylish apparel published and/or distributed by AK Press.

Cover design by Kate Khatib | manifestor.org/design
Printed in the USA on acid-free paper.

Dedication

This book is dedicated to the unknown Russian POW who was caught 'urging the women workers to work more slowly' and, when challenged by a fascist lackey, became 'abusive and threatened him with his fists'.

He was charged with sabotage, threatening behaviour and assault.

His fate is unknown but is not hard to guess.

And to Militant Anti-Fascists

Around the World.

CONTENTS

Acknowledgements

Anti-fascists from all over the UK and beyond helped us out with information and personal accounts, all inspiring, some hilarious, and others unprintable. Our thanks go out to: AFA Ireland, the 'Archivist' at AFA Archive online, Bish, 'Brenda', Callum, Matt Collins, Simon Davies, EDL News, Sonia Gable (62 Group), Tony Greenstein, Larry O'Hara, Rachael Horwitz, Steve L., Matt, LiamO, Louise P., the Red Action archive online, 'Rosa', *TAL Fanzine*, Top Cat, Steve Tilzey, Liam Turbett, and especially John Penney for his time, input, and contributions. Thanks to the hundreds of people who supported the blog. And many apologies if we forgot anyone.

Preface

The aim of this book is to give an overview of anti-fascist activity in mainland Europe from the late-nineteenth century to 1945, and in the UK from the 1920s to 2014. The book is for contemporary anti-fascists who want to increase their knowledge of the subject, those who may not be aware of the long history of resistance that they are part of, and especially the new generation of anti-fascists who have mobilised against the English Defence League and their splinter groupuscules. It is also for those studying the subject in an academic context as well as those who have been active against fascism for some time. We hope that the victories and struggles of anti-fascists past and present can inspire and energise militants.

The book aims to show the how the racism, misogyny, anti-Semitism, gangsterism, homophobia, militarism and essentially anti-working-class nature of fascist and ultra-nationalist organizations, are adapted by different organizations, as well as their opportunist collaborations with bourgeois democrats.

Unlike some of the (all too few) books on militant anti-fascism in the UK, such as *Beating The Fascists* (both versions), *No Retreat*, *Physical Resistance*, and *Anti-Fascist*, this book offers a broader historical context for militant anti-fascists by initially looking to other countries outside the UK and over a longer period of time.

We have admittedly given a 'subjective overview' of militant working-class opposition to fascism. Martha Gellhorn, an anti-fascist who wrote about her experiences during the Spanish Civil War as well as the Second World War, once stated that she had no time for 'all that objectivity shit'. There is no point in denying our bias here: how can we be objective about fascism and what it ultimately leads to?

Militants are often criticised by liberal anti-fascists for 'being as bad as the fascists', and we do not deny our support for the use of violence, but only when necessary and as a tactic along with the dissemination of information, organization inside the workplace and outside, and the defence of our communities from the divisive actions of the far right.

Militant anti-fascism is often a defensive strategy, although it can quickly mobilise numbers to take the initiative, denying political space for fascists. In the times when fascism is in temporary abeyance, as Red Action once said, 'instead of being wound up, it was more pragmatic to wind [militant anti-fascism] down to a level appropriate to the nature of the challenge now being offered by the far right'.[1] Something that the sudden emergence of the English Defence League and the relatively slow organization of militant anti-fascists demonstrated all too well. We learn from our histories.

Finally, we are hoping that this book will be augmented by a second volume on anti-fascism post-1945 in the USA and Canada, as well as on mainland Europe, especially in Greece, Hungary and Russia where militant opposition to fascism can become a matter of life and death.

M. Testa, 2014.

1   Sean Birchall, *Beating the Fascists: The Untold Story of Anti-Fascist Action* (London: Freedom Press, 2010), 88.

Introduction

This history of militant anti-fascism has, in part, been excavated from the orthodox histories of fascism in order to produce a coherent anti-fascist narrative. We celebrate the activities and achievements of militants in Europe from the late-nineteenth century to the present day, and we make no apologies for advocating the use of physical force as part of a political strategy. Anti-fascism can be proactive as well as defensive, and we have, with considerable help from militants past and present, identified three of the successful elements in the century of struggle against fascism: physical resistance, political organization and propaganda. The use of physical activity to confront or pre-empt fascist activity, along with organization within the workplace, local communities, and links with other working-class organizations, can present a successful opposition. The maintenance of an anti-fascist media presence, particularly in the digital realm, to put forward the arguments for militancy, to publicise activities and successes, to expose fascists, and to encourage others to join the struggle, be it in print media, music, or social networking sites on the net, all are important. We do not advocate one form of action above another; people must use whatever tactics they see as appropriate. Militant anti-fascism also argues for a non-partisan approach wherever possible whilst recognising that popular fronts have met with mixed success and that liberal anti-fascists cannot be relied on most of the time. Neither can the law.

Anti-fascism

There are several identifiable kinds of 'anti-fascism': militant, state legislative, and liberal. Militants cannot rely on state legislation against fascism, as it will inevitably be used against anti-fascists; urging the state to ban far-right groups and activities merely supplies a pretext for banning radical left ones. The state, in its bid for self-preservation, legislates against extremism of any kind. Anti-fascists need to organise themselves to defend against fascist incursions into their communities, not ring the cops.

Liberal anti-fascism is useful at times, for political connections, denigration of fascist activity in the mainstream press and mobilising numbers. Liberal anti-fascism is 'respectable' and has the backing of MPs, and political, religious, and community groups, as well as the ear of the mainstream media. The liberal hope of trying to 'understand fascists' or 'convince them that they are wrong' is appeasement that has had a less than successful history—as Neville Chamberlain found out. Fraser quotes the ironic slogan of German liberals before the Nazis took over: 'We are so liberal that we even grant the freedom to destroy liberty', and Goebbels made his intentions perfectly clear: 'We have come to the Reichstag in order to destroy it. If democracy is stupid enough to reward us for doing this, this is the problem of democracy.' [1] Unfortunately, many anti-fascists can testify to occasions when liberals have identified militants to the police, which have resulted in time-consuming court cases. In times of difficulty, liberal anti-fascists tend to gravitate towards police protection, which militants cannot do.

It is possible for different kinds of anti-fascists to work together successfully, be they community groups, liberals, or militants, and anyway, the far right views opposition as all the same and does not differentiate between the array of political opponents. The massed and mainly peaceful blocking of fascist march routes by anti-fascists proved to be a very successful tactic against the English Defence League in Brighton, Bristol, and Walthamstow in 2012. This frustrates the fascists, hinders the progress of their marches, and sends a clear signal that they are not welcome in our communities—which seriously demoralises them. Birchall writes, in *Beating The Fascists*, that 'I had no problem with the use of political violence, it was the fighting I didn't like'. [2]

---

1   Nicholas Fraser, *The Voice Of Modern Hatred: Encounters with Europe's New Right* (London: Picador, 2000), 75.

2   Birchall, *Beating the Fascists*, 314.

Fascism is imbued with violence and secures itself politically through the use or threat of it, so it is inevitable that anti-fascists have to countenance some involvement in violence themselves during the struggle. This is not to say that anti-fascists should like violence or seek it out in the manner of political hooligans. Far from it, but it is true to say that for many militant anti-fascists violence is an unpleasant method to achieve a greater political goal. It is not fetishized the way that fascism fetishizes violence, and it would be much more preferable to rely on passive resistance, but we cannot guarantee that what Trotsky referred to as 'flabby pacifism' will effectively inhibit fascist encroachment. Fascism views passivity as weakness, not as a political strategy; it will crush peaceful protests and the will to resist, and their violence must be met head on. In Italy, socialists, communists, and anarchists organized against the increasing violence of Mussolini's *squadristi* and met force with force in order to protect their institutions. In Germany, fascism was met with equal violence by communist militants who at first responded defensively to intimidation but eventually used violence as a preventative strategy in a bid for self-preservation. In Spain, the militias of anarchists and socialists who fought back against Franco's coup attempt would view non-violence with immense scepticism. What else could they do? Resort to sarcasm?

This is not to say that violence is the only option for anti-fascists. Physical resistance is not simply hitting someone with a plank. Physical resistance means blocking routes, picketing meetings, and turning up to oppose fascism on the streets. It means being there. This is only one element of anti-fascist strategy. Anti-fascists need to respond politically to the socio-economic conditions that birth fascism, and maintain a strong presence on the streets in demonstrations, in counter-demonstrations, and wherever else fascist groups attempt to organise.

The physical force tactics that Anti-Fascist Action used so well in the 1980s and '90s are difficult to employ against the Euro-fascist entryism of the BNP and other 'respectable' fascist outfits. However, with the recent rise and fall of the English Defence Leagues and their splinter groupuscules, a physical counter-presence has played an effective part in demoralising them. The large amount of police from many different forces, the CCTV, the DNA samples, the FIT squads, and the harsh legislation mean that violent opposition remains mostly opportunistic, but a mass physical presence preventing fascist marches can be just as effective.

Fascism[3]

This book is for and about militant anti-fascists, so we are not overtly concerned with an analysis of the various ideological and practical differences between the European fascist, national socialist, and ultra-nationalist organizations. There have been a wide variety of 'fascisms' over the years that have embraced all, or most of, the following ideas.

The Fuhrer Principle is an absolute subservience to, and belief in, a leader, like Hitler and Mussolini, whose mediocrity was shrouded in mystique as the figurehead of a nation. Fascism excludes minority groups, whether Jews, Muslims, or Roma, whilst claiming that these 'others' receive preferential treatment regarding access to money, housing, or work.

Members of political, ethnic, or religious groups are blamed for the greater problems of capitalism and are removed from positions of power or influence—for example, doctors or teachers. Other points of view apart from the leader's are excised.

This kind of exclusionism is used to further belief in the purity of race and genetic superiority whilst traditional gender roles are enforced: women are seen as mothers of workers rather than workers themselves (although this is not exclusive); non-reproductive sex is seen as decadent; and the family unit is sacred. Fear of the sexual prowess of the other is propagated along with unsubstantiated myths like 'they're taking our women' and the indigenous culture being 'outbred.' Heterosexuality is normalised and the preservation of the gene pool is a priority.

This kind of nationalism desires a new 'Golden Era' and the destruction of diversity, degeneracy, and decadence. Cultural work is

---

3   Many thanks to Rachael Horwitz who wrote most of the section on fascism.

state-sanctioned, and although there were often fascist intellectuals (Gentile, Marinetti, Speer), anti-intellectualism is stressed: the material over the abstract, action over ideas, and belief over knowledge. Mass media are controlled and the state determines cultural discourse: cabarets are closed, newspapers are silenced, music is state sanctioned, jokes and certain writers are banned. Fascism emphasizes the glorification of violence as a method of achievement and empowerment, and this idea is represented in both militarism and para-militarism. National security is prioritised with a build-up of armed forces to protect territories, take over new ones (the Nazi Lebensraum), or encroach on 'lost' ones (Mussolini's Abyssinia). The military is used to secure power whilst the paramilitaries maintain their threatening presence on the streets through 'extra-legal' endeavours, or gangsterism. A hard line on crime and punishment is pursued but only for select criminals. Industry is focussed on building military strength, the corporate state benefits big business, and the state adopts capitalism when it is suitable. Working-class organizations are suppressed, unions are banned or controlled by the state, and workers are forced to collaborate. Whether they call themselves fascists, national socialists, nationalists, or patriots, fascist organizations embrace some or all of these principles, and anti-fascists must recognise and respond to them.

This book is divided into two parts and examines how anti-fascists have organised against fascist aggression in the hope of drawing lessons for the future.

Pre-Fascist Parties and Fascism in Europe

The first section of this book looks at the growth of ultra-nationalism and fascism across Europe from the late-nineteenth century to the 1940s. Italy, Austria, Germany, and Spain became fascist states whilst Hungary, Romania, Poland and France experienced an upsurge of fascist violence, and militants were forced to organise and counter this, with varying success. In all these countries, anti-fascists fought and died to protect their communities and institutions. The situation for anti-fascists in 1930s England was less drastic, and certainly less murderous, but still saw anti-fascists meeting violence with violence. It is surprising how few fatalities there have been in the battles pre-1939 and post-1945 in the UK.

Post-War British Anti-Fascism

The second part of the book specifically looks at anti-fascism in Britain and Ireland following 1945 when, despite the defeat of the fascist bloc (excluding Spain, of course), fascists still maintained a presence on the streets. Several waves of post-war fascism in Britain have been successfully countered by one of the strongest and most successful anti-fascist movements in Europe. The confrontations with Mosley, the NF, the BNP's street campaign and the EDL are all testimony to a tradition of anti-fascism that is too little acknowledged, let alone documented, by political historians. But, as ever, even though the fascists may be defeated, they never really go away, and as we have seen so many times they merely reinvent themselves whilst their poisonous ideology remains relatively unchanged.

PART I

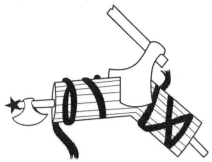

Italy: No Flowers For Mussolini

The concept of a united front of the more 'subversive' groups—socialists, communists, republicans and anarchists—[was] put forward by the anarchist Malatesta.[1]

On 11th September 1926, Gino Lucetti, an Italian anarchist, attempted to assassinate fascist dictator Benito Mussolini. As the dictator known as *Il Duce* drove past him, Lucetti threw a grenade, which bounced off the windscreen and exploded nearby, injuring several pedestrians. Lucetti, who was hiding in a doorway, was pounced upon by Il Duce's bodyguards and severely beaten. He was found to be in possession of another grenade, a revolver loaded with dum-dum bullets, and a knife. As he was arrested, Lucetti said defiantly, 'I did not come with a bouquet of flowers for Mussolini. I also meant to use my revolver if I failed to achieve my purpose with the bomb'.[2] With his usual self-aggrandisement, Mussolini later claimed that the grenade had landed in the car and he had scooped it up and thrown it back at Lucetti before it exploded, but witnesses in the car stated that the windows were closed and Il Duce was most shaken by the event.[3]

After strenuous interrogation, during which he confused the police with a false name, Lucetti was sentenced to thirty years. His accomplices, Leandro Sorio, a waiter, and Stefano Vatteroni, a tinsmith, were sentenced to nineteen and twenty years respectively. Vatteroni

---

1   David Forgas in *Rethinking Italian Fascism: Capitalism, Populism and Culture* (London: Lawrence and Wishart, 1986), 74.

2   Maura de Agostini, *Prisoners & Partisans: Italian Anarchists in the Struggle Against Fascism* (London: Kate Sharpley Library, 1999), 4.

3   Frances Stonor Saunders, *The Woman Who Shot Mussolini* (London: Faber and Faber, 2010), 218–219.

served his first three years in solitary confinement. Lucetti, a lifelong anarchist and anti-fascist activist had been shot in the neck by a fascist during an altercation in a bar, and Perfetti, the fascist, was shot in the ear. Lucetti was unable to find sympathetic medical treatment so was smuggled onto a ship heading for France, where he plotted with exiled anti-fascist comrades to kill Il Duce. The plot had been approved by the influential anarchist Errico Malatesta, and it was agreed that the assassin would allow himself to be arrested, presumably to avoid the fascists rounding up 'the usual suspects.' This was not to be: hundreds of anarchists were arrested in reprisals.

Italian anti-fascists have speculated on what would have happened if Lucetti had been successful, but it is clear that the attempt had significant symbolic value: one writer said, 'It is utterly pointless to debate what the assassination bids might have brought the country to...[but it] helped to keep public opinion alert and to give heart to anti-fascists and to the labour movement opposed to the regime'.[4] Lucetti was in prison until September 1943, when he was killed by a shell after escaping.

Lucetti was not the only one intent on killing Mussolini. Shortly after this first attempt on Il Duce, Anteo Zamboni, the fifteen-year-old son of Bolognese anarchists, was stabbed then shot to death by fascist bodyguards under dubious circumstances. He had been accused of shooting at Mussolini, although the shot may have been fired by one of the dictator's own entourage, extremist fascists who intended to force Mussolini's hand. As Mussolini was standing in the back of an open topped car the bullet hit him in the chest. In typical style, he later claimed that 'Nothing can hurt me!' adding the story to his personal mythology. He forgot to mention the small and not insignificant matter of the bullet proof vest he wore beneath his uniform.[5]

In 1931, Michele Schirru and Angelo Sbardelotto were arrested before they could even attempt their assassination plan on Il Duce. Schirru was tried and sentenced to be shot. Sbardelotto was caught later and faced the same death sentence. Even approving of an assassination attempt could have severe consequences: after Lucetti's

4   de Agostini, *Prisoners & Partisans*, 5.
5   Saunders, *The Woman Who Shot Mussolini*, 225.

attempt, two Roman workers were jailed for nine months for allegedly commenting that 'they still haven't managed to kill him'.[6]

Contemporary militant anti-fascists probably see the assassination of their foes as a tad extreme, but Italian fascism was founded in a climate of political violence, and anti-fascists had to resort to the most extreme measures as murders, beatings, arrests, and torturing escalated. Given such a situation, the assassination attempts by Lucetti and others become more understandable.

Italian Fascism

It is Mussolini himself who dates the beginning of fascism in 1914 after he had broken with the socialists and 'was caught surprisingly off-guard when, during "Red Week" in June 1914, Italy came close to a real revolution with a million people taking to the streets'.[7] Martin Pugh writes that 'the Italian fascisti first appeared during the autumn of 1914. They were largely recruited from patriotic former Socialists who were determined their country should enter the First World War'.[8]

Although the war caused a political hiatus, by 1919 Italy had become increasingly unstable with factory occupations, the rise of 'Bolshevism', and increased militant working-class activity. Opposed to this were the bourgeois and church-based parties, the industrial aristocracy, royalists, mainstream politicians and opportunists like Mussolini who moved from socialism to fascism. The Russian Revolution had frightened European capitalists, the bourgeoisie and the clergy, so raising the spectre of communism served as a useful tool for the right wing: Mussolini talked up the 'Red Peril' to justify strike-breaking and violence against workers. Following the syndicalist factory occupations of 1920, which some saw as a precursor to social revolution, fascism seemed to present a solution for the Italian mainstream against increased working-class militancy: in September, half a million workers had occupied the factories. Mussolini's skill as

---

6   Ibid., 242.
7   Denis Mack Smith, *Mussolini: A Biography* (London: Granada, 1983), 28.
8   Martin Pugh, *'Hurrah for the Blackshirts!' Fascists and Fascism in Britain Between the Wars* (London: Pimlico, 2006), 37.

an orator and propagandist (he was a journalist by trade), combined with his natural charisma, gave the impression of a strong man who could lead Italy into the future and away from the disruption.

Mussolini's fascism was essentially placatory, attempting to appease church, state and crown, as well as the bourgeoisie and working class. There was less a rigid ideology and more of a set of multilateral platitudes that Mussolini used with some dexterity to appeal to all those who felt strongly about unity and nation and feared the 'Red Terror'. He was not exempt from utilising socialist and anti-capitalist rhetoric to appeal to the sections of the working class who felt disenfranchised by the triumvirate of God, government and sovereign as and when appropriate. Early fascism attracted professional soldiers, students who had missed out on the fun of war and the Italian futurist art movement (whose Russian counterparts were, on the contrary, pro-Bolshevik), alongside shopkeepers, smaller business owners and some factory bosses. They were initially attracted to fascism's simple answers dressed up in fancy hats with the chance of a bit of argy-bargy. There was also a strong criminal element, not just the violent, that were attracted (then as now) to fascism, which was exemplified in the later gangsterism of local fascist leaders. Mussolini realised the youthful and adventurist appeal of fascism and began to organize the Squadristi, a fascist militia, into a national organization that eventually usurped local government, police and military control in certain towns and cities. Armed with their *manganello* clubs, the Squadristi were free to attack the members and organizations of the left.

The years 1919 and 1920 were the years of factory occupations and militant working-class opposition by anarchists, syndicalists, communists and socialists. These became known as the *Biennia Rosso*, the Red Years, and along with post-war scarcity and unrest, inflation, increased working-class agitation for better working conditions, and the fear of Red Revolution, enflamed the consternation of the bourgeois and capitalist classes. Fascism played on this and presented a strong-armed, patriotic response, an ideology of action not words. Many of the workers' concerns were economic, but given the strength of militant organizations they took on a revolutionary aspect, particularly 'by the Anarchist and Anarcho-syndicalists where they were influential in the labour movement in Liguria, Tuscany and the Marche'.[9] The factory council movements in militant cities like Milan and Turin also presented a threat to the ownership of the means of production. The most prominent working-class organizations were the Socialist Party of Italy (PSI), the council communists, and the anarchists and syndicalists, whose voices were heard in Antonio Gramsci's newspaper *L'Ordine Nuovo* (New Order) and Malatesta's *Umanita Nova*, and it was the latter who said prophetically, 'if we do not go on to the end we shall pay with bloody tears for the fears we are now causing the bourgeoisie'.[10] The industrial class and other concerned affected parties, such as farmers and landowners, helped finance the fascist organization who also had the tacit backing of the church, state and crown against the rise of 'Godless Bolshevism'.

Fascism benefits from either real or perceived crises and plays on the fears of the bourgeoisie and leaders of capital, and Mussolini played on these fears, presenting himself as an antidote to both social and industrial unrest. Political aggression was fetishized by Mussolini and was an inherent part of his fascist ideology of action, of taking control of the situation using might rather than 'right', and of attracting moderates and right wingers who were scared of the 'crisis in law and order and by the increase in violence. On the left, this took the traditional forms of intimidation, connected with strikes, riots and protests in the piazza.'[11] The factory occupations of 1920 had proved to be a pivotal moment for the working-class movement, which could not transform the situation into a full-blown revolution. Mussolini capitalised on this as proof of the Bolshevist threat, and the failure of the anarchists, syndicalists and socialists proved to be decisive (the communists were yet to split away from the PSI and were not yet influential in the syndicates).

---

9   Philip Morgan, *Italian Fascism 1919–1945* (London: Macmillan, 1995), 23.
10   Ibid., 34.
11   Adrian Lyttelton, *The Seizure of Power: Fascism in Italy, 1919–1929* (London: Weidenfeld, 1987), 35.

Although the squads were not overtly active as strike-breakers in this instance it was something they would later become professional at, thus emphasising the anti-working-class nature of fascism. The fascist squads involved themselves in labour disputes, protecting scabs and intimidating socialist councils and other organizations. The squads were active against syndicalists in Genoa in 1922 and broke the union hold over the docks in order to implement scab labour, something that the ship owners no doubt welcomed with relief. In 1922, the Socialists called a general strike, which again roused bourgeois fears of working-class revolt and saw Squadristi actions against militants.

The Squadristi

The whole espirit de corps of the blackshirts was concentrated in the squad.

—Adrian Lyttelton in *The Seizure of Power*

It is unlikely that Mussolini would have achieved his political success without the use of violent gangs to intimidate the opposition. He had always seen political violence as some sort of redemptive medicine, and this reached its apotheosis in the Squadristi who operated in a gangster, extra-legal manner and became answerable only to the local leaders.

After Mussolini took power in 1923, the squads operated as a paramilitary force to implement the fascist programme—a programme that seemed vague at best and opportunistic and contradictory at worst. Italian fascism, it would seem, was whatever Mussolini wanted it to be at any given point.

The squads were led by the *Ras* (after the Ethiopian term for boss) and grew in such strength that their local power eclipsed institutional power. Even sympathisers, including Mussolini, worried about their autonomy and had difficulty controlling their violent excesses. The squads organized 'punitive expeditions,' usually in trucks lent by military or police sympathisers, against political opposition, and eventually controlled their locality through intimidation and often murder. The squads also occupied socialist cooperatives and forced peasants out of their collectives and back into the hands of the landowners. Typical squad members were students, ex-soldiers and tradesmen, as well as professional criminals, and there was often 'a loose, informal relationship between a group of adolescents, somewhat resembling that of a youth gang'.[12] The squads represented the idealization of fascist action and the embodiment of the political violence that was so central to Mussolini's ideas—at meetings Mussolini would boast that he preferred weaponry and thuggishness to the more legitimate ballot. However, once the 'Red Threat' had been pacified, the Squadristi turned to more lucrative ventures such as extortion, blackmail and drugs.

AVANTI!

One of the Squadristi's first acts of outright political violence, led by Marinetti, the Futurist polemicist, was the burning of the socialist *Avanti* newspaper offices in Milan in 1919. The printing presses were destroyed and this arson attack operated as crude censorship as well as violent intimidation. *Avanti* was the newspaper at which Mussolini himself had worked between 1912 and 1914 before he donned the black shirt of fascism. A fascist group also attacked a socialist parade with bombs, and the police did very little to stop it: '[Mussolini] took good note that when the victims of street violence were on the extreme left the police would intervene very little if at all.'[13]

Many students were attracted to the excitement of fascism and Marimotti, the president of the student's union, was killed in the fascist attack on Turin in 1921. These student groups would smash up the lectures of those they disagreed with and they benefited from the nepotism of right-wing academics who sided with them. They were also involved in violence in Bologna, a socialist stronghold, whose bourgeoisie relied on the support of the student-dominated squads and their 'departure from legality and the repudiation of the liberal mentality'.[14] On May Day, 1920, fascist patrols took to the Bolognese

---

12 Lyttelton, *The Seizure of Power*, 244.
13 Smith, *Mussolini*, 42–45.
14 Lyttelton, *The Seizure of Power*, 59.

streets, facing no resistance, and later that year joined members of other 'patriotic' organizations to oppose 'the acts of violence which the extremists of the PSU [socialists] and the anarchists were committing in the city'.[15]

As 1921 progressed, Mussolini's squads became more openly violent, intimidating socialists, communists and anarchists and continuing to attack their institutions, burning buildings and destroying printing presses. This was seen as acceptable by the state and the bourgeois in order to keep the 'Reds' in hand; the industrial class saw fascism as effective against union militancy; and the landowners saw it as a way to suppress the peasants agitating for land reforms. The activities of the squads were very rarely punished by the police, military, government or courts. Sympathetic members of the military trained or armed them, and the police supplied vehicles for the roving squads to attack political opponents. As the Ras became increasingly powerful locally, the squads, which tended to include youthful students or the unemployed, soon became sanctuaries for misfits and criminals, as well as the fiefdoms of gangsters.

Gangsterism and Squadrismo

Moves by the fascist leadership to control the excesses of the squads were met with resistance. Once in control of a town, the fascists could attack with impunity anyone whom they saw as enemies, political or otherwise, and the Ras used the squads to consolidate their local power, so they were hardly likely to give it up. One notorious Ras was Ricci whose squad controlled Massa-Carrara. Ricci had his own private squad, 'an armed and organized unit of blackshirts, with a uniform elegantly edged in white thread, and supported by another unit of cavalry'.[16] This was used to intimidate the local prefect (the highest position of local authority) who turned 'a blind eye to what is happening in the province...he denies the existence of the disperta (Ricci's private squad)...he is unable to find those responsible for murders.'[17]

The Ras were often involved in feuds, and squad members were

---

15   Ibid., 60.
16   Ibid., 168.
17   Ibid., 163.

8

used to assassinating local rivals. The Ras also created a system of cronyism, and anyone who enjoyed their protection could almost guarantee their immunity from persecution. Local landowners and farmers were forced into protection rackets and, if they refused, they would be beaten up. The Ras also intimidated voters in order to deliver the results that Mussolini and the city fascists required from the regions. As Lyttelton succinctly notes, 'Patronage and intimidation were mutually reinforcing; the Ras could threaten their enemies because they could reward their friends.'[18] In certain areas both fascist and nationalist organizations sought 'an alliance between the politicians and the forces of organized crime'.[19] The centralization of violence and a flexible morality over whom they collaborated with was a characteristic of fascism, and many squads openly recruited known criminals and bored hooligans, despite a warning by fascist leader Achille Starace in 1922: 'Do not let yourself be led astray by the stupid prejudice that the convicted criminal dressed in a blackshirt is an element of strength.'[20]

Faint-Hearted Fascism?

The Ras were often caught between their dedication to fascism and their pursuit of local profits and power. Whilst Mussolini sought to placate his political opponents over the direction of fascism, the rural squads remained at liberty to carry on as they pleased and the more faint-hearted fascists increased their demands that these local power bases be curtailed. After the violent incidents in Turin in 1922, even fascist leaders condemned the squads who were involved in the murder of eleven workers. On 18th December, fascists attacked Turin, beating workers and smashing homes. Some anti-fascists were seized, put in trucks, taken away and beaten up. The anarchist Ferrero, who had been involved in the factory occupations, was tied by his feet to a truck, dragged through the streets, and dumped by the roadside. The anarchist Mari had better 'luck': he was bound and thrown into the river Po but managed to get back

18   Ibid., 169.
19   Ibid., 189.
20   Ibid.

21

to safety. The incident became known by militants as the massacre of Turin.

These attacks on individual anti-fascists often led to fatalities. There are many examples of fascist violence, both frequent and horrific, which never saw any legal redress. In 1921 in Sarzana, Dante Raspolini was beaten with clubs by a fascist gang, then tied to the back of a car and dragged for several miles. Ten years later, his son, the anarchist Doro Raspolini, shot at the fascist boss he held responsible. Doro was arrested and tortured to death. Even when exiled, militants still faced fascist violence: in Paris in September 1923, the anarchist Mario Castagna was attacked by a goon squad although he killed one during the fight. The following February, the anarchist Ernesto Bonomini assassinated a fascist journalist in a restaurant. Years later, Carlo Rosselli, an anti-fascist who had gone on to fight in Spain, was assassinated in France along with his brother. It was the second attempt on his life.

Arditi del Popolo

In the face of such violence, anti-fascists were forced to respond more aggressively, and many organized and fought back. Locally, coalitions of socialists, communists, anarchists and syndicalists organized together in the Arditi del Popolo (People's Army) and political differences were temporarily put aside. However, in 1921, the leadership of the socialists (PSI) signed the Pact of Conciliation with the fascists, which led to many socialists withdrawing from the anti-fascist militias, although many independent-minded socialists stayed. The newly formed Italian Communist Party (PCI) feared the autonomy of local militants siding with syndicalists and anarchists, and ordered communists to withdraw from the fray, thus fragmenting and weakening resistance to fascist provocation. Gramsci later justified the withdrawal of communist militants from the Arditi del Popolo, thus 'the tactic…corresponded to the need to prevent the party membership being controlled by a leadership that was not the party leadership'.[21] The communist move away from non-partisan militant anti-fascism

21 Anarchist Federation, *Resistance to Nazism* (London: AFED, 2008), 26.

can only have hastened the success of Italian fascism. Anti-fascism is at its most effective when ideological differences are subjugated to the more important overall struggle.

Working-class militants, then as now, could not rely on the reformist party's opposition to fascism or on the police, and had to defend themselves from fascist violence. They set up militias to protect their printing presses, union meetings and social clubs. In Cremona, the fascists led by Farinacci had mobilised against the socialist city council attacking people and property. Parliamentary opposition to fascism proved inadequate and anti-fascist deputies (MPs) were heavily outnumbered.

In 1922, the Alliance of Labour, an anti-fascist organization that had the support of socialists, communists and anarchists, called a general strike in opposition to fascism, but this turned out to benefit no one but the fascists, confirming the allegations they had made to the middle and upper classes that a Red Italy was just around the corner. The Alliance also saw the fascist squads mobilise to suppress the strike, thus securing the favours of the local boss class.

Working-class organizations were soon put under pressure to fight back against fascist gangsterism. In his essay 'The Rise of Fascism in an Industrial City', Tobias Abse describes the Arditi del Popolo as 'this mass violent resistance to fascism on the part of the urban workers and sections of the petit bourgeois' and that, perhaps optimistically, Italian fascism could have been defeated 'if only the leadership of the left parties at the national level had been more responsive'.[22] Abse cites the example of Parma in 1922 and 'the total humiliation of thousands of Italo Babo's Squadristi by a couple of hundred Arditi del Popolo'.[23] Abse is critical of the leadership of both the PCI and PSI for not backing the anarchist militant Malatesta in his call for a united front in the Italian towns and cities where the anarchists had a strong influence, such as Livorno. The communists formed their own defence squads. According to Abse, the Arditi 'exemplified the most organized, coherent and militant phase in the Livornese working class's

22   Forgas, *Rethinking Italian Fascism*, 56.
23   Ibid.

resistance to fascism'.[24] The Arditi had a strong connection with the working-class movement and worked with—and were from—local communities engaged in the militant anti-fascist struggle, employing offensive as well as defensive actions. Abse describes them as 'formidable' and says they numbered three hundred in Pisa, five hundred in Piombino and eight hundred in Livorno.[25]

Anti-fascists launched a 'dramatic attack' on the Livornese fascists who 'anxious to retaliate against the Arditi, mounted a punitive expedition'.[26] Although the local *carbinieri*, or police militia, tried to maintain neutrality, they unsurprisingly sided with the fascists, which led to a general strike and more violence. Livorno already had a tradition of militant non-sectarian anti-fascism with the League of Subversive Students (anarchists, socialists and communists) and their Arditi del Popolo dished out a few beatings to recalcitrant fascists in the area. In 1921, local anarchists defended 'the 17th National Congress of the Socialist Party (at which the Communist Party of Italy was to break away)…by beating off fascist gangs aimed at preventing it'.[27] After the fall of Mussolini, anarchists again worked with all organizations who were anti-fascist, including the communists, socialists, and republicans.

Sarzana

In 1921, anti-fascists lived under the constant threat of violence. In Sarzana, fascist squads attacked a meeting place for workers and trade unionists; the following day they murdered an anarchist, and then attacked his funeral a few days after that. Militants began to organize themselves against the increasing savagery of these 'punitive expeditions' that targeted working-class organizations. Although the police rarely did much to prevent fascist violence (and militants should never rely on the police to do so), there were occasional deviations from this, such as in June 1921, when the fascist gang leader Ticci was arrested after anti-fascists had repulsed an attack on their

24   Ibid., 73–74.
25   Ibid., 75.
26   Ibid.
27   de Agostini, *Prisoners & Partisans*, 7.

organizations in Sarzana. The fascists attempted to release him and wreak revenge on anti-fascist militants, but on arrival they were confronted by the carabinieri who shot at them and told them to leave as it was 'in their own interests'.[28] As the fascists withdrew, they were attacked by a section of the Arditi del Popolo led by local anarchists, and whose ranks had increased with workers and anti-fascists; the attack led to at least twenty fascist fatalities and numerous injuries.

The fascist humiliation at Sarzana led to countrywide reprisals that ended with murder. In Pisa, a fascist gang attacked an anti-fascist area but were beaten back. They stopped at a restaurant and murdered an anarchist named Benvenuti. In the ensuing fracas, two fascists were also killed. The squad fled only to return later in a truck supplied by the local carabinieri. They stabbed an anti-fascist's son to death and threw his body in the river, then set fire to Benvenuti's house where his two children were sleeping. Other incidents in Pisa included the murder and mutilation of an anarchist printer and the murder of an anarchist schoolteacher. Although the killers were caught, they were later acquitted.

Imola

Imola is another example of anarchists and socialists working together to combat early fascist violence. Anarchists had led an unsuccessful assassination attempt on Dino Grandi, the notorious fascist, earlier in 1920, and the fascists found it initially difficult to suppress militant opposition: 'the local fascists were squalid figures and in some cases outright lunatics. They found support among the farmers, who praised them and made them drunk with wine and bribes.'[29] Anarchists, socialists, and communists had formed Red Guards in order to prevent fascist provocation. On 14th December, trucks filled with fascist thugs descended on Imola and were met by well-organized opposition. Red Guards had occupied strategic points, and anarchist machine guns guarded the entrance to the town. The fascists were persuaded to withdraw by the mayor who feared serious bloodshed.

---

28 Rivista Anarchica, *Red Years, Black Years: Anarchist Resistance to Fascism in Italy* (London: ASP, 1989), 6.
29 Ibid., 19.

The fascist squads later returned to Imola and their violence increased. They shot up a socialist meeting, injuring several people, and they attempted to assassinate the anarchist Bassi, but accidentally killed a bystander (a murder for which they tried to frame Bassi). The incident had started with a fascist attack on a local worker who escaped into the pub where Bassi was drinking. The gang followed him in and attacked Bassi, who recalled that 'the fascist Casella, gun in hand, was almost on top of me and I drew my pistol from the belt of my trousers and shot at him, hitting him in the leg.'[30] Although Bassi was wounded he was arrested by the carabinieri and beaten, although he was better off than the fascist in the pub who had been seriously wounded and died.[31] This led to armed fascist gangs running through the streets and burning the local offices of anarchists and syndicalists; an anarchist was arrested for shooting a local fascist, and a communist party member was shot in the chest. Shortly after this, a fascist gang attacked an anarchist named Banega in a bar and shot him. Two comrades who were with him escaped, and Banega killed his would-be assassin, 'a professional thief'.[32] This led to more fascist intimidation: they attacked union offices and murdered a disabled anarchist war veteran. Anti-fascists were imprisoned and continuously harassed as organization was made increasingly difficult. Bassi was sentenced to twenty years.

Trieste

By 1920 in Trieste, fascist activity had increased with the local *fasci* recruiting from the unemployed and disenfranchised, buying their favours with money and cocaine.[33] These new members joined the fascists on their days out, attacking militants and destroying offices and printing presses. In Trieste the fascists feared the reaction from the significant Slavic population, the anarchists and the communists, so, with the aid of lorries supplied by sympathetic local military, they began to take the initiative. In 1920, using the killing of two

30   Ibid., 20.
31   Ibid.
32   Ibid., 21.
33   Ibid., 35.

officers as a convenient excuse, the fascists torched the Balkan Hotel, which housed the Slavs' headquarters, then attacked the local communist party newspaper offices. In response, anti-fascists started a fire at the local shipyard. Other smaller incidents continued to keep anti-fascists busy, such as when fascists tried to storm an anarchist's house but fled when fired upon. The fascists also tried to take over the Casa del Populo (the People's House, a leftist meeting place), but were forced to flee yet again after anarchists hastily gathered stashed weapons to rebuff them. In August 1922, fascists attacked an anarchist meeting by throwing two bombs into a café, but they failed to explode. Anti-fascists could also take the initiative, and in July 1921, a group of anarchists and communists attacked a fascist gang with bombs, wounding twenty-eight of them.

Anti-fascists realised that the use of propaganda, along with union organization and strikes, was essential to countering fascist activity, but so, too, was 'direct action against the gangs and against the rise of fascism'.[34] The anti-fascists took militant action against scab labour and shopkeepers who were trying to break strikes. Strike action soon became the only recourse for militant anti-fascism but, with the passing of emergency laws against such activity, these eventually dwindled.

Trieste established a pattern of operation for the squads: mobilization, then provocation, followed by violent action and destruction of leftist infrastructures and organizations. This was wholly connived by the police and local industrialists who supported such operations and thus facilitated the rise of violent fascism in the city. Being better funded and more numerous than the anti-fascists, the fascist gangs soon took control of the streets in Trieste, which led to mass arrests of militants and many anti-fascists going into exile to escape fascist retaliation.

Piombino

Fascism developed more slowly in the militant town of Piombino, where anarchists and anarcho-syndicalists were well organized and

---

34   Ibid.

made retaliatory attacks on local fascists after Squadristi violence in places like Pisa. The 144th Battalion of the Arditi del Popolo was launched with anarchist, communist and socialist militants to the fore. Following an assassination attempt on a socialist in 1921, militants from the Arditi attacked the local fascists. The Royal Guard came to the fascists' aid but were disarmed and the Arditi controlled the city for several days. As elsewhere, the Pact of Pacification that the socialist leadership signed with the fascist government fractured anti-fascist militants, weakened the Arditi del Popolo, and ultimately only aided fascism.

The anarchist Morelli was putting up posters against the pact when fascists attacked him. Despite firing back, he was killed. Police arrested two hundred anarchists that night, many of them Arditi militants. The fascists realised their chance and attacked opposition printing presses and offices, only to be confronted by militant anti-fascists and rescued by the ever-sympathetic police. In 1922, fascists again tried to take Piombino but were again repulsed by the well-organized Arditi. In June, using a fascist funeral as a pretext, Squadristi, with Royal Guards from Pisa, destroyed socialist offices and meeting places (despite the pact). They attempted to occupy union offices and the anarchist printers but faced militant responses for a day and a half before taking over the city. Many more anti-fascists faced a future in exile.

The year 1922 was that of Mussolini's fabled March on Rome, which was accompanied by Il Duce's declaration that he was prepared to rule by machine gun if need be. Mussolini himself did not march to Rome but caught the train. Fascist violence erupted in the capital, with attacks on radical newspapers and bookshops and with public book-burning. Squadristi attacks on opposition media and their printing presses ensured a one-sided account of events the following day.

Fascist violence continued with the murder of three opposition MPs and savage beatings given out to other opponents. Following the kidnapping, beating and murder of the socialist parliamentarian Matteoti by fascists in 1924, which nearly united oppositional forces against Mussolini, Il Duce increased his control over social and political life in Italy. Socialist and communist deputies such as Gramsci were arrested and their parties banned, so activists were forced to work covertly. Organizations and clubs were illegal 'and even wine shops suspected of serving as meeting places for "subversives" were closed down'.[35] All of these police actions were enthusiastically accompanied by Blackshirt fascist squads and meant that any consolidated anti-fascist activity was going to be extremely difficult in a one-party state.

The consolidation of power by Mussolini did not mean the squads went away, and, in fact, they still proved to be uncontrollable in some parts of the country. Once in power, the fascist squads had no one left to fight, their *raison d'etre* had vanished, and they resorted to either infighting or found new enemies to bully, which enervated a movement at risk of becoming stale. Some squads were dissolved following party discipline, whilst others simply disguised themselves as leisure associations. Many Squadristi had been calling for a second wave of violence, more out of adventure than political expediency it seems, so they selected new targets in the shape of catholic institutions and freemasons. Leading fascists such as Farinacci wanted to maintain the squads as a bulwark against any possible anti-fascist or industrial agitation as well as to maintain a vital symbol of fascist ideology. However, given the mounting evidence of corruption, blackmail and extortion coming in from the provinces, Farinacci had a difficult case to make; it was obvious to many party functionaries that the Ras were a law unto themselves and very keen on maintaining the status that had elevated them from nowhere men to political somebodies. However, Farinacci, under pressure from Mussolini, was forced to curb the influence of the squads and made moves to suppress them, although, in some areas, they were still used in their traditional scab role of intimidating workers and suppressing working-class organization.

By the 1930s, Mussolini, although hardly exporting fascism in any great measure, was supporting fascist organizations in other

---

35   Lyttelton, *The Seizure of Power*, 267.

countries: the British Union of Fascists benefited from his patronage, as did the Croatian fascists led by Anton Pavelic. In the 1930s. Mussolini supplied men and materiel to Franco during the Spanish Civil War, and he demanded that any captured Italian anti-fascists be deported and executed. Italian fascist mercenaries were humiliated by anti-fascist forces, including Italians at Guadalajara, which proved most embarrassing for Il Duce. He had to satisfy himself by torpedoing neutral ships that he suspected were carrying supplies to the Spanish Republic.

From Prisoners to Partisans!

The anti-fascists who were lucky enough to escape from Italy to France, or even further to America, avoided arrest and imprisonment, whilst those who remained often faced heavy sentences and regular persecution. Many anti-fascists were interned under new provisions for containment of political opposition and were exiled to islands in the Mediterranean. Relations in these camps between anarchists and communists were often fractious, especially with the commencement of the Spanish Civil War. Isolated and in bad conditions, many anti-fascists were stuck there for the rest of their sentences; some had their tariffs extended due to violent insubordination, whilst others remained in the camps until 1943 and the collapse of Mussolini's regime.

Italian anti-fascists in France faced mixed fortunes: many were arrested and deported back to Italy and the camps, some went to fight in Spain, and others managed to live clandestinely in Vichy after 1941. The difficulty of political activity and life under fascism and in exile is illustrated by the case of Egidio Fossi, an anarchist who, in 1920, was sentenced to twelve years, the first two of which were spent in solitary confinement. Released under a general amnesty in 1925, he was continually harassed by fascists until he escaped to France where he was pursued by the police. Fossi left to fight in Spain in 1936, and in 1940 he was arrested and sent to a German labour brigade. Freed in 1943, he returned to Piombino to join the anarchist struggle. In 1920, another anarchist, Adriano Vanni, was tried with Fossi and, after the general amnesty, fascists attacked him, so left for exile in France. Finding life just as hard there, he returned to Italy where fascist persecution continued. In September 1943, when Italy surrendered, Fossi was a key anarchist organizer in the partisans, and after the liberation he confronted the fascist thugs who had harassed him previously. Incredibly, he did not seek the ultimate retribution.

Pietro Bruzzi was a Milanese anarchist who had lived in Russia and France before fighting in the Spanish Civil War. He was deported from France and spent five years on the isle of Ponza. The deposition of Mussolini and his replacement by the Badoglio regime did not mean instant liberation for anti-fascists, especially anarchist ones, and Bruzzi remained in internment. Like others though, he escaped and joined an anarchist partisan group back in Milan, only to be betrayed, arrested and tortured 'with such ferocity that his face was completely smashed. He gave no information to the Nazis and was subsequently shot. Before dying he still had the strength to shout, "Viva l'anarchia!"'[36] Following his death, Milanese anarchists formed the Malatesta and Bruzzi Brigades and fought alongside the socialist Matteoti Brigade to liberate the city. As the partisan struggle intensified in 1943, the local anti-fascists seized weapons including 'a small calibre piece of artillery,' which was put to good use by destroying a German truck.[37] The Germans eventually took control of the city, but anti-fascists had seized all the weapons from the barracks and the partisan fightback continued for several days. Organization became more difficult as the fascists evacuated the city centre, so partisans moved to the outskirts where farmland made guerrilla activity unfeasible. The partisans formed the revolutionary Livorno Garibaldi Division and continued their armed struggle against fascism. When the American army arrived they demanded that the partisans disarm, which the anarchists refused to do and then 'set about the elimination of fascist criminals and collaborationists'.[38]

In 1943, Mussolini established his Salo Republic and adopted a pseudo-radical programme that reverted to the political, anti-capitalist radicalism that Italian fascism had used as a tactic earlier on.

36   Rivista Anarchica, *Red Years, Black Years*, 43.
37   de Agostini, *Prisoners & Partisans*, 8.
38   Ibid., 11.

According to Deakin, 'the new regime was republican, but also socialist and revolutionary'.[39] Mack Smith stated that

> The Mussolini of 1944 reasserted the socialist beliefs of his youth because he now felt that he had been cheated by the world of finance and industry.... To maintain some intellectual coherence he tried to pretend that, notwithstanding appearances, he had never deserted the socialist programme he had put forward for fascism in 1919.[40]

Hitler was under-impressed and stated that 'our Italian ally has embarrassed us everywhere'.[41] By 1943, it was obvious that the Axis powers could not win the war, and the Italians lost faith in Mussolini who was deposed and arrested as Italy changed sides. Mussolini was rescued from his mountain retreat by a Nazi squad sent by Hitler and led by Skorzeny, a fascist who remained active long after the war. Mussolini's much reduced empire faced opposition on several fronts: not only were the Allied forces knocking on the door, but on a local level the partisan struggle was intensifying and industrial action was increasing as Mussolini's power waned. The partisans, often communist-led, began to use more violent terror tactics against the fascist infrastructure, whilst on an industrial level, in November 1943, Turin communists brought out 50,000 workers on strike. The German occupiers could not cope with a city of over 200,000 workers, and many of them aggrieved. A Nazi missive to the beleaguered cops read, 'The Fuehrer further empowers you to arrest ringleaders and shoot them out of hand as communists.'[42] In other cities, clandestine communist squads were active, attacking fascist officials, twenty-eight of whom were assassinated. Reprisals were frequent and brutal. When a leading fascist was assassinated in Ferrara, squads were sent in to exact revenge. Seventeen anti-fascists held in jail were executed.

---

39   F.W. Deakin, *The Last Days of Mussolini* (Harmondsworth: Penguin, 1962), 167.
40   Smith, *Mussolini*, 362.
41   Deakin, *The Last Days of Mussolini*, 207.
42   Ibid., 156.

Anti-fascists fired upon the funeral of another fascist assassinated by the communists, to which the fascists retaliated with five thousand rounds of ammunition. To make matters worse for the Axis, deserters and draft-evaders were taking to the hills and swelling the ranks of the partisans waiting there.

In 1944, communist-led strikes in Turin, where the Fiat factories were, spread to Milan and Genoa, and a general strike in March was coordinated with resistance activities and sabotage on the railways that prevented workers from getting to the morning shift. It was a success. The German occupiers recognised the strike was political rather than economic in character and arrested hundreds of strikers. Hitler was so angered that he insisted that twenty percent of all strikers should be deported to Germany. For Deakin, the strikes were a revelation 'of the extent of progress made by...the National Liberation Committee of the partisan movement, and of the leading part played by the communists'.[43] In Turin, the militants continued to have the upper hand and organized further strikes in June. In retaliation for increasing worker and partisan militancy, fascist repercussions maintained their usual brutality: 'in the valleys infested by the partisans, good results had been achieved by deporting the entire male population'.[44] The Nazi Marshall Kesserling issued orders that included:

2. Every act of violence must be followed immediately by counter-measures.

3. If there are a large number of bands in a district, then in every single case a certain percentage of the male population of the place must be arrested, and, in cases of violence, shot.

4. If German soldiers are fired at in villages, the village must be burnt. The criminals or else the leaders must be publicly hanged.[45]

Killing Mussolini

From his radically diminished powerbase, Mussolini and his remaining sycophants also ordered harsh justice against anti-fascist

43   Ibid., 177.
44   Ibid., 187.
45   Ibid., 221.

partisans, demanding that ten should be killed for every dead fascist. As usual, a militia was gathered around the ex-Duce who continued in the remaining territory with 'a dozen squads…operating in Milan, some of them in receipt of government funds, some composed of criminals running various kinds of protection rackets, some with their own private prisons and torture chambers'.[46] Criminality, sadism, and fascism seem to be vicious and frequent fascist bedfellows. One squad, led by Koch, had its own instruments of torture and had profited from their involvement in hard drugs. They were eventually suppressed by the use of the equally psychotic Muti gang whom Mussolini made 'a fascist legion because of its usefulness in suppressing strikes in a number of factories'.[47] In Milan, fifteen people were executed in revenge by the Muti gang for a bomb attack on a fascist truck. After being told they were being deported to Germany, the anti-fascists realised that this was not the case and they attempted to escape but were shot down and left in the sun. The partisans exacted bloody revenge on forty-five Italian and German prisoners. The war was clearly not going to Mussolini's plan despite his use of the paramilitary Black Brigades, who were 'an auxiliary corps of Black Shirts composed of Action Squads'.[48] These brigades quickly gained a reputation for brutality against political opponents as partisan activity became increasingly successful. Mussolini also encouraged reprisals against partisans and the execution of Italian women and children as well.

Bombast, hyperbole and fabrication were hardly underused by Il Duce, and near the end of 1944 he wrote to Hitler, 'Even the anti-fascists are no longer waiting with their former enthusiasm… the partisan phenomenon is dying out.'[49] It is assumed he meant the partisans that arrested and executed him shortly after. Mussolini's entourage, and those few willing to fight for him, fled on 28th April 1945 with Il Duce disguised in the back of a truck heading for Austria. He was apprehended on the road by partisans of the

46   Smith, *Mussolini*, 357.
47   Ibid.
48   Deakin, *The Last Days of Mussolini*, 199.
49   Ibid., 234.

(communist) 52nd Garibaldi Brigade led by a Colonel 'Valerio,' who recognised and then arrested them near the amusingly named Dongo. Il Duce, along with his long-term mistress Clara Petacci, and fascist thugs like Farinacci and Starace, were executed by anti-fascists near a village called Mezzegra. Nearby, another group of fleeing fascists were also executed. The bodies of twenty-three fascists were taken back to Milan where they were strung up by the heels in the Piazza Loreto, a symbolic and violent end for a regime that prided itself on its own brutality.

Following the fall of fascism, socialists and communists became assimilated into the democratic political process, and prisoners from these organizations were freed from the islands and camps first. The anarchists were often still detained. During the partisan struggle the allies refused to arm the autonomous anarchist groups, though many anarchists fought side by side with others in groups like the socialist Matteoti Brigade and the communist-dominated Garibaldi Brigade, in addition to forming their own units named after Lucetti and Schirru. The allies also knew that the anarchists would want no part in the organization of the future government, whilst the anarchists did not trust allied command and were rightly mistrustful of the reformist socialists and especially the Stalinist communists following the debacle in Spain. During internment on the island of Ventotene in 1943, the communist leadership had denounced the anarchists for hindering unification of a popular anti-fascist front and as 'enemies of proletarian unity'.[50] Clearly, the communists had little understanding of the reasons why.

---

50   de Agostini, *Prisoners & Partisans*, 32.

France: A New Acceptance of Violence

The brutalization of political life in many parts of Europe was accompanied by a new acceptance of violence.
—Stanley G. Payne in *A History of Fascism 1914–45*

Fascism did not spring out of nowhere in the aftermath of the First World War but had clear precedents in a number of groups across Europe that were authoritarian, anti-Semitic, racist, ultra-nationalist and violent in various degrees. The ideas represented by these groups along with the effects of the First World War helped create the early fascist parties. The fetishism of uniforms, war and patriotism alongside borrowings from syndicalism, socialism, republicanism and monarchism presented a fetid potpourri of possibilities for disillusioned ex-soldiers who added national grievances and personal bitterness to these often contrary ideologies. The successes and failures of these parties varied in some countries, like France and Romania, some being particularly strong and other groups being co-opted or suppressed by governments.

In France, Le Faisceau was founded by Georges Valois, a former member of Action Française (AF) who eventually moved to the Resistance and died in a concentration camp: in a rather grim irony, the fascism that he sought to establish eventually did him in. Members of Le Faisceau were subject to violent assaults from the left but also from AF, which ran a vehement campaign against them. On one occasion the AF stormed a meeting and attacked Valois putting him on his arse. The Patriot Youth were a ten-thousand-strong right-wing movement that emerged around 1924 and, after a large and bloody clash with the communists in 1925, ended up with four fatalities, creating martyrs for the sake of increased Patriot Youth membership. In the 1930s, there was militant opposition to right-wing events in France and 'because of frequent violent clashes provoked by the presence of counter demonstrators at such political rallies, the police occasionally banned public meetings or parades where the threat of violence was great'.[1] Several extremists displayed the usual far-right-wing penchant for individual terrorism and were caught up in bomb plots and illegal arms caches with the Cagoule group. Various other patriotic leagues and organizations subsequently formed and faded, all agitating for an authoritarian regime and culminating in mass riots in Paris in 1934 with largely negative results: 'the result of the scare, however, was to magnify French anti-fascism...[which] became the dominant political fact in France and led to the election of the Popular Front in 1936.'[2]

Following the end of the Spanish Civil War, more than half a million Republican refugees headed for France. Having been ill-supported by Leon Blum and the Popular Front government, they could hardly expect to be received with much sympathy. Many were interned in 'refugee camps' that were little better than concentration camps: 'Communists [and] anarchists had been sent to special disciplinary camps,' some of which were in North Africa. French authorities tried to repatriate many republicans, whilst other 'battle-hardened Spanish veterans' were viewed as useful and encouraged to join the Foreign Legion. The International Brigaders from fascist-dominated countries could hardly expect to go home and were treated appallingly. However, the militant spirit in some veterans was not crushed, particularly the 'many Spanish republicans [who] disappeared from labor camps in the Auvergne and joined French maquis groups or formed their own Spanish resistance units. One such group participated in the liberation of Montlucon'.[3]

Many French anti-fascists continued their propaganda activities, whether chalking anti-Vichy slogans on a wall or distributing leaflets

---

1   John F. Sweets, *Choices in Vichy France: The French Under Nazi Occupation* (Oxford: University Press, 1994), 85.
2   Stanley G. Payne, *A History of Fascism, 1914–1945* (London: UCL, 1995), 294.
3   Sweets, *Choices in Vichy France*, 112–115.

in the workplace. The communist resistance paper *L'Humanite* was produced under severe duress. Other resistance propaganda supported the exiled De Gaulle and there was suspicion and mistrust between camps: the left saw De Gaulle as an imperialist stooge and the right saw the communists as Soviet agents. Whatever political bias, acquiring material for such propaganda was difficult, dangerous, and closely monitored. The Vichy police 'considered Gaullist resisters to be misguided patriots, but were unwilling to extend such "tolerance" to the Communists'.[4] There could be moments of community resistance such as on Bastille Day and May Day in 1942 when demonstrators took to the streets. In one town 'no one had been arrested thanks in part to the vigorous reaction of several armed men who were former volunteers for the International Brigades in Spain'—something that was contradicted in the following day's police report.[5] Resistance took place in the workplace with sabotage, absenteeism and violence against collaborators, as well as 'thefts of equipment, clothing, ration coupons, and other resources needed to supply the Maquis'.[6]

Under the Vichy regime, armed and pro-fascist militias joined in anti-resistance activities whilst simultaneously exploiting their positions of power, their motto being 'To save France from Bolshevism'.[7] As in Italy and Germany, extremist militia members indulged in gangsterism and 'had a direct hand in the robberies, murders, deportations, and torture for which the Milice were justly notorious in the region…their actions could hardly be distinguished from those of common criminals—extortion, robbery, acts of vengeance against rivals, and much seemingly senseless violence'.[8]

---

4   Ibid., 205.
5   Ibid., 209.
6   Ibid., 213.
7   Ibid., 108.
8   Ibid., 95.

Austria: Fascist Violence Could Only Be Met by Violence

In 1918, far right nationalism was hardly a new concept in Austria: in the 1880s Georg Ritter von Schönerer, a fervent nationalist who Hitler mentioned in *Mein Kampf*, was agitating for the unification of the German-speaking peoples. He was both anti-Semitic and anti-Slavic and referred to his compatriots as 'racial comrades.' In 1885, Schönerer backed the 'Linz Programme', which pledged to 'eliminate Jewish influence from all spheres of public life' and later, in 1887, urged that the 'unproductive and obnoxious behaviour of many Russian Jews' fleeing the pogroms be confined to the ghettos. Along with his anti-Semitic ultra-nationalism, Schönerer also appeared to sympathise with the worker and middle-class fears of 'big capitalism' and urged the nationalization of the Viennese railway as well as a limit on working hours. The socialist Karl Kautsky warned about these groups whose 'appearance is oppositional and democratic thus appealing to the workers instincts' as well as their anti-Semitism.[1]

It seems that wherever this strain of ultra-nationalism appears it is inevitably followed with violent reinforcement. In 1888, after the erroneous reporting of the emperor's death, Schönerer and a gang of heavies barged into a newspaper's offices demanding the supplication of the journalists, with unforeseen results: The journalists called in some printers for support and 'a free fight developed in which the anti-Semites used beer glasses and walking sticks, but after some minutes were put to flight by the printers. Schönerer was put on trial

---

1   F.L. Carsten, *Fascist Movements in Austria* (London: Sage, 1977), 12–16.

for public violence and forcible entry'.[2] It is tempting to view this incident as the first successful militant anti-fascist action.

Previously, in 1887, Schönerer took his followers to the streets to protest a bill that institutionalised the Czech language, thus equating the Teutonic with the Slav. There were violent confrontations between Schönerer's supporters and the police, and in Graz, one student protester died. When parliament accepted the bill, further violence erupted in the chamber and demonstrations and riots broke out in several cities. By 1913, Schönerer's political career had passed, but his anti-big business, anti-Semitic, anti-Slavic nationalism preceded Hitler's by several decades, as did the use—albeit more spontaneously in Austria—of political violence to push forward their programme.

In 1918, Austria was no more exempt from the fear of 'Red Revolution' than any other country in Europe. Following the dissolution of the Austro-Hungarian empire, the rise of traditional nationalism, anti-clericalism (i.e., Rome) and anti-Semitism, there was also resentment over the Social Democrats' 'Red Vienna' and their political reforms. Following the uprising in Munich in 1919, Bavarian defence units were set up, which forwarded large amounts of weapons to the Austrian Heimwehr, 'the paramilitary force of the extreme right',[3] to bolster protection from the possible spread of malign Viennese and Hungarian Bolshevism which could link up with the north and Berlin in particular. This was all fuelled by the fear of 'Asiatic hordes in the form of Bolshevism under Jewish leadership, against German culture'.[4]

The Heimwehr

The Heimwehr were the Austrian version of the German Freikorps, anti-communist authoritarians who lacked the organizational rigidity of their German counterparts, and in 1920 they announced a 'shooting festival' in the Tyrol, which the Viennese Social Democrats (SD) opposed. A strike was called and the SD and armed workers

---

2   Ibid., 20.
3   Martin Kitchen, *The Coming of Austrian Fascism* (London: Croom Helm, 1980), 3.
4   Carsten, *Fascist Movements in Austria*, 47.

prevented support from Bavarian units crossing the border. The rally still took place with speakers issuing dire warnings to Vienna. Thus the Heimwehr, a German-funded and heavily armed militia also supported by sympathetic industrialists, grew relatively unopposed under a Social Democratic government and were vocal over armed resistance should the 'Red Revolution' occur. Which it didn't. The SD and Independents kept a curb on the growth of the communists, who remained small.

Elements of the Heimwehr were becoming even more provocative, and they not only advocated a coup but also organized 'terror groups' that were to be used as strike-breakers. Clearly things threatened to escalate and catch the socialists unprepared. In Styria in 1922, socialists confiscated the weapons of the Heimwehr, which they retaliated by arresting the SD leaders. In protest, three thousand steel workers came out on strike and confronted 'a large-scale mobilization of the Styrian Heimwehren' operating in a strike-breaking capacity for one of the first (but by no means last) times.[5] In 1923, the Viennese SD ordered the formation of a Republican Defence Corps (RDC), which drew on socialists and workers and led to the inevitable clashes. In October, a Heimwehr squad attacked a socialist in Klagenfurt. A forty-strong group of RDC arrived to confront them but the Heimwehr had gone, only to return the following day to conduct intimidating house searches of workers. The RDC arrived again in greater numbers and the Heimwehr swiftly exited. Humiliated, the local Heimwehr then demanded the arrests of the leading RDC involved and threatened retribution against a workers' demonstration, to no avail. Shortly after, the Heimwehr took over an inn and began firing at police, who subsequently disbanded them.

Despite its funding and materiel, the regional Heimwehr were too disputatious and remained a potentially powerful but disunited force. As the threat of 'Red Revolution' receded, they became less active—although in 1926 at a rally of right-wing paramilitaries, one speaker described the SD as 'the representative of the most radical socialism of a Marxist colour outside Soviet Russia', proving that paranoia

5   Ibid., 66.

and bluster were just as prevalent as anti-working-class activity. The speaker was convinced that the socialists could only be stopped by armed resistance or, echoing Hitler, 'national revolution'. Clearly some of the Heimwehr leadership harboured grander ambitions despite their declining influence. The right-wing Frontkampferbund had also begun to organize in some socialist strongholds; these socialists responded by mobilising the previously dormant RDC.[6]

In 1927, Styrian unions called a general strike and, aware of the right-wing militias' strike-breaking history, called in the RDC to protect the workers. Superior numbers of Heimwehr surrounded the area to cut off food supplies and force the strikers to back down. The Heimwehr was being used as a political paramilitary force, but so was the RDC. The RDC was only strong in certain areas, most notably Vienna and other centres of industry, and although it was up against the far right Heimwehr, it was answerable to the SD and sent in against rioting Viennese workers. At one point in 1928, nineteen thousand Heimwehr marched, and the SD mobilised the RDC and its socialist supporters, although violent conflict was ultimately avoided. By 1929, the Heimwehr had started holding provocative demonstrations in socialist-dominated areas in a show of strength. In 1929, ten thousand right-wing paramilitaries marched in Vienna. Not only was the Heimwehr involved in physical strike-breaking, but they also organized 'independent' trade unions to undermine the working-class movement with the backing of certain employers. This reduced the ability of the general strike to be an effective political weapon. The Heimwehr were being manipulated by political and industrial figures in a virulently anti-socialist direction.

The Rise of Austrian Fascism

The main pre-conditions for Austrian fascism were the resentment of the Social Democrats' 'Red Vienna', a popular desire for *Anschluss* (the annexation of Austria by Germany), a tendency for authoritarian government, and a predominant and institutionalised anti-Semitism. The two fascist parties vying for electoral respectability were the

---

6   Ibid., 107.

Heimwehr and the National Socialists. The Heimwehr had benefited and grown when the 'conflict between the right and the Socialists first peaked in 1927, enabling the Heimwehr to gain recruits as an alternative to the party systems'.[7] They were indirectly funded by Mussolini who, in his later 'anti-German phase of 1934–35',[8] wanted to curb German influence by curtailing the Anschluss. The Austrian Nazis were backed by Hitler but initially lacked a powerbase because voting loyalties were fairly intractable in many communities; the workers tended towards socialism, and voters in the rural areas tended towards the Christian Social Party. The Nazis agitated strongly for the Anschluss, in addition to propagating their usual anti-Semitism in order to gain favour. The Nazis attempted a putsch in 1934, which failed and led to their temporary suppression.

Jewish Resistance in Austria

Austrian working-class resistance was weakened due to their smaller infrastructures and organizations and a lack of militant leadership, whereas the Jewish militant resistance was small if not determined. After the 1925 anti-Semitic riots, newspapers wrote that 'the violence was the work of "Jewish and Communist provocateurs" who tried to provoke the crowds'.[9] Anti-Semitic right-wing students attacked Jewish and socialist meetings. The fact that socialist student groups, as well as the Social Democrats, all featured prominent Jewish figures meant that the two were unified, which fomented hostility from the right and anxiety amongst bourgeois and orthodox Jews: 'The more Jews there are among the leaders of Social Democracy, the stronger the desire will become to square accounts through a show of anti-Semitism'.[10]

The League of Jewish Front Soldiers was the biggest organization; it was created in 1932 in reaction to Nazi electoral successes to

7   Payne, *A History of Fascism*, 246.
8   Philip Morgan, *Fascism in Europe, 1919–1945* (London: Routledge, 2003), 16.
9   Bruce F. Pauley, *From Prejudice to Persecution: A History of Austrian Anti-Semitism* (Chapel Hill: University of North Carolina Press, 1992), 113.
10   Ibid., 266.

'protect the honour and respect of the Jews living in Austria'.[11] The League was a militant organization and followed from the earlier City Guard, Self-Defence Force and Protection Corps, and the later Jewish Armed Sporting and Defence Association, and the Jewish Protection League. In the face of anti-Semitic organizations like the Heimwehr, which was also made up of ex-soldiers, the non-partisan League had around eight thousand members in the main cities as well as its own newspaper and 'young people would not only acquire military discipline but would also learn not to tolerate the insults of anti-Semites'.[12] The Jewish Protection League offered physical opposition against Nazi aggression, responded to anti-Jewish propaganda and organized large demonstrations. They also linked up with non-Jewish veterans and the worldwide Jewish Front Fighters who held a meeting in Vienna in 1936, which the League stewarded and, unsurprisingly, the Nazis chose not to attack. Their entreaties to the more orthodox Jewish organization to form a united front did not succeed and internal differences created factional problems.

The Schutzbund

> The strength of the Schutzbund lay...in its political convictions and its relationship to the labour movement.
> —Martin Kitchen in *The Coming of Austrian Fascism*

Political street violence was prevalent and the parties organized militias to defend against provocation: 'The Socialists (like their counterparts elsewhere in central and southern Europe) had long had [militia]'.[13] This was the Schutzbund, whose militancy was quelled by the Social Democrat Party (SPD) leadership, which 'abhorred violence and were a truly humanitarian party'. In 1927, 'workers launched a spontaneous demonstration to protest the acquittal of Heimwehr members who had been accused of murdering a member of the Schutzbundler and a child', when the Schattendorf jury returned a not-guilty verdict. The SPD leadership considered using

11   Ibid., 248.
12   Ibid.
13   Payne, *A History of Fascism*, 248.

the Schutzbund against strikers, although militants within the Bund were amongst the demonstrators. The Palace of Justice, the police station and a newspaper office were all burnt down. The police opened fire on the strikers and unarmed Schutzbundlers and were subsequently viewed in some quarters as being anti-worker. Fighting with the police led to ninety-four deaths. The Schutzbund ended up policing its own militants, and although accused by the right of agitating for a civil war, they clearly were not. The Schutzbund and the SPD leadership were not nearly militant enough and the Bund's job was to protect the Republic from left and right extremists alike.[14]

However, despite the overt caution by the Schutzbund, violence between them and the Heimwehr did occur. In 1929, 'a fight that resulted in four deaths and some sixty injured, was taken by the Schutzbund leadership as triumphant proof that, even when outnumbered the Social Democrats were more than a match for the Heimwehr and that any attempt to launch a "March on Vienna" was bound to fail'.[15] The Schutzbund at times seemed immobilised by weak leadership and a lack of militancy, despite pressure from hostile forces and at one point being 'more concerned about the workers' Olympics than...the possibility of a fascist coup'.[16] The police raided the Schutzbund on government orders, hoping to find stockpiled weapons that would assist them in a civil war, but it came to nothing.

In Simmering in October 1932, the Schutzbund fought the Nazis when the latter attacked their centre, leaving two fascists and one policeman dead. When the authoritarian leader, Engelbert Dolfuss closed parliament in March 1933, the Schutzbund leadership prevaricated; units waited to be mobilised against the move but eventually stood down. Dolfuss subsequently banned the Schutzbund. As with many organizations made illegal, the more active members rebuilt, forming the Young Front for anti-Nazi activity. Despite this, many militants left, angered at the leadership's failure to mobilise in March.

14   Larry Ceplair, *Under the Shadow of War: Fascism, Anti-Fascism, and Marxists, 1918–1939* (New York: Columbia University Press, 1987), 68.
15   Kitchen, *The Coming of Austrian Fascism*, 128.
16   Ibid., 133.

As they watched the erosion of social democracy, the ex-Bunders were still subject to police harassment.

The Socialist leadership kept the Schutzbund on a short leash, opting for a general strike rather than full-on street warfare. This was to prove mostly ineffective and they 'tried to ignore their Leftists' insistent demand for militant activity'.[17] The leadership also acted weakly when the chancellor, Dolfuss, attacked workers' organizations and printing presses. Mussolini urged for the final destruction of the socialists, so the diminutive Dolfuss unleashed the 'police and military forces to crush what had been the best-organized and most solidly entrenched Socialist party in Europe'[18] in 1934, which saw the workers take 'up arms to resist months of unlawful, arbitrary measures aimed at crushing the labor movement'.[19] After four days of street violence and shooting in the industrial cities, two hundred people had been killed, ten prominent activists had been hanged, hundreds had been jailed and thousands lost their jobs.

In February 1934, Austria erupted into violence when heavily armed members of the Schutzbund ended up in a shootout with cops in a Linz hotel. The situation escalated as news reached Vienna. Viennese workers immediately went on strike in support, and the Schutzbund occupied strategic positions in a long-delayed confrontation with reactionary forces. Workers occupied a major bakery and kept it running as a cooperative, with a machine gun on the roof to scare off the Heimwehr. The Schutzbund barricaded the workers' area and took control of the trams—though, crucially, not the entire railway network, which was used to transport more troops into the city, as the government grabbed the opportunity to violently suppress the organized working class. Government forces also fired artillery into the Karl-Marx-Hof workers' housing complex; Dolfuss considered using poison gas, but it was rejected for fear of 'a most unfortunate international incident'. The fighting continued from early on the

---

17   Ceplair, *Under the Shadow of War*, 68.
18   Ibid.
19   Evan Burr Bukey, *Hitler's Austria: Popular Sentiment in the Nazi Era 1938–1945* (Chapel Hill: University of North Carolina Press, 2000), 15.

12th February until nearly midnight on the 15th. Repercussions were harsh, with the bakery workers receiving long sentences and other militants arrested and jailed. Many workers died.

The SPD had been a considerable organization, but once they were banned following the February uprising, their property was seized and redistributed and their leaders and prominent members were subjected to repression and 'any leaders of the party or the Schutzbund, any prominent agitators or radicals, journalists or lawyers who defended leftists should be sent to concentration camps'.[20] In Austria, as elsewhere, funerals turned into sites of resistance, and every flower placed on the grave of the executed radical Georg Weissel became a symbol of silent dissent. In the aftermath, the exiled socialists finally realised that 'fascist violence could only be met by violence'[21] and that what had been needed was 'an anti-fascist front among widely different political groupings which could not simply be denounced as agents of fascism',[22] and 'in the face of fascism an offensive not a defensive strategy was needed'.[23] Keeping the RDC and Schutzbund on short orders, plus the lack of militant leadership seizing the initiative, had led to disaster.

Later that year, Austrian Nazis assassinated Dolfuss, which led to more violence, which was eventually suppressed by the Austrian army. When the Nazis marched into Austria, they were met with an enthusiasm that transformed into mass outbreaks of anti-Semitic violence, with 'young toughs heaving paving blocks into the windows of Jewish shops'.[24] This was not just a few local fascists: 'The Nazi brawlers—tens of thousands of them—fanned out into Jewish neighbourhoods, looting shops and beating hapless passers-by.'[25] As with much anti-Semitic violence, it had as much to do with jealousy and theft as intolerance. As the National Assembly voted for the Anschluss, gangs of storm troopers and vigilantes emerged to settle

---

20 Kitchen, *The Coming of Austrian Fascism*, 247.
21 Ibid., 257.
22 Ibid., 258.
23 Ibid., 261.
24 Bukey, *Hitler's Austria*, 27.
25 Ibid., 28.

accounts with Hitler's opponents, both real and imagined, including Jews, communists and socialists. Leading Nazi Heinrich Himmler arrived with forty thousand police in tow, and the Gestapo techniques of rounding up and arresting political opponents proceeded to channel at least twenty thousand into concentration camps to uncertain fates.

Resistance

Anti-fascist resistance became less prominent and the workers movement had been weakened, badly affected by mass unemployment (a third of the population was jobless) and the rise in the cost of living. Following the February uprising, left-wing activists had gone 'underground' and the far right absorbed some of the socialists' votes. By the summer of 1938, shortages were affecting morale and Vienna saw much 'lawlessness accompanied by violence, perpetrated by marauding Nazi malcontents' in Jewish areas.[26] Also, Austrian Nazis were being usurped by their more efficient German counterparts. Although active resistance was slight, workers still dissented: the communist underground paper *Rote Fahne* reported that workers had gone on strike for better wages and that there was unrest throughout industry. In Vienna in 1939, dissatisfaction was widespread and anti-German sentiment was expressed as the communist underground spread further, distributing propaganda and encouraging sabotage.[27] The Nazis responded with more surveillance and arrests and ordered the police to arrest 'all persons of Marxist persuasion—Communists, Revolutionary Socialists and so forth—who might be suspected of undermining the leadership of the National Socialist state'.[28] The communists still maintained cells in industry and propaganda activities whilst 'socialist railwaymen solicited contributions, set up safe houses, and established links with like-minded groups in Bavaria'.[29] It was not without risk, and 250 Salzburg railway workers were arrested by the Gestapo alone.

---

26 Ibid., 56.
27 Ibid., 84.
28 Ibid., 87.
29 Ibid., 90.

Schlurfs: Youth Against Fascism

The most prominent resistance came from the youth with 'a growing number of scuffles between teenage gangs of Schlurfs and the Hitler Youth.... [The Schlurfs were] composed largely of working-class boys'.[30] Their numbers were increased by other disenfranchised young people, 'apprentices, armament workers..."some misfits" and cripples'.[31] They modelled loud suits, quiffs and arrogance, listening and dancing to jazz in bars with girls, or Schlurf Kittens, and 'they directed their hostility against the Hitler Youth, whose formations they ridiculed for compulsory drills, senseless discipline, and mindless conformity'.[32] Himmler ordered a clampdown, and the police attacked the Schlurfs in their bars and forcibly cut their hair. This did not deter their 'anti-social' activities and 'over the course of the years clashes between Schlurfs and Hitler Youth escalated sharply. There were rumbles in Wienar-Atzgerdorf, muggings in the Prater, and stone throwing attacks on various Hitler Youth neighbourhood quarters.'[33] They also smashed up a Hitler Youth dormitory and, despite the punitive measures against sexual liaisons, a Nazi reported that one women entertained several wayward youths at home where 'they make noise and howl, play the gramophone, dance or play music until two in the morning.... Mrs G [was] sitting stark naked on the toilet with the door wide open!'[34] In these small ways did people resist.

War fatigue, shortages, low wages and general dissatisfaction continued throughout the early 1940s. Anti-German sentiment was expressed at football matches in 'a series of soccer riots that culminated in a wild melee.... Young toughs stoned and pummelled Gauleiter Schirach's limousine, shattering its windows and slashing its tires,'[35] which was comparatively mild hooliganism given later UK standards. Over two thousand per month were arrested for a variety of offences, including 'insubordination, disruptive behaviour, or

---

30   Ibid., 195
31   Ibid.
32   Ibid., 199.
33   Ibid., 196.
34   Ibid.
35   Ibid., 189.

refusal to work'.[36] There was 'an upsurge of Communist violence in Salzburg and in railway yards in Styria and Carthinia',[37] and by 1943, 'there were "daily executions of ten to fifteen anti-Nazis" in Josefstadt'.[38] By 1944, communists, socialists, and moderate conservatives joined with O5, the resistance movement who, by the time the war was over, could claim 100,000 members. For others, an era of collective amnesia began.

The violence in Austria was not as prominent as in Germany; during the entire conflict between the left and the fascists, the attempted socialist uprising in 1934 and the subsequent failed Nazi coup, 567 people died—significantly less than in Germany. The far-right militia operated in an anti-working-class capacity, something that was repeated many times in many countries, and anti-fascists were moved towards militancy through provocation by the Heimwehr. The relatively small communist party, the moderation of the SD, the inherent conservatism of the Austrian people and the acceptance of an authoritarian government did not create the climate for militant anti-fascism. After the Anschluss, communists and more radical workers maintained propaganda work and communication with the outside world, in particular the American Office of Strategic Services (OSS). The Gestapo arrested many workers, who met uncertain though no-doubt horrific fates. That the Schlurfs dissented and physically attacked the Hitler Youth is reassuring. As the war progressed, ordinary Austrians, having faced hardship, shortages and external pressures, saw through the Nazi programme—but this in no way explains the barbarity of certain right-wing Austrians and their violent anti-Semitism.

---

36   Ibid., 205.
37   Ibid., 170.
38   Ibid., 188.

Germany: Beat the Fascists Wherever You Meet Them

Struggle, violence and war were at the centre of Nazi ideology and for years the Nazi storm troopers, the SA, had been engaged in a campaign of politically motivated street fighting which left hundreds dead and thousands injured during the final years of the Weimar Republic.

—Richard Bessel in *Life in the Third Reich*

On January 15, 1919, Rosa Luxemburg and Karl Liebknecht, the Spartacist leaders of the Berlin uprising, were taken from police custody, assaulted and murdered by the proto-fascist Freikorps. Their bodies were dumped in the Landwehr Canal near where the Bauhaus Archive and the museum to German anti-Nazi resistance now stand. Luxemburg and Liebknecht had split away from the reformist socialists (SPD), to lead the Spartakists and form the German Communist Party (KPD). The socialist Ebert, leader of the government coalition, was seen as being too weak by independent socialists, communists, and worker's and soldier's councils who were agitating for a revolution. Violence between the left and the Freikorps escalated. The Freikorps were a reactionary street force that mobilised against the growing rebellion, 'volunteer units raised by the old Army Command and paid by the Prussian War Ministry...[and] led by Imperial officers'.[1] Freikorps members were ex-soldiers nostalgic for the camaraderie of the trenches and angry over the 'stab in the back' by the politicians who had signed the armistice in 1918; they were also unemployed adventurists seeking excitement and a sense of certainty

1   A.J. Nicholls, *Weimar and the Rise of Hitler* (London: Macmillan, 1968), 23.

and belonging; and, as with the Italian fascist squads, Freikorps members were also violent criminals. Like the Italian squads, the Freikorps' lack of answerability was a cause of worry to watery-kneed conservatives. Political assassinations were to become a characteristic of this proto-fascist activity: Kurt Eisner, who had led the Munich uprising, was murdered in February 1919 by the Freikorps, as were the politicians Matthias Erzberger and Walter Rahtenhau, the ex-foreign minister. Nichols writes that 'most victims of such violence were men of the left. [Defence minister] Noske's forces freed Berlin from the fear of a Communist insurrection, but at the expense of working class unity'.[2] The police turned a blind eye and the courts were lenient when the subjects of the Freikorps enthusiasms were militant leftists, and few Freikorps faced the consequences: 'Attempted counter-revolution, political murder and libellous publications were often connived at in the courts because the judges thought the perpetrators more "patriotic".'[3]

Via the legal system, political pressure was exerted against militant workers whilst the murderers of Luxemburg and Liebknecht and leading figures of the Freikorps got away with lighter sentences: 'Yet thousands of workers who had been involved in the fights in the Ruhr and in Central Germany were sentenced to extremely long terms of imprisonment and hard labour'.[4]

Berlin was not the only city to witness reactionary violence: on 7th April 1919, revolutionaries in Munich proclaimed a Soviet Republic and organized a Red Army as a defence measure. However, on the symbolic 1st of May, the defence minister Noske sent in troops who brutally suppressed the Soviets and imprisoned and executed many revolutionaries without trial. Berlin and Munich were only two of the cities where working-class militancy faced state-sanctioned violence.

In 1919, the Freikorps continued with their 'punitive expeditions' against left militants, and thousands were kills in street battles. In Munich on May Day, 1919, workers fought pitched battles with

---

2   Ibid., 24.
3   Ibid., 47.
4   Evelyn Anderson, *Hammer or Anvil: The Story of the German Working Class Movement* (London: Victor Gollancz, 1945), 86.

soldiers: 'About 1,000 people were killed during the battle. Between 100 and 200 revolutionaries were murdered'.[5] In the Ruhr, workers armed themselves against proto-fascist militias and 'the Red Brigades drove the Free Corps and Reichswehr troops out of the district. A united front of all socialist parties and Free Trade Unions was formed'.[6] The mix of unity, organized workers, and militancy was seen as key in successful anti-fascist struggle. The Freikorps engaged in scab action against working-class organizations, and in 1921, when Berlin workers went on strike, they acted in a predictable manner: 'ultra-Right wing students, young engineers and former officers' formed into strike-breaking Technical Emergency Squads that were maintained and 'in later years [they were] often used to break the organized resistance of labour'.[7]

The association with gangster-like behaviour recurs throughout fascist history. Anderson states that the Freikorps were responsible for attacks on and murders of radical workers and 'were comparable to organized gangsterism in America, except they were much more dangerous'. They made public calls for the executions of prominent radicals on posters reading, 'Kill their leaders. Kill Liebknecht!'[8]

After Russia, Germany had the largest working class in the world, and Stephen J. Lee illustrates the left-wing power base in 1920 thusly: 'Challenges came in 1920 from rail and miner's strikes, mass demonstrations by the USPD [Independent Social Democrats] and uprisings in the Ruhr from a variety of groups ranging from workers' self-defence units, USPD activists, syndicalists and communists.'[9]

The SPD unions were well institutionalised in the factories and they had the advantage over the communists: the KPD had 300,000 members but 80–90 percent of them were unemployed so they lacked the syndicalist potential of the socialists—although the reformist nature of the SPD meant that the syndicalist approach of politically motivated strikes would be used infrequently. The KPD's forces

---

5   Ibid., 60.
6   Ibid., 74–75.
7   Ibid., 85.
8   Ibid., 53–4.
9   Stephen J. Lee, *The Weimar Republic* (London: Routledge, 1998), 52.

were best mobilised on the streets. Both the communists and fascists realised there was a potential force otherwise unengaged in the ranks of the jobless, and they both vied for members from there, organizing propaganda that dealt specifically with unemployment issues: 'the increasing competition between Nazis and Communists to woo those who were out of work led to severe clashes between both sets of activists in front of the unemployment offices'.[10] The KPD identified anger and dissatisfaction amidst the ranks of the unemployed and saw that the young were the worst-affected of all. The KPD recruited at the offices where the unemployed attended twice weekly with considerable success: 'A Red Help organization, special unemployment committees and the Revolutionary Trade Union Opposition (RGO) recruited large numbers'.[11]

In 1920, left-wing militancy increased and there was fear of a communist coup: 'A spontaneous strike broke out in the Ruhr in which Independent Social Democrats, anarcho-syndicalists and some supporters of the Majority Social Democrat Party were as important as the Communists. Arms were distributed and barricades erected'.[12] Again, the reformist SPD sent in forces to crush the rebellion (which would have a long-term effect on relations with KPD militants).

Despite moves to dissolve the Freikorps following the Munich uprising, the remaining groups who had not been assimilated into formal military structures like the Reichswehr still benefited from the protection of the reinstated Bavarian government. They began operating as Patriotic Leagues, and the army and police supplied weapons, ignoring the typical fascist gangsterism, and protected such murder gangs. The paralegal status of reactionary militias is a constant feature of fascism's spotty complexion, given to political thuggery and intimidation with the tacit (and not so tacit) support of the state. This was something that Hitler capitalised on, and in 1921, the SA squads were formed and specialised in intimidating

10 C.C.W. Szejnmann, *Nazism in Central Germany: The Brownshirts in 'Red' Saxony* (New York: Berghahn Publishers, 1999), 62.
11 Peter H. Merkl, *The Making of a Stormtrooper* (Princeton: Princeton University Press, 1980), 11.
12 Nicholls, *Weimar and the Rise of Hitler*, 72.

workers' demonstrations, in street violence and in the protection of fascist meetings. Ernst Rohm also bolstered the ranks of the SA with unreformed Freikorps and the disbanded Defence Leagues. Hitler needed to defend his activities against attacks from political opponents and he drew on 'comrades who had seen active service with [him;] others were young Party members' for security; he also believed that 'the best means of defence is to attack, and the reputation of our hall-guard squads stamped us as a political fighting force and not as a debating society'. The SA was used to attack the opposition members and smash up meetings, although they were not the only ones: in Munich in 1921, there was a mass battle as left-wing opposition attacked a Nazi meeting, 'which was built up into a Party legend'. The SA also continued Mussolini's tradition of violent censorship and targeted left-wing printing presses and newspapers. Like other fascist leaders, Hitler centralised violence within his ideology, as and when apposite, and the more public the better. This organized violence amplified the physical aspect of the Nazis along with their uniforms, marches, flags and tedious martial music on city streets.[13]

Militants clearly had to organize physical opposition in order to counter and defeat this concerted right-wing violence, so in 1923 the KPD organized the Proletarian Hundreds, which consisted of 'several hundred thousand men...ready for the next wave of revolution'.[14] SPD members also joined in 'the setting up of the Proletarian Hundreds in Saxony—these were unarmed contingents which were manned by SPD and KPD activists and were formed to defend Republican institutions against counter-revolutionary activities from the far right'.[15] The Proletarian Hundreds also 'disrupted conservative and nationalist celebrations', and on one occasion, 'more than 100 persons from Chemnitz disrupted the parade. Knife fights took place. One of the injured had to go to hospital'.[16] The Proletarian Hundreds were eventually outlawed.

---

13   Alan Bullock, *Hitler: A Study in Tyranny* (London: Penguin Books, 1962), 72–73.

14   Merkl, *The Making of a Stormtrooper*, 36.

15   Szejnmann, *Nazism in Central Germany*, 16.

16   Ibid., 154.

In 1923, the SA planned to attack the annual left-wing May Day demonstrations in Munich, partly as a publicity stunt: after all, what use is political violence if no one notices? The SA were armed with machine guns and rifles and this was meant to be more than the routine street fights that many were used to; it was to be a major statement of Hitler's intentions. However, they were routed by a small detachment of troops and police; so embarrassed was the future Fuhrer that he disappeared from sight for several months after it. After emerging from his self-imposed exile in November 1923, Hitler became the leader of the Kampfbund, a formation of Freikorps, Patriotic Leagues and assorted other violent groupuscules, which he then led into the middle of Munich in an attempted putsch. State forces in much smaller numbers rebuffed them again and they dispersed, only to be reorganized in greater numbers through Nazi mythmaking. Hitler fled the scene, leaving several of his comrades dead on the paving stones.

Anti-Fascist Action

> But among the dead were people from the Reichsbanner as well as
> people of ours,
> So we said to the comrades of the SPD:
> Are we to stand by while they murder our comrades?
> Fight alongside us in the Anti-Fascist Front!
> —Bertolt Brecht, 'When the Fascists Keep Getting Stronger'

Anti-fascist activity was widespread and violent from the start of the Republic. In 1923, fascists 'faced persistent pressure from the workers' movement who searched suspects for weapons and disrupted or broke up Nazi meetings'.[17] In the town of Werdau, 'Communists forced their way' into a Nazi meeting and 'beat up the National Socialists with clubs and sticks'.[18] In Zschopau, in 1930, a Nazi meeting attracted 550 attendees, four hundred of whom were anti-fascists. As tensions increased, 'the Communists demanded to stay in the hall. At this moment a beer glass flew from the middle of the hall to the stage where

17   Ibid., 27.
18   Ibid.

the stewards were. A few Stormtroopers grabbed chairs to use them as protection against projectiles. When the brawl started, both sides used chairs, part of chairs, beer glasses, coffee cups, etc. to beat or throw'. The room and many participants ended much the worse for wear.[19]

The principle anti-fascist groups were Roter Frontkämpferbund (RFB, Red Front Fighters), AJG (Anti-Fascist Youth Guards), the Fighting Leagues and Anti-Fascist Action (AFA), all operating in a militant capacity, all aligned with the KPD. The Proletarian Hundreds had been operating since 1923. These groups also worked as propaganda units. The Brownshirts of the SA were also built up, and they increased their policy of encroachment in 'Red' areas. In May 1924, the Nazis staged a demonstration in Halle, and despite the Proletarian Hundreds and Red Front Fighters being banned, communist demonstrators violently engaged with the police, leading to several fatalities and the KPD 'calling on the workers to seek more confrontations with "the fascists".'[20] In a show of strength, the KPD could also mobilise between '20,000 and 40,000 uniformed RFB members' dressed in 'green Russian shirts, jackboots, army belts, and caps with the red star'.[21]

The youth wing, Young Red Front (YRF), could mobilise an equal amount and were well-known for their over-enthusiastic approach regarding both cops and fascists during 'street patrols.' There was also a 'straight-edge' aspect to the YRF, with a ban on cinema, drinking, smoking and pornography. According to Merkl,

> The Communists needed a new and more centralized paramilitary organization that could protect their rallies and speakers, demonstrate in the streets, engage in canvassing and propaganda during elections, and, most of all, stand its ground against the paramilitary shock troops of the right.[22]

In 1924, realising the escalation of paramilitary organizations

---

19   Ibid., 269.
20   Merkl, *The Making of a Stormtrooper*, 53.
21   Ibid., 55.
22   Ibid., 52.

on both sides, the SPD organized the Reichsbanner, a physical defence force that recruited members from outside the SPD and grew to a million strong. The Reichsbanner proved to be an effective organization but one whose fortunes varied and were dependent on the political motives of the SPD of the time. By 1928, however, the Reichsbanner had gained a sense of militancy and 'prepared to wage a much more vigorous battle against Hitler's SA'.[23] And they needed to.

The Reichsbanner 'was the largest paramilitary army of its time, with between 1.5 and 3.5 million members' and was set up initially to protect the Republic, as the SPD government could not trust the Reichswehr, the regular army, which was rife with reactionary and conservative forces.[24] As things became more violent, the Reichsbanner had to raise their game and 'organized an elite Protective Formation (Schufo), which could stand up to the Stormtroopers in street fighting and meeting-hall battles', although they remained unarmed.[25] The tone of the SPD's Iron Front propaganda also shifted focus from defending the Republic to the 'defense of working class interests.'[26]

Red Berlin

> All through our red Berlin the Nazis strutted, in fours and fives,
> In their new uniforms, murdering
> Our comrades.
>
> —Bertolt Brecht, 'When the Fascists Keep Getting Stronger'

Not all towns succumbed to Nazi provocation or their attempts to organize: 'in 1926, the Nazis in Freiburg admitted that their SA was not able to protect two local party meetings.... Instead the SA was beaten up twice on these occasions by Marxist followers.'[27] The Nazis found it hard to make inroads into the working-class areas that were

---

23   Nicholls, *Weimar and the Rise of Hitler*, 150.
24   Merkl, *The Making of a Stormtrooper*, 49.
25   Ibid., 76.
26   Ibid., 78.
27   Szejnmann, *Nazism in Central Germany*, 109.

predominantly aligned to left-wing parties. In 'Red' Saxony in Central Germany, militant anti-fascism was a considerable force up until 1934. A typical provocation occurred when Nazi fanatic Joseph Goebbels held a meeting in a KPD beer hall in Wedding, which led to fighting in the streets in early 1927. Shortly after, on a train, a brawl erupted between SA and RFB men which destroyed the carriage and led to confrontations throughout the night. The SA suffered a temporary ban.

Control of the Streets

> In and around Leipzig...the clashes were at their most severe and took the heaviest toll of human life.
>
> —C.W.W. Szejnmann in *Nazism in Central Germany*

Nazis faced violent opposition when trying to organize activities in 'Red' Leipzig, which 'tended to turn into wild brawls between the SA and Marxist supporters and the Nazis had to leave again, highly frustrated'.[28] Facing either well-organized or violent opposition in the workplaces, the Nazis looked to 'the home front' in their recruiting drives: 'In places where they faced overwhelming resistance they often avoided outright confrontation. As parades or public meetings in the west of Leipzig only fuelled tough resistance from Marxist activists, they preferred to be active "beneath the surface"'.[29] Fascists organized a surprise march through Plauen, which meant that the left-wing residents 'could not demonstrate their skill in building street barricades and limited themselves to throwing beer bottles...[and] the usual shouting of "Red Front!" and "Down! Down! Down!"'[30] Even as Hitler edged closer to power, working-class resistance remained strong with one organizer reporting,

> The fight in our district is incredibly hard. Marxism defends it as its rightful domain. SA members who walk home alone are attacked; party members, as soon as they are known as such, are

28 Ibid., 114.
29 Ibid., 116.
30 Ibid., 115.

watched every step they make; their family members are hounded, even children suffer due to the terror of the red comrades; business people are boycotted...the pack does not even shrink from attacks in apartments.[31]

On the May Day demonstrations in Wedding in 1928, the SDP police chief demanded that KPD demonstrators disperse; this led to pitched battles and several days of rioting, leaving twenty-five people dead and 160 seriously injured. The RFB were banned. As with most proscribed militant organizations, they simply reformed under another name but also lost significant membership numbers. Following May Day 1928, the SA attempted to march through Wedding and were met with fury. The police stepped in at the last moment to prevent the leftists from attacking the interlopers. Merkl describes the repercussions thus:

> There followed other clashes, such as a half-hour street battle involving 100 to 150 Red Fronters near their Sturmlokales Volksgarten and two trucks of SA returning from a campaign in small towns outside Berlin. Pavement stones, beer steins, fence poles, garden furniture, and flag poles served both sides until the Volksgarten was totally demolished, with beer gushing from the smashed counter.[32]

The Nazis attempted to march through Neukoln in a provocative gesture. The workers reacted with violence, leaving the fascists with serious injuries. Although they were initially repulsed, it was only the beginning of a Nazi incursion into 'Red' territory, and in 1928, the SA started setting up the first Sturmlokales, public bars or meeting places in the area. Communists responded by occupying Nazi meeting halls, which caused the predictable battles and also replicated the intrusion tactics of the Nazis: 'Three times in one week, they tried to storm the Treptow Sturmlokale of the SA, the second time allegedly with 180 men of the elite Liebknecht Hundreds, and under police protection.

31   Ibid.
32   Merkl, *The Making of a Stormtrooper*, 168.

The third time the RFB completely destroyed the SA hangout.'[33]

On May Day in 1929, the KPD staged an illegal demonstration, which was attacked by baton-wielding riot police. Hundreds of arrests and many beatings were reported as the police imposed quasi-martial law. Thirty people were killed. The KPD called a general strike for the following day and, in response to this, the RFB, the AJG youth wing, and the newspaper were banned. The KPD viewed this outrage as a 'confrontation between Social Democrat police and Communist workers'.[34] KPD resentment of the socialists was also guided by the rapidly changing and opportunistic foreign policy objectives of Stalin, which lay behind the increased use of the 'social fascist' insult, and that culminated in the disastrous ultra-left 'third period' strategy, where the KPD saw Social Democracy as no different from the Nazis.

By 1929, KPD leader Ernst Thaelmann and others had increased recruitment amongst the unemployed at the labour exchanges where thousands gathered every day, despite the reservation of the Moscow-dominated Communist International. The SPD was frequently disparaging about the KPD, referring to their 'Bolshevism, the militarism of the loafers', and pointing out the fact that 80–90 percent of the communists were unemployed and that the party was not as politically effective in the workplace as the SPD was.[35] The KPD was increasingly competing with the Nazis who, being better funded, could offer temporary work for the unemployed. The KPD organized 'proletarian shopping trips', where unemployed workers would raid stores and take goods *gratis*. There was some discussion over how much was being taken and of what kind and if this was a political or a more dubious act: Walter Ulbricht, later leading figure of the DDR and Stalinist henchman in Spain, described these missions, quaintly, as 'self-help'.

Initially, for the most part, the KPD was involved in defensive

33   Ibid., 169.
34   Eve Rosenhaft, *Beating the Fascists?: The German Communists and Political Violence, 1929–1933* (Cambridge: Cambridge University Press, 2008), 35.
35   John Hiden, *Republican and Fascist Germany: Themes and Variations in the History of Weimar and the Third Reich, 1918–1945* (London: Longman, 1996), 63.

rather than offensive violence but soon realised that 'pre-emptive strikes' could be politically effective. Defection to the Nazis was not looked upon lightly, and KPD militants often identified transgressors for 'special treatment'. The violence was not exclusively left/right but also factional. In Leipzig in 1930, a 1,500-strong meeting of the SAJ (Socialist Working Class Youth) was disrupted by two hundred KPD militants. The SPD was also losing members who defected to the KPD, the SAP (Socialist Workers Party) or the Nazis. Not only were the political organizations competing for members, but also 'the KPD, NSDAP and the Reichsbanner were competing against each other regarding party publicity and propaganda activities. Fighting parades, red days, propaganda rallies...minor incidents often led to clashes'.[36] Not all areas were as divided: in Auerbach 'in contrast to most other places, Social Democrats and Communists often cooperated to secure a socialist majority in the town council or to fight the growing threat of the Nazis'.[37]

By 1930, both the KPD and Nazis realised that the violence could have a negative impact on electoral returns (although it certainly helped recruitment on the streets). The KPD leadership argued for the cessation of violence between political gangs in the street and was uneasy over socialist/communist alliances engaged in attacks on political opponents at the local level rather than consolidated mass action. The militants felt confident that they could beat the fascists; the youth wing sided with the militants as leadership figures started agitating for the closure of the fighting bodies. Dismantling the militias would leave individuals vulnerable to fascist violence in the streets, but the leadership wanted to rein in any autonomous activities that these non-partisan groups may be carrying out. The KPD eventually reorganized the fighting groups to consolidate militants under a different name but to operate in a similar capacity as before.

In the 1930 election, the KPD received 13.1 percent of the vote and the SPD 24.5 percent, so a potential anti-fascist vote was 37.6 percent in total, but the ideological schisms between the two left-wing

---

36   Szejnmann, *Nazism in Central Germany*, 54.
37   Ibid., 108.

parties were deep and savage.[38] For some, the fragmentation amongst the left was a defining factor in their defeat: 'Any realistic chance of winning a physical confrontation with Nazism was destroyed by the lack of a united front on the left, and the fact that the overwhelming majority of the Social Democrats stuck to legal means and tried to avoid any confrontation on the streets.'[39]

By 1931, the SA had 300,000 uniformed members ready to confront anti-fascist opponents on the streets. The Reichsbanner, representatives of the governing party, began to liaise with police in order to prevent a Nazi coup. In the long term, although there were many militants in the Reichsbanner, it was subject to political machinations out of its control and was neither properly trained nor properly armed. By 1931, the unions had also organized their muscle as the 'Hammerschaften, strong-fisted teams of workers in the major plants who would enforce a general strike against management resistance or Communist interference if necessary'.[40]

Protection of meetings and demonstrations was paramount and the use of firearms became an issue following the May Day violence. In 1931, a Comintern handbook recommended

> knives, brass knuckles, oil-soaked rags, axes, bricks, boiling water to pour on the police-beasts raging in the streets of the workers' quarters, simple hand-grenades made of dynamite, to emphasise only the most primitive of the infinite and ubiquitous possibilities of arming the proletariat.[41]

Physical resistance and militant street activity was crucial: political dialogue was futile, as evidenced by the fateful meeting when Ulbricht confronted Goebbels on the platform of a Berlin meeting in 1931, which rapidly descended into chaos and 'which really served to kick off a gigantic meeting-hall battle that three hundred policemen

---

38   Detlev J.K. Peukert, *Inside Nazi Germany: Conformity, Opposition, and Racism in Everyday Life* (London: Penguin, 1987), 101.
39   Szejnmann, *Nazism in Central Germany*, 82.
40   Merkl, *The Making of a Stormtrooper*, 81.
41   Rosenhaft, *Beating the Fascists?*, 40.

were unable to stop'.[42] In the Landtag, the regional parliament, fighting broke out between KPD and NSDAP members and, with superior numbers, the Nazis came out best. Anti-Fascist Action was launched shortly after this with the intention of uniting socialist and communist militants in self-defence of working-class communities, but it was to prove an uphill struggle. Violence increased and according to Szejnmann it was

> a crucial part of Nazi, but also of Communist, propaganda… after 1929 the amount of violence between political opponents (particularly between Nazis and Communists), and clashes between demonstrators and police (mainly with Communists) clearly increased. The growing use of knives and firearms made the nature of these fights more and more brutal: twelve demonstrators and two policemen lost their lives in confrontations in northwest Saxony in 1930 and five people died in clashes between political opponents in…1931 alone.[43]

Control of the streets has always been central to fascist strategy, and the SA's slogan was 'Possession of the streets is the key to power in the State'. As the 1930s began, 'the Communists marched in formation singing down the streets, broke up rival political meetings, beat up opponents, and raided each other's "territory"'.[44] As did the Nazis. The violence had intensified beyond control: 'Ordinary brawls had given way to murderous attacks. Knives, blackjacks, and revolvers had replaced political arguments. Terror was rampant'.[45]

In the early 1930s, an era of mass uncertainty and high unemployment, the SA offered potential recruits violent excitement, food, a uniform and even a place to stay in the 'Brown House' headquarters. For a few marks, a potential fascist Stormtrooper 'could sleep and eat in these hostels, which varied widely…. Some of the largest…housed

---

42   Ibid., 173.
43   Szejnmann, *Nazism in Central Germany*, 83.
44   Alan Bullock, *Hitler: A Study in Tyranny* (London: Penguin, 1962), 167–68.
45   Merkl, *The Making of a Stormtrooper*, 95.

250 SA men', and many were paid for by 'sympathetic businessmen'. A good place for total indoctrination and a free sandwich:

> Unemployed young males were put up in dormitories (SA Heime), where they received shelter and food in exchange for their full-time services as marchers and fighters for the brown cause.[46]

When the SA was suppressed in 1932, many ended up homeless. As usual, the violence was an attraction for many, and it was in the interests of both the KPD and NSDAP to maintain public visibility and, most of all, street victories to maintain and boost membership. For Merkl, '[The] street battles of the S.A., the monster rallies with Nazi speakers, and the meeting-hall battles of the Stormtroopers… uniforms, disciplined marching, flags, and quasi-military behaviour may have been as attractive as witnessing the violent encounters with Communists and the Reichsbanner'.[47]

The hard core of SA membership 'consisted of unemployed men who lived in SA messes and barracks'.[48] The Nazis continued to set up 'Sturmlokales' in 'Red areas', which were 'part dormitory, part soup kitchen, part guardhouse'.[49] The Nazis also started to intrude on 'Red pubs', which pushed the KPD's unemployed street fighters out due to their low or no income. Saturation patronage by the Nazis meant that they could take over a tavern and, through economic superiority, guarantee the consumption of so many barrels of beer a week. The owners where unlikely to refuse increased revenue in such dire times, and thus the SA began to take over more venues, whilst the owner could either close in protest or accept the new clientele and their cash.

During the run-up to the election in 1930, street fighting and political agitation increased significantly:

> Political mobilization frequently exploded into violence,

---

46   Ibid., 12.
47   Ibid., 250.
48   Bullock, *Hitler*, 242.
49   Hiden, *Republican and Fascist Germany*, 68.

especially between Nazis and Communists. In late September 1930 there was a typical clash between both sides in Eibenstock: a local Nazi leader had called on his followers to demonstrate against Communist terror. When the 150 Nazis who had turned up met an even larger group of Communists who came marching down the street, a brutal fight developed with stones and picket fences. In the end, there were many injured and a few seriously wounded.[50]

Smashing up meetings, storming opponents' pubs, and street brawling were daily occurrences: in 1930 alone there were 23,946 demonstrations, which drew in 25 million people: 'There was also a dramatic increase in violent incidents: there were 351 reported clashes and verbal abuses in Leipzig alone between 1 August and 20 November, 1932'.[51] The scale of activity and associated violence is difficult to imagine: Merkl puts the body count in the hundreds between 1923 and 1933, with many others seriously injured. More specialised and expertly targeted violence was required and hit squads were formed and were involved in activities outside their local areas to avoid identification:

> The Stormtroopers were combat units who aimed at defeating their opponents in street battles.... The Communist hardcore reacted to this challenge by taking the counter-offensive with their slogan, 'Beat the fascists wherever you meet them'.

The SA had grown to over 400,000 members: 'many hundreds of thousands of SA and SS men every day have to mount on their lorries, protect meetings, undertake marches, sacrifice themselves night after night'.[52] Complete control over the SA was something Hitler coveted, and splits amongst the Nazi hierarchy over their function intensified: Hitler, as supreme leader, ordered the SA to avoid street fighting and was keen to stay inside the law in order to avoid being

50 Szejnmann, *Nazism in Central Germany*, 53.
51 Ibid., 32.
52 Bullock, *Hitler*, 199.

discredited prior to securing political victory. No doubt wealthy sponsors would be getting nervous over continuous political brawling and murder. Given this restriction, the SA, organized as a violent political force, laid mainly idle and without the relief of exciting confrontation. In September 1930, the restless SA smashed their Berlin headquarters over grievances, including pay and political direction, which led Hitler to personally appease their desire for violent action. A few months later it happened again. When the government finally moved in 1931 and banned private armies, Hitler forced the SA to comply in accordance with his new 'legal' stance. This was not to last and the ban was lifted again in 1932, which 'caused an immediate and alarming upsurge in violence. Murderous encounters took place, especially between Nazis and Communists. Deaths were frequent'.[53] The record is appalling: the police reported 461 political riots in six weeks with over eighty people killed and many more seriously injured. In 1932, 'pitched battles took place on Sunday 10 July in which eighteen people were killed. The next Sunday, the 17th, saw the worst riot of the summer, at Altona, near "Red" Hamburg, where the Nazis under police escort staged a march through the working class districts of the town and were met by a fusillade of shots from the roofs and the windows'.[54] Nineteen people died and many were seriously wounded. Never being one to miss an opportunity to make propaganda, Goebbels staged large and public funerals of the Nazis killed by anti-fascist actions, using the usual mix of sacrifice and martyrdom to stir his followers' patriotic blood.

The police operating against the fascists was a relative rarity as they were naturally more sympathetic to the authoritarian Nazis and viewed the left as their main threat, with one noting 'that the KPD was prepared and determined to use violence right from the start in order to prevent the infiltration of fascists into working-class districts'.[55] Not only that, but 'large sections of the police sympathised with their cause, the Nazis wore down Marxist followers in a brutal

---

53 Nicholls, *Weimar and the Rise of Hitler*, 161.
54 Bullock, *Hitler*, 214.
55 Szejnmann, *Nazism in Central Germany*, 82.

battle for control of the streets by the end of 1931'.[56]

In 1932, despite the changing face of public support for fascism, anti-fascists retained their militancy: 'Political opponents clashed more frequently too, particularly in strongholds of the KPD and SPD where Nazis faced stiff resistance. For instance, two Nazis were seriously wounded by activists of the Reichsbanner and KPD in Lossnitz, a Marxist bastion'.[57] When Nazis tried to march through Red Altona in July 1932, the KPD fired on them, causing an armed police response. The KPD built barricades and the violence ended with eighteen dead, sixty-eight injured and 150 arrested. Later in July, a newspaper reported a clash between KPD and Nazis, which left 'one of the SA men stabbed to death; another seriously injured'.[58] The same paper reported SA men invading an SPD meeting, which turned into a mass brawl as the police completely lost control. In 1932, violence escalated and newspapers reported 'daily, and even nightly clashes, brawls, assaults, and shootings amongst the huge private armies that has been assembled'.[59] The KPD's hatred of the Nazis was exacerbated by those supporters who had been part of the Freikorps and violently put down workers' organizations. The KPD had been continually involved in savage and fatal brawls with these fascists for over a decade and 'armed raids of Nazi formations on political meetings of opponents or on workers' settlements had become an almost daily occurrence.'[60]

In Berlin in 1933, KPD and NSDAP continued the attacks on each other's meeting places and pubs. Guns were increasingly used with attendant fatalities. This was now a coordinated policy of 'mass terror' rather than individual terror, ordered by the KPD leadership and responded to in kind by the Nazis. It was a deliberate and violent escalation in response to the failure of communist 'mass action' and strikes to make a significant political impact. Factory agitation increased, and workers mobilised and initiated a united front policy

57 Ibid., 57.
58 Merkl, *The Making of a Stormtrooper*, 22.
59 Ibid., 26.
60 Anderson, *Hammer or Anvil*, 148.

with the SPD, formerly 'social fascists'.

As Hitler was aware, these outbreaks of violent disorder and the expression of more extreme sentiments were doing little to assure the bourgeoisie electorate of Nazi respectability or their suitability to govern. Incidents like that of five SA members kicking a communist miner to death in front of his mother were neither endearing nor placatory. The five were initially sentenced to death although this was later commuted to life imprisonment. Despite their bid for respectability and Hitler's public entreaties, the Nazis were still openly provocative and sought to control their turf through violent means. In January 1933, they demonstrated outside Berlin's communist headquarters with Goebbels saying, 'We shall stake everything on one throw to win back the streets of Berlin.'[61] Again, protected by armed police, several thousand fascists held a march through Berlin which culminated in a speech by Hitler. The communists had been banned from counter-demonstrating.

Of all the European street confrontations between anti-fascists and their opponents, the Germans counted the most fatalities and, apart from the state-sanctioned violence of Mussolini's fascists, made places like the UK seem very modest in their affairs. Hundreds of deaths were recorded and large-scale street clashes were a regular occurrence. Between 1925 and 1933 there were hundreds of violent confrontations between left-wing militants, Nazis and the police, with most occurring in Berlin. By the end of 1933, Hitler became chancellor.

1933 & Beyond

After Hitler seized power in 1933, the police and SA began to seal off workers' strongholds and carry out mass arrests and house searches for KPD members, weapons and propaganda. When KPD leader August Saihof's house was searched, a gun and bullets, as well as KPD propaganda 'of a highly treasonable nature and Bolshevist content' were found.[62] This meant immediate detention. It became

---

61   Bullock, *Hitler*, 245.
62   Martyn Housden, *Resistance and Conformity in the Third Reich* (London: Routledge, 1997), 26.

increasingly difficult and dangerous for anti-fascists to operate. Once arrested, they could hardly expect tea and sympathy, and many died under torture, which was apparently only used selectively; 'Under the circumstances, the sharpened interrogation may be applied only against Communists, Marxists, members of the Bible Research Sect, saboteurs, terrorists, members of the resistance movement, parachute agents, asocial persons, Polish or Soviet prisoners who refuse to work or idlers'.[63] This list doesn't leave many out.

By 1935, fourteen thousand communists were in confinement with many more to follow: there were few alternatives to arbitrary arrest apart from fleeing and going into hiding. By 1945, between 25,000 and 30,000 KPD members had either died in the camps or been murdered or executed. The paramilitary nature of the state was enforced by the SA, SS and the regular police. The violence and suppression meted out towards the radical left (KPD, USPD) was soon focussed on moderate socialist organizations and their assets, such as property and printing presses, which were seized by the Nazis. Meetings were forbidden and the Reichsbanner was forced to disband. All political opposition was made illegal, co-operatives and clubs were outlawed, newspapers were banned, and mass repression began. The SA had been sitting on their truncheons for some time, having been bound by Hitler's bid for legality, but now they could wreak havoc on opponents, real or imagined. The SA had set up improvised concentration camps and many anti-fascists were abducted, beaten and murdered with the usual fascist mix of sadism and criminality: 'In Berlin's Columbia cinema, in Stettin's Vulkan docks, and in countless other places enemies were incarcerated and tortured in a microcosm of the hell that was to come'.[64] This in addition to the setting up of 'legal' concentration camps and the activities of the Gestapo (which, according to Eatwell, was set up by leading Nazi Hermann Goering to monitor his rival's activities). The Nazi strategy legitimised institutional violence and the mass arrests of left-wingers (which led to torture and incarceration in 1933) was overlooked by many voters as it was represented as a determined

63   Ibid., 8.
64   Roger Eatwell, *Fascism: A History* (London: Chatto and Windus, 1995), 111.

response to republicanism and the Red Menace.

Local fascists sought revenge on militant anti-fascists who had beaten them from the streets previously. Guilty by association, attacks on families and violent reactions were frequent:

> These planned raids, together with threats, insults, beatings and arbitrary arrests, and the spontaneous acts of vengeance and terrorist onslaughts carried out by local SA groups which set up their own 'private' concentration camps, created an atmosphere of insecurity and helplessness even in working class strongholds.[65]

According to Szejnmann, 'The persecution of Marxists was particularly ruthless in Saxony: more than one sixth of all concentration camps were on Saxon soil in 1933.'[66]

Shortly after Hitler assumed power, communists organized demonstrations. In Breslau, a general strike was ordered but the SA occupied the muster point and, together with the police, attacked the strikers: 'the communists scattered, some running up nearby streets and smashing windows of shops selling Nazi uniforms'.[67] One communist was killed and subsequent demonstrations were banned. Continued sporadic resistance was evident: shortly after the riot in Breslau, militants fired on the SA from a trade union headquarters, which led to further violence against workers' organizations.

With the KPD, USPD, SPD, and working-class organizations drastically suppressed, supporters of the left grew demoralised. Remarkably, physical opposition still remained in places:

> Approximately 2,000 members of the Kampfstaffeln (Fighting Units) in Leipzig—an SPD organization which had been set up to combat the Nazis by violent means—were prepared to occupy streets and public buildings. After the March 1933 elections, however, they waited in vain for three days for a signal to strike

65   Peukert, *Inside Nazi Germany*, 104.
66   Szejnmann, *Nazism in Central Germany*, 22.
67   Richard Bessel, ed., *Life in the Third Reich* (Oxford: Oxford University Press, 1987), 2.

because their party leadership had decided against the use of violence.[68]

Organization became ever difficult as the arrests increased. Although the Nazis systematically destroyed all established working-class organizations, they remained concerned that, as a class, workers benefited least from fascism whilst the regime entirely depended on their output in order to maintain itself. According to Tim Mason in *Nazis, Fascism and the Working Class*, 'it is not wholly surprising that the regime should have enjoyed the active or passive consent of most sections of the middle class and of the power elites,' whereas 'the only tangible benefit for the working class was the increase in employment'—which after years of uncertainty and unemployment was no doubt welcome. Whilst a small percentage of workers did benefit, the vast majority were just able to manage. Increasing rearmament depended on consistent production, and Hitler needed the workers onside. However, work itself had transformed from 'a social activity into a political duty' and became ideological— as well as alienated—labour supporting a system that consistently disenfranchised those who maintained it.[69]

Fascist gangsterism and opportunism was not far behind with many chancers scrambling for positions and seeking influence in the new infrastructures. Nazi purges were carried out: many liberals and leftists were removed from positions of office; cultural and educational institutions, such as the Bauhaus, were closed; and fascist sycophants were all eager to profit from the new Germany. Members of the SA, some of whom had been around since the days of the Freikorps, also sought their rewards, knowing they had a potent militia of nearly three million at their disposal. However, they were resistant to being assimilated into the hierarchy of the regular military, which would rob them of their positions of power. This was not a satisfactory situation for Hitler who now wanted rid of the SA and 'the "old fighters" who had been useful enough for

---

68   Szejnmann, *Nazism in Central Germany*, 123–124.
69   Timothy Mason, *Nazis, Fascism and the Working Class* (Cambridge: Cambridge University Press, 1996), 232–233.

street brawling, but for whom the party had no further use.'[70] On the night of 30th June 1934, the leadership of the SA were assassinated in the Night of the Long Knives, leaving the way clear for the black-shirted SS.

Resistance

> Socialists and communists did maintain a clandestine resistance, and though their acts of sabotage achieved little, the latter did develop an effective espionage system.
>
> —Stanley G. Payne in *A History of Fascism 1914–45*

Given the severe duress under which anti-fascists operated, much activity was concerned with either secretive propaganda distribution or a limited strategy of sabotage, opportunist or otherwise, in the factories. Spies in the workplace and the union hierarchy meant that organization became increasingly difficult, but individual acts of resistance continued. Many people expressed their dissent through apathy at work, slow production, sick leave and absenteeism.

Rote Kapelle (Red Chapel) activists were active in passing information to the Russians and, although for a time it was relatively successful, the group was betrayed by a Russian contact, leading to the execution of seventy-eight anti-fascists. It was not unknown for communists to infiltrate the Gestapo, but the Gestapo more successfully infiltrated the communists and their secret organizations, which led to more arrests and executions. Many militants joined the resistance, and those who did not or could not, according to Detley J.K. Peukert, 'kept an attitude of sullen refusal which on many cases led to positive acts of opposition'. Peukert also states that three kinds of resistance developed in the early years of Nazi domination: 'resistance in order to preserve traditions, opinions and cohesion (informal discussion groups, camouflaged clubs and associations); resistance in order to devise plans for a post-fascist democratic state; and resistance in the sense of immediate action…(strike and sabotage)'.[71]

Adam Wolfram was a salesman who kept in contact with trade

---

70   Bullock, *Hitler*, 286.
71   Peukert, *Inside Nazi Germany*, 118–120.

unionists and socialists on his travels, collecting and passing on intelligence, a job that was not without danger:

> Side by side with this there were also active resistance groups which, at great risk to themselves, distributed information, leaflets and newspapers among the population. Unfortunately, Gestapo spies managed to track down these groups, round up the participants, torture them and send them to prisons and concentration camps.[72]

Political opponents were not only concentrated in the camps: forced labour and prisoners of war faced unimagined brutality, and punishments were carried out for even the most minor infraction. One unfortunate was caught with ten tins of boot polish whilst others were caught carrying 15 kg of venison and a bag of rabbit fur.[73] Others resisted physically: one Russian POW was caught 'urging the women workers to work more slowly' and, when reprimanded, the fascist lackey said the POW became 'abusive and threatened him with his fists…[and] he jumped at me and threw me to the ground.'[74] This unknown worker was charged with sabotage, threatening behaviour, physical assault and undermining the guard's authority. His fate is unknown but it is not hard to guess. German workers were also known to defend foreign workers: at the Duisburg colliery a worker defended a Russian prisoner from harassment by an overseer: '[he] turned on the foreman and defended the POW in a manner such as to encourage the latter to strike the foreman on the head with his lamp…. [He] received a gaping wound on the face which has required stitches.'[75] The German miner had already spent time in a concentration camp and when reprimanded, boldly stated that he would carry on intervening. These were small acts of resistance but remarkable given the possible consequences.

Far be it from militant anti-fascists to take succour in the words

---

72   Ibid., 121.
73   Ibid., 131–132.
74   Ibid., 141.
75   Ibid., 142.

of a former CIA director, but Allen Welsh Dulles supplied information on allied relations to anti-fascists both in exile and within Nazi
Germany. Exiled socialists worked with Allied intelligence in addition to supplying propaganda, advice and money to their comrades:
SPD, KPD, and other socialist militants maintained links with those
still under the Nazi regime. One striking example was the charismatic
Carlo Merendorff, a journalist who 'studied, wrote, worked, laughed,
slaved, fought, drank and loved through many a German landscape
and was viewed by the fascists as a dangerous influence'.[76] He spent
between 1935 and 1937 in a concentration camp, but on his release
continued his subversive activities before being killed in an air raid in
1941. Merendorff worked with Theodor Haubach, who co-founded
of the Reichsbanner, the socialist militia who had once 'pledged to
uphold the Weimar constitution and defend the government against
both communists and Nazis'. Merendorff and Haubach had agitated
for a united front with syndicalists to oppose the Nazis.[77]

Informal networks continued even if party organizations were
severely compromised by arrests and informants. However unfortunate, a funeral could become the site of resistance and a show of
solidarity for anti-fascists: 1,200 showed up in solidarity at the funeral of a prominent member of the SPD who had died after release
from a concentration camp. Adam Schaeffer had been imprisoned
for political reasons and died in Dachau after attacking an SS guard.
He was allegedly shot, although rumours grew that he had been
beaten to death, hence the closed casket. Eight hundred people
turned up at the funeral, mainly SPD and KPD members and sympathisers. Minor acts of resistance and sabotage affected production:
the Albert Baum Group had thirty-two members, many of them
KPD, who campaigned over work conditions, spread propaganda,
and created informal networks. They had even disguised themselves
in stolen Gestapo uniforms in order to confiscate items from the
Berlin homes of the rich. Together with other Jewish anti-fascists,
they destroyed one of Goebbels's propaganda exhibits. Baum and

76   Allen Welsh Dulles, *Germany's Underground: The Anti-Nazi Resistance*
      (New York: Da Capo Press, 2000), 104.
77   Ibid.

others were later arrested, and although Baum was tortured, he never revealed who his accomplices were. Although Mason concedes that many acts of resistance did take place', he also asks why did it not take place on a larger scale. Workers often enough displayed their lack of enthusiasm for the mass demonstrations of the Third Reich, but they never translated a May Day assembly into a street battle.[78] Local circumstances, degrees of solidarity, organization, and opportunism were factors in resistance, but there was also the mitigating factor of terror, the fear of what may happen based on threats, and the knowledge of what had happened to other dissenters and their families. This fear became a pre-emptive tool and enforced compliancy to a regime that gave few concessions to the working class. Demoralization, disorganization and dread became an effective triumvirate to suppress rebellion.

In her autobiography *One Life Is Not Enough*, Lore Wolf recounts her life as a member of the KPD resistance: 'I have been called "the White Raven of the Communists". As a resistance fighter and a refugee I—like many others—always stood with one foot in prison. Twenty times I was caught, nineteen times I got away.'[79]

After 1933:

> Red Aid of Germany was the organization of the oppressed. It cared for the dependents of the politically persecuted and the prisoners, it carried out solidarity actions for the suffering working-class, it agitated, made propaganda and spread information by means of leaflets and illegal newspapers.[80]

They printed thousands of clandestine newspapers per month and 'often a single copy went through half the factory—each of the readers contributing some money'.[81] They could be caught any time with the papers or be informed on and, although only simple

---

78 Mason, *Nazis, Fascism and the Working Class*, 234.
79 Lore Wolf, *One Life is Not Enough: A German Woman's Antifascist Fight* (Newcastle: People's Publishers, 1982), 7
80 Ibid., 24.
81 Ibid., 27.

propaganda, they could be subjected to the same punishment as for any other anti-fascist activity: arrest, torture, murder or starvation in a camp. Producing the leaflets was difficult, and paper was bought in many different shops to avoid suspicion. Some were passed on more secretively. In Wolf's words, 'there was a tobacco shop near the main station where we could also store brochures and other materials. Close co-operators who bought their cigarettes there collected the texts in small packs and passed them on to trusted colleagues.'[82]

In 1934, the police called for 'ruthless suppression of the intense Communist activity promoting propaganda', the Gestapo warned that the Red Front Line Fighters were reorganizing, and Gestapo goon Reynard Heydrich demanded 'particular attention to the efforts of Red Aid'.[83] The group was ultimately betrayed, and Wolf fled to France and then to Switzerland where she was arrested and deported. Red Aid continued in exile, helping homeless anti-fascist exiles and distributing information. Wolf worked as a courier in Paris until the 1939 mass round-ups of German communists and anti-fascists. She was sent back to Germany to a concentration camp until the end of the war. Wolf's story is an exemplary account of selfless anti-fascist activity. Despite all the hardships, she retained her sense of dignity and solidarity. It is only one story of many.

Edelweiss Pirates and Others

> Now look at the youngsters growing up! They give in to every desire and craving, puffing away at English cigarettes, buy the first tasty titbit, dance, and throw away every activity that requires some effort.
> —C.W.W. Szejnmann in *Nazism in Central Germany*

It is, perhaps, the youth who could often express dissent more effectively, away from illegal political organizations, and remain unknown to the authorities. The enforced tedium of the Hitler Youth with its uniforms, daft songs and marching about was obviously anathema to disenfranchised and more independently minded youths. The compulsory sublimation of sexual appetites—boys separate from

82   Ibid., 31.
83   Ibid., 33.

girls—whilst fetishizing flags and lederhosen was understandably repellent to many. Smoking cigarettes, getting prematurely drunk, listening to contemporary music and sexual cavorting has always been the prerogative of youth, much more than callisthenics and accordions—as has a natural anti-authoritarianism. The worldview that the Hitler Youth was putting forward was likewise unappetising to many with its focus on war as a natural state, hailing to the leader, and the subordination of individuality. It was inevitable that some youths would rebel.

> Reports of brawls with members of the Hitler Youth (especially the disciplinary patrols), of assaults on uniformed personnel, and of jeers and insults aimed at Nazi dignitaries are legion.
>
> —Detley J.K. Peukert in *Inside Nazi Germany*

Throughout the 1930s, reports of gangs or 'cliques' proliferated. They were often comprised of runaways who were avoiding the Hitler Youth or compulsory work schemes: Berlin police patrols would 'periodically round up whole lorry-loads of youth…. There is a section of youth that wants the romantic life. Bundles of trashy literature have been found in small caves. Apprentices too are disappearing from home much more frequently and are drifting in the hurly-burly of the big cities'.[84] It was a common phenomenon and one that worried the fascist establishment who warned that 'a serious risk of political, moral and criminal breakdown of youth must be said to exist.'[85] The spontaneity and informality of these gangs made them difficult to monitor and, as time went on, they became increasingly widespread, militant, and violent.

> Get out your cudgels and come into town
> And smash the skulls of the bosses in brown.
>
> —Pirate song

The Edelweiss Pirates, the Kittelbach Pirates and the Navajos were all informal gangs that indulged in the standard deviations of sex, drinking, dodging work and avoiding the tedious adult authoritarians. The

84 Peukert, *Inside Nazi Germany*, 153.
85 Ibid.

Edelweiss Pirates started at the end of the 1930s, wore distinctive outfits and emblems, and spent time escaping to the relative freedom of the countryside to party at weekends. Other gangs soon grew to prominence and were tied to a particular area: 'groups from the whole region met up, pitched their tents, sang, talked and together "clobbered" Hitler Youth patrols doing their rounds'.[86] In 1941, one mining instructor reported, 'They beat up the patrols, because there are so many of them. They never take no for an answer. They don't go to work either, they are always down by the canal.'[87] Compulsive work was viewed negatively by the Pirates and 'something to be evaded as much as possible by "skiving off," idling and causing trouble'.[88] Work was war work, and the Nazis knew that absence directly affected production; the Pirates could exploit this.

According to Mason,

> The few direct armed attacks mounted by German resistance fighters against the hated Gestapo were the achievement of scattered gangs of 'Edelweiss pirates': groups of young people, utterly cut off from the inherited organizations and values of the working class movement, who in the last years of the war spontaneously developed into violent anti-fascist assault troops.[89]

On their rural sojourns, the Pirate gangs could relax, away from the pressure of everyday life, 'though always on the watch for Hitler Youth patrols, whom they either sought to avoid, or taunted and fell upon with relish'.[90] Although not ideologically aligned, the natural anti-authoritarianism of the Pirates began to take on political meaning: everything the Pirates wanted—freedom of assembly, sex, drink, music, travel—was seriously curtailed under the Nazis. If we are defined by our desires, then the Pirates were anti-Nazi by definition. In some cities, once the air-raid sirens had gone off and civilians sought

86   Ibid., 154.
87   Ibid., 155.
88   Ibid., 171.
89   Mason, *Nazis, Fascism and the Working Class*, 237.
90   Peukert, *Inside Nazi Germany*, 156.

shelter, many young people met up to continue the same kind of activities as at the weekend, unsupervised. These were moments of temporary freedom.

Other gangs were similar to the Pirates, only more politicised from the outset. In Leipzig between 1937 and 1938, working-class youth had been much more influenced by the socialist and communist climate of their communities and took pleasure in 'their acts of provocation against the Hitler Youth.' They were given to 'speculations about the day when the violent overthrow of the regime would come'.[91] Provocation was a political tactic at street level for the irate Pirates as they 'looked for a new hangout in the reddest part of town…there were often massive clashes, and we were exposed to many a danger'.[92]

> When the knives flash
> And the Polish coffins whizz past
> And the Edelweiss Pirates attack!
>
> —Martyn Housden in *Resistance and Conformity in the Third Reich*

The Pirates were hardly simple street-corner gangs, and punishment for membership was severe. In 1940, the Gestapo in Cologne arrested 130 Navajos; elsewhere other Pirates were hanged; and in Düsseldorf, 739 were arrested. Also in Düsseldorf, the Edelweiss Pirates battled so frequently with Hitler Youth that in 1942 the latter reported no-go areas. In 1944, the ring-leaders of one Cologne gang were publicly hanged. The Gestapo raided the gangs on Himmler's orders and arrested hundreds of youths who ended up in special courts, but runaways and deserters increased the ranks of the Pirates as the war went on. In Cologne in 1945, there were reports of twenty groups over one-hundred-strong who raided food stores and attacked and killed fascists. As the war neared its end, some Pirates joined with the resistance, along with anti-Nazi deserters and escapees: 'They got supplies by making armed raids on military depots, made direct assaults on Nazis, and took part in quasi-partisan fighting. Indeed the chief of the Cologne Gestapo fell victim to

---

91 Ibid., 165.
92 Merkl, *The Making of a Stormtrooper*, 243.

one of these attacks.'[93]

Students also engaged in acts of resistance. Hans and Sophie Scholl organized a small group to distribute anti-fascist leaflets at Munich University, whose alumni mainly consisted of, according to Dulles, 'girls, cripples and Nazi "student leaders"'.[94] They became known as the White Rose group and built a propaganda network in nearby cities as well. The principal protagonists, the Scholls, were caught and executed, and the bravery of these young anti-fascists has been commemorated by a Berlin school and a film. Others fared slightly better on arrest: Anton Saefkow was a member of the communist resistance and a friend of Ernst Thaelmann who was arrested in 1933 and almost tortured to death. Saefkow then spent the next ten years in a camp until he escaped and became a leading figure in the anti-fascist underground.

> Make sure you're really casual, singing or whistling English hits all the time, absolutely smashed and always surrounded by really amazing women.
>
> —Detley J.K. Peukert in *Inside Nazi Germany*

The Swing Youth were upper-middle-class jazz enthusiasts given over to eccentric dress, a heightened appreciation of the trombone, and resistance through rhythm. Jazz was strictly *verboten* under Hitler who detested 'negro music' and its African-American origins, so adherence to it became a political statement. They faced opposition from the Hitler Youth who reported their 'long hair flopping into the face…they all "jitterbugged" on the stage like wild creatures. Several boys could be observed dancing together, always with two cigarettes in their mouths'.[95] Not only was the music viewed as outlandish but so were the clothes of the Swing Youth: 'English sports jackets, shoes with thick light crepe soles, showy scarves, Anthony Eden hats, an umbrella on the arm whatever the weather'.[96]

---

93 Peukert, *Inside Nazi Germany*, 164.
94 Dulles, *Germany's Underground*, 120.
95 Peukert, *Inside Nazi Germany*, 167.
96 Ibid., 168.

KPD vs. SPD

One of the most contentious issues in Germany was the relationship between the KPD and the SPD. Both had nothing to gain from the electoral success of the Nazis other than arrest, torture, imprisonment, and death. In 1922, the combined vote of the SPD and KPD was 52.3 percent, which (although dropping later due to rising unemployment, shortage of food and bourgeois reaction) was surely an indication of the potential of left-wing and anti-fascist sentiment. The KPD was opposed to the SPD because the communists were agitating for a revolution, whereas the socialists were in government and had sanctioned state violence to suppress revolutionary activity. It was difficult for KPD to side with the reformist SPD when the socialists had used the police to break strikes and attack workers. During the violence on May Day 1929, the police opened fire on unarmed demonstrators. Not only did this result in twenty-five workers being killed, but it widened the gap between the socialists and communists and saw the communists gain more votes. The SPD police chief was blamed, although it was the police boss on the demo that gave the order to fire.

The split between the SPD and KPD was cultural as much as ideological: it was along lines of unemployed and worker, revolutionary and reformist, younger generation and older, and so on. Members of the KPD were often on the fringes of electoral politics and, like the Nazis, had a particular attraction for the younger and more rebellious elements—something that John Hiden confirms in *Republican and Fascist Germany*: 'The KPD supporter was more likely than the SPD follower to be young, unskilled and above all unemployed.'[97] These are some of the reasons that a hoped-for left-wing block vote against the Nazis failed to happen.

---

97   Hiden, *Republican and Fascist Germany*, 63.

Spain: 'The Spanish Anarchist Lives for Liberty, Virtue, and Dignity': The Spanish Civil War

Introduction

Despite the scope of its subject, this chapter has been kept relatively brief for several reasons, the principle one being that we have little new or original material to contribute. The Spanish Civil War is one of the most well documented and important periods in the history of anti-fascism, but being a full-scale war—as opposed to political resistance under tyrannical regimes or fighting on 'the streets of democracy'—it moves slightly beyond the remit of this current volume. It has also been done far better in other volumes.

'Spain 1936' retains a particular attraction for anti-fascists everywhere and anarchists in particular. The struggle has been articulated by hundreds of images, thousands of words, and half a million lives lost. The idea of an embattled republic defended by inexperienced, under-supplied militias made up of young, motivated volunteers who fought against the odds with small chance of survival is a powerful one. The very fact that untrained militias of Spanish workers and peasants were fighting against a professional army handsomely equipped by Hitler and Mussolini, whilst 'civilised countries' stood by, demands outrage. The murderous internal civil war, the Stalinist's manipulation of events and the conflict being a precursor to the next world war, continues its fascinations and frustrations.

The Popular Front

Before the 1930s, Spain was a strictly conservative monarchy with an authoritarian church and strong military presence, a place that modernity, with all its gains and faults, had eluded. It was practically a feudal society with an impoverished peasantry, a slow pattern of industrialization and strong regional identities. There was the growing influence of syndicalism and the concept of the political strike, after the French syndicalists, and anarchism had found support with many industrial and agrarian workers. The socialists' influence was predominantly in industrial centres. By 1934, the Confederación Nacional del Trabajo (CNT, the National Confederation of Workers), the anarcho-syndicalist union, and the socialist Unión General de Trabajadores (UGT, the General Union of Workers) had over three million members between them. Political disputes were frequently resolved by the gun: the bosses were not beyond hiring *pistoleros* to shoot political activists, and the CNT were not shy of responding likewise. Strikes and civil uprisings were met with force by the Assault Guards (the state militia), and when things got too bad the government sent in the military. After a failed mass rebellion across the country in 1934, the Asturian miners' uprising was crushed with particular brutality by the army under the command of one Francisco Franco: a warning of things to come.

The CNT and their militant wing—the Federación Anarquista Ibérica (FAI, the Federation of Iberian Anarchists)—the orthodox socialists (Partit Socialista Unificat de Catalunya [PSUC], the United Socialist Party of Catalonia), the communists (Partido Comunista de España, PCE), and the Partido Obrero de Unificación Marxista (POUM, the Workers Party of Marxist Unification), as well as republican and various regional parties, all increased in numbers after the election of the Popular Front government in 1936. Some had already organized militias in response to increased political violence, and armed groups were formed to defend workers' organizations from attack. These militias were to be in the forefront of the struggle against fascist aggression, playing decisive roles in protecting working-class institutions after the military coup.

The Falange

Middle class youth flooded into the Falange, an openly fascist party,

86

which increasingly engaged the left on the streets in armed clashes.

—Charlie Hore in *Spain, 1936: Popular Front or Workers' Power.*

The Falange were the main physical force on the right that sided with ultra-conservative Catholics and ardent monarchists, united in their fear of a 'Jewish-Bolshevik-Masonic conspiracy' and a hatred of the Republic and the Popular Front.[1] Like so many other proto-fascist groups, they attacked working-class organizations, violently opposed strikes and assassinated union members: 'On 1 June 70,000 Madrid building workers began a joint UGT-CNT strike. Falangists machine gunned the pickets from cars in hit-and-run raids or attacked isolated workers'.[2] Elsewhere, 'Falangists drove at top speed through working-class districts shooting people indiscriminately. There were bomb attacks on newspaper offices and Falangists shot down a judge who had sentenced one of their number to 30 years imprisonment for murder'.[3] Although there is little doubt that a large percentage of the Falange were politically motivated and determined to stamp out the Republic, 'the rest simply seemed to find sanctified gangsterism appealing'.[4] Paul Preston records that 'Falangist terror squads, trained in street fighting and assassination attempts, worked hard to create an atmosphere of disorder which would justify the imposition of an authoritarian regime.'[5]

When Franco led the attempted coup in 1936, the Falangists were on hand in a supporting role and continued to pursue an appalling revenge against pro-Republicans. Although Franco did not call himself a fascist, he was a virulent nationalist and his militarism, chauvinism and anti-communism equated with Hitler and Mussolini ideologically enough for them to guarantee supplies of arms and men.

1   Paul Preston, *The Spanish Civil War: 1936–1939* (London: Weidenfeld and Nicolson, 1990), 33.
2   Antony Beevor, *The Spanish Civil War: The Spanish Civil War, 1936–1939* (London: Cassell, 1999), 65.
3   Ibid., 66.
4   Ibid., 111.
5   Preston, *The Spanish Civil War*, 41.

The Coup

On the morning of 18ᵗʰ July 1936, Franco and other military leaders instigated a coup, an uprising that surprised the Republican government, who were in a state of chaos and disunity, and was only partially suppressed. In certain towns like Granada, the coup was swift and successful:

> The working-class district of Albaicin was shelled and bombed. When control of the city was assured, the military authorities allowed the Falangist 'Black Squad' to sow panic among the population by taking leftists from their homes at night and shooting them in the cemetery. In the course of the war about 5,000 civilians were shot in Granada.[6]

Brennan remarks on the enthusiastic butchery by the right-wing militias and 'the eruption of the Falange and Carlist militias, with their previously prepared lists of victims' and whose scale of executions 'exceeded all precedent'.[7] The immediate government and working-class parties' response was insufficient: 'Posters were put up ordering the summary execution of these gangsters who were engaged in these murders.'[8]

In the working-class strongholds of Madrid or Barcelona, the workers' militias routed the rebels but not without difficulties. Despite being numerous and used to street fighting, the party militias were badly equipped to repulse an armed insurrection. The government refused to arm the workers, fearing that the weapons may be turned against them by openly revolutionary organizations like the CNT/FAI. The attitudes of the various governors determined which towns fell to the coup and which ones effectively resisted. Despite their differing ideologies, the communists, socialists and anarchists all had everything to lose under Franco. In certain places

---

6   Ibid., 55.
7   Gerald Brennan, *The Spanish Labyrinth: An Account of the Social and Political Background of the Spanish Civil War* (Cambridge: Cambridge University Press, 1971), 321–322.
8   Ibid., 323.

resistance grew and barricades were built despite the workers being poorly armed, if at all, and many were effectively massacred in the streets or, if the military had gained control of the town, arrested and then murdered.

The government wasted forty-eight hours before finally allowing the militias access to the guns; the CNT and UGT called a general strike, and the militias began recovering their own hidden weaponry. In Madrid, finally, sixty thousand rifles were released to the CNT and UGT but only five thousand were actually usable. Elsewhere, the CNT took matters into their own hands: they raided arsenals and armed themselves whilst commandeering vehicles and daubing them with their party's initials.[9] Key to whether a town stayed loyal to the Republic was whether the local armed forces sided with the coup or not. Barracks that did not stay loyal were besieged. In Barcelona, the anarchists under Durutti stormed the Atarzanas barricades in a bravely foolhardy charge, which led to many unnecessary losses. In what was to become almost a motif for the entire civil war, no prisoners were taken and political opponents were shot. By the end of the war, thousands of prisoners had been killed.

The Militias

> Arms, arms, let's have arms for Saragossa—what's your idiot of a republic doing, starving us of arms?
>
> —Miguel Garcia in *Miguel Garcia's Story*

The workers' militias were the first line of defence against the insurgents, and they fought bravely, often losing many members in the initial battles, and only later being supported by anti-fascist volunteers who began pouring into Spain to augment their ranks. The militias operated politically: saluting officers and other time-wasting army rigmaroles were avoided in favour of political-awareness raising and fairly minimal weapons-training, then mobilization for the front or to patrol the towns and cities. The main militias were aligned with the

---

9   After the initial violence, it was estimated that the Barcelona anarchists had accumulated forty thousand rifles. See Beevor, *The Spanish Civil War*, 127.

anarchist CNT/FAI, the Marxist POUM and the socialists. Durruti's column with several thousand anarchist militants in the ranks was the most popular. The anarchists also had female combatants, many from the Mujeres Libres organization, who took up arms fully aware of the revolutionary potential for dismantling patriarchy: 'Mujeres Libres rapidly grew into a federation of over 30,000 women. By the end of September it had seven union sections—Transport, Public Services, Nursing, Textiles, Mobile Brigades for non-specialists, and brigades able to substitute for men fighting the war.'[10]

They also worked to convince prostitutes to give up their trade. The Mujeres Libres organization was de-escalated over time and, with the formation of the Popular Army, women were pushed behind the lines and eventually ousted completely from the combat zone. Antony Beevor writes that 'there were probably fewer than 1,000 women at the front. There were, however, several thousand under arms in the rear areas and a woman's battalion took part in the defence of Madrid.'[11]

It was a military conflict as well as an ideological one and a thorough knowledge of Marx or Bakunin was no match for heavy artillery. The Francoists may not have been as politically committed but they were better fed and equipped. A voluntary militia, no matter how idealistic, is going to face difficulties fighting a professional army containing Moroccan mercenaries and supplied with superior materiel. The militias delayed and defended against the Francoist offensives, despite lacking formal military skill and weaponry, and fought back hard with much to lose.

The Non-Intervention

When the civil war broke out, Britain had declared neutrality, and despite the fact that France was being governed by a Popular Front, the socialist leader Leon Blum also proposed 'non-intervention'. Spain was looking increasingly vulnerable. Although Mexico did send some munitions, the only serious ally for the Republicans was

10   Tower Hamlets DAM, The Spanish Revolution: Anarchism in Action (London: ASP, nd), 27.
11   Beevor, The Spanish Civil War, 129.

Stalin, and the Spanish government traded their gold with Russia for arms, which, on arrival, were worth scarcely a fraction of the cost. Such supplies were supplemented by clandestine deals with foreign armament companies: these were often inadequate with outdated rifles of different calibres, poor ammunition, a lack of artillery and aeroplanes, and a shortage of vehicles and petrol. Capitalist countries were hardly willing to supply the ailing Republic, which was seriously under-prepared for a civil war. The Francoists, who were also generously supplied by other fascist states, had seized much of the decent materiel in Spain.

By the 1930s, the Third International, or the Comintern, had been launched by Stalin and the line was 'socialism in one country', as opposed to Trotsky's 'permanent revolution'. Through this, Stalin ensured that all communist parties were under his control and would not upset his diplomatic relations. The delay in Stalin's support proved crucial. And deliberate. He did not want the Spanish revolution to succeed and took measures to make sure it didn't. As part of his shifting foreign policy, Stalin initially prevaricated for fear of angering Hitler and alienating France and Britain. The arms he did covertly supply were conditional on extending his influence in the Republic and were distributed selectively—that is, to the PCE. The PCE had also been 'guided' towards the Popular Front with social democrats in order to negate fascism but also to keep a lid on the demands of the anarchists and radical left by suppressing the revolution. The KPD's struggle with the SPD was also forgotten as Stalin exercised an adjustable political amnesia, dropped the 'social fascism' insult, and cozied up to social democracy as an expedient. Stalin did not want democratic capitalist countries to be driven into the fascist camp through fear of a socialist victory in Spain. The Spanish people were simply 'politically expendable'.

When the civil war exploded, the anarchists felt that revolution was possible and began to collectivise industries in their strongholds: places like Barcelona were radically transformed and run by the working class. The CNT believed that the fascists could be defeated, the working class could control the cities and the peasantry could collectivise the land—as manifested in their 'make revolution to win the war' slogan. This was anathema to the communist line, the disingenuous 'win the war, then the revolution', which Stalin had no intention of carrying out. The anarchist position was further undermined by reformists within the CNT, who, in the name of unity, called for a retreat from confronting the Stalinists and then called for joining the government. Anarchists at the front were denied Russian weapons, the POUM was smeared as 'Trotskyite Fascists' and the Spanish communists sided with, and eventually dominated, the moderates of the government. The first Russian aid reached the Republic in October 1936, and according to Gabrielle Ranzato, 'as late as the middle of January 1939, when the situation could be considered desperate, a vast quantity of armaments arrived from the Soviet Union: 400 aircraft, 400,000 rifles, 10,000 machine guns (though a considerable part was blocked at the French border'.[12] Few, if any, were ever sent to anarchist or POUM frontlines.

The arming of the Republic by Stalin boosted the ranks of the communist party which started attracting bourgeois careerists who, afraid of an anarchist take-over, hoped that the PCE could contain them. Before the civil war, the communists were a relatively small party, much mistrusted by the CNT/FAI who had learned of the treatment of anarchists after the Russian Revolution, so the enmity between the two organizations escalated. On May Day 1937 the outbreak of fighting between the anarchists and POUM on one side and the communists and Republicans on the other threatened to disrupt the war effort and saw many militants disappear off the streets and into Stalinist dungeons.

The Volunteers

The Spanish Civil War volunteers have been romanticised to an extent by anti-fascists, and a negative view that all volunteers were adventurous, naïve, or bored and terminally unemployed has been perpetuated by others. In his book *British Volunteers in the Spanish Civil War*, Richard Baxell strongly refutes these claims with

12 Gabrielle Ranzato, *The Spanish Civil War* (Gloucester: Windrush, 1999), 105.

empirical data on the political backgrounds and professions of re-
gistered volunteers that negates 'the myth that the Brigades were
made up of large numbers of intellectuals [and] the "vague notion
that everyone in the brigades was a poet or writer"'.[13] This negative image badly serves the anti-fascist men and women who went
to Spain through political conviction. However different the backgrounds of the volunteers may have been, their motivations were
similar: Mosley, Mussolini, Hitler and the spread of fascism; the
non-intervention stance of their own countries; mass unemployment; and anger over Franco's attempted military coup were all
factors. The volunteers were aged in general between early twen-
ties and mid-thirties, and the majority arrived in December 1936
and January 1937, with an additional influx in early 1938. Many
but not all were communist party members and there were also
many unaligned workers and trade unionists, the largest percentage being miners and labourers. Many volunteers saw the Spanish
Civil War as a continuation of the class struggle only in a different context: Welsh miners had obviously felt solidarity with the
Asturian miners who were so brutally suppressed in 1934. Some
had particularly impressive CVs: one British volunteer was in the
Young Communist League (YCL), was thrown out of Mosely's Albert Hall rally, had been at the Olympia and Hyde Park events
and was on the barricades at Cable Street. There were others, like
Emilio Canzi: an Italian anarchist, Canzi had been a soldier and a
trainer in the Arditi del Popolo; he was exiled from Italy and joined
with the French anarchists before ending up in Ascasos's anarchist
division in September 1936. He was in Barcelona in May 1937, but
later left for Paris, where he was eventually arrested by the Gestapo.
He was sent to a camp in Italy and finally joined the partisans.
Canzi died in 1945 in a mysterious traffic accident but had lived a
life of anti-fascist commitment.[14]

---

13   Richard Baxell, *British Volunteers in the Spanish Civil War: The British
      Batallion in the International Brigades, 1936–1939* (Torfaen: Warren
      and Pell, 2007), 54.
14   Paolo Finzi, *Emilio Canzi: An Anarchist Partisan in Italy and Spain*
      (London: Kate Sharpley, 2007).

The International Brigades

The volunteers preceded the International Brigades, who later absorbed the militias and 'unaligned' fighters and were usually formed on a national basis. The organization of the International Brigades was done clandestinely by communist parties throughout the world due to the non-intervention pact between Western governments, which made support for the Republic illegal. Volunteers could be arrested en route and imprisoned before being forcibly repatriated. In Paris, one of the main communist recruitment centres, volunteers had to adhere to strict party discipline and, whilst awaiting departure, they had their money confiscated to prevent them spending it in bars and brothels—although 'each man had ten francs a day doled out to him, enough to buy cigarettes and possibly two bocks [beers]'.[15] From there, they took a train south, trying to be as incognito as a varied bunch of foreigners could hope to be, to cross the Pyrenees on foot.

The International Brigaders who fought and often died selflessly in the fight against fascism were not immune to behind-the-scenes political manipulation. According to W.G. Krivitsky, Stalin saw the opportunity for a bit of political spring-cleaning in Moscow: exiled and unwanted foreign communists were sent to Spain to join the International Brigades. (There were Russians in Spain but they were forbidden from fighting—'Stay out of range of the artillery fire', Stalin is rumoured to have said.[16]) Along with the Popular Army, the brigades would try to usurp the last autonomous anarchist and POUM militias and 'were to be used as a means of prolonging the war while restricting the revolution'.[17]

The first International Brigade was formed in October 1936, and was sent to defend Madrid where it was welcomed enthusiastically by the Madrilènes, and successfully prevented fascist incursion into the city. The Brigades were more formal than the workers' militias

---

15   Vincent Brome, *The International Brigades: Spain 1936–1937* (London: Mayflower-Dell, 1967), 32.

16   W.G. Krivitsky, *In Stalin's Secret Service: Memoirs of the First Soviet Master Spy to Defect* (New York: Enigma, 2000), 67.

17   Charlie Hore, *Spain, 1936: Popular Front or Workers' Power* (London: Socialist Workers Party, 1986), 23.

and were modelled on the Red Army, with a command structure and political commissars. Madrid did not fall despite air raids and continuous bombardment. The failure to take the capital proved to be a prolonged embarrassment for Franco as the Republican slogan '*No Pasaran*' was realised.

Although the Republicans did thwart Franco's army at various places, they never made the decisive move that would determine the ultimate outcome of the war. In many instances, the Republicans were operating in a strictly defensive—though no less heroic or dangerous—position, but there were early initiatives. In 1937, Republican forces defeated Franco at the battle of Jarama and Guadalajara, and they beat back Franco's attempt on Madrid and held it for two more years. The bombing of Guernica in May 1937 was a humanitarian disaster with negative political consequences for Franco, whilst the battles of Brunette and Belchite in July and August 1937 did not make the necessary impact against the fascists. The Republic was seriously damaged when it was split in two by the Francoists in March 1938. The battle of Ebro saw a retreat and then, after this, the International Brigaders were repatriated, and it was inevitable that Barcelona and then Madrid would fall.

The Prisoners

One of the contentious points of the Spanish Civil War was the treatment of prisoners by both sides. As Franco advanced through Spain, peasant anarchists and left-wing industrial workers were executed. The Republicans were also guilty of such indiscriminate killings, although at times the execution of local landowners, clerics and police by those whom they had brutally oppressed is a bit more understandable though still reprehensible. Ranzato blames the 'uncontrollables', the anarchist militia 'who operated at the edge or outside of political and union organizations' for some of the atrocities.[18] This is something that an 'uncontrollable' from the Iron Column describes in his memoir as a 'black legend' that was used to discredit the militias that had been the first to oppose the Francoists. These militias passed

---

18   Ranzato, *The Spanish Civil War*, 91.

though the villages, liberating them from the grip of cleric and cop alike. The 'uncontrollable' wrote,

> After expropriating the fascists, we changed the mode of life in the villages through which we passed—annihilating the brutal political bosses who had robbed and tormented the peasants and placing their wealth in the hands of the only ones who knew how to create it: the workers.[19]

There were few prisoners. Manzanera mentions that several gangsters, using the Iron Column's name, were entering 'villages to loot homes, stealing money from the inhabitants', so, 'wasting no time, the Committee despatched a squad of young men to track down these low-lifes who were killing and carrying out dirty deeds in our name. They were soon run to ground'.[20]

Throughout 1937, the communists increased their power base and started arresting and executing non-communist militia members, anarchist militants and supporters of 'dissident' parties like the POUM. These prisoners suffered as they would have under Franco. Rudolf Rocker writes that in April 1937, 'the CNT succeeded in uncovering a Chekist cell in Murcia and in arresting its most important members. For months the populace had been alarmed by the sudden disappearance of residents, a large number who belonged to the CNT'.[21] Bookchin writes that 'by August, the notorious Military Investigation Service was formed under Negrin's premiership to intensify the Stalinist terror inflicted on militant anarcho-syndicalists and POUMistas. In the same month, the Moscow-trained thug Enrique Lister…"[shot] all the anarchists [he] had to"'.[22] George Orwell, who fought for the POUM, records the conditions under which political opponents were held in *Homage to Catalonia*, in addition to

19 An 'Uncontrollable' from the Iron Column, *A Day Mournful and Overcast* (London: Black Cross, 1993), 6–7.
20 Elias Manzanera, *The Iron Column: Testament of a Revolutionary* (London: Kate Sharpley, 2006), 15.
21 Rudolf Rocker, *The Tragedy of Spain* (London: ASP, 1986), 33.
22 Murray Bookchin, *To Remember Spain* (Edinburgh: AK Press, 1994), 62.

recording his own successful evasion of the Stalinist police after the May Day events.[23]

The Exodus

The Republic gradually acceded territory throughout 1937 and 1938, and in September 1938, the International Brigades were disbanded and a mass sending off parade was organized. Martha Gellhorn witnessed it:

> Women threw flowers and wept, and all the Spanish people thanked them.... The Internationals looked very dirty and weary and young and many of them had no country to go back to. The German and Italian anti-fascists were already refugees; the Hungarians had no home either. Leaving Spain, for most of the European volunteers, was to go into exile.[24]

As Franco's forces sliced Republican territory in half, many would be captured and executed. By the end of 1938, those in the North who managed to escape headed to France; others who were less lucky, having nowhere to go nor the means to get there, awaited their fates expecting little clemency. The Spanish anarchist Miguel Garcia recalls being imprisoned after the fall of the Republic: 'Trials condemning 30 or 40 people to death were quite frequent. The [prison], built to take 1,000 men, was at bursting point with 14,000...people were automatically locked up for nothing more than having a union card.'[25]

An exodus of thousands of militia members, anarchists, socialists, syndicalists and peasants headed back over the Pyrenees to the 'safety' of France, only to be interned in makeshift camps and treated like prisoners of war. The luckier volunteers, such as the Americans, British or French, headed back to their homes, where many carried

---

23   George Orwell, *Homage to Catalonia* (Harmondsworth: Penquin, 1979), 206.

24   Martha Gellhorn, *The Face of War* (London: Virago, 1986), 44.

25   Miguel Garcia, *Looking Back After Twenty Years of Jail* (London: Kate Sharpley, 2005), 6.

on the fight against fascism in the streets, although many remained behind as prisoners.

But for others, home was hostile territory under fascist control and they remained exiled, joined the resistance in France or conducted clandestine actions in Francoist Spain. The anarchist Francisco Sabate Llopart had been in the FAI, fought in the militias and at the Aragon front with the Durutti Column, and then after being in a concentration camp in France, joined the resistance and spent fifteen years fighting against the fascist regime in Spain, where he was ultimately killed in 1960. There were many more militant anti-fascists like him.

Hungary, Romania and Poland: 'To Arms! To Arms!'

In some countries, authoritarian right-wing governments curtailed the development of fascism and simultaneously curtailed the growth of anti-fascism and socialism. In Hungary, Bela Kun, who had been in the Russian Revolution and in the Red Guard, led a Soviet regime in 1919, which was eventually violently suppressed. Kun was amongst many dissatisfied soldiers, unemployed and workers amongst the communists, the radical left and splinter factions from the socialists, who took part in mass political action. Soviets ran factory occupations, and the socialists and communists formed a coalition, demanding a republic to maintain Hungary's territorial integrity. The Hungarian Red Army was formed on Soviet lines with recruits from organized labour and with political commissars.

International pressure, shortages and violence led to the dissolution of the Soviet experiment as Romanian troops invaded. Austria refused to help and Russia could not, besieged as it was by White and Allied aggressors following the revolution. The collapse of communist power saw many Hungarian leaders arrested after a violent demonstration that ended with several policemen dead. There followed ruthless persecution, as 'White Terror' sought revenge on left-wingers (both real and imagined) and those who had taken part in the soviet. There was also a resurgence of anti-Semitism under the new right-wing Horthy regime, which was fired by the usual fears of 'Jewish Bolshevism', as many communists and socialists were Jewish. This led to an authoritarian, anti-Semitic right-wing regime where political opposition had been destroyed. At least five thousand were killed with many more held in concentration camps and prisons. The communist party was banned, its leaders exiled in Austria and Russia, and there was little underground organization.

With a racist, anti-Semitic, antisocialist nationalist at the head of the country, fringe fascist groups were thus denied the political space and support that they were usually able to operate with, unlike in Germany and Austria. The fascist leader and Hitler sympathiser, Gyula Gömbös, had organized sixty thousand vanguard fighters in his Party of Racial Defence in order to protect the 'Greater Hungary,' but this was proscribed by the Horthy regime to the satisfaction of Hitler, who did not want renegade fascists upsetting the running of countries to which he had economic ties.[1] As Philip Morgan notes in *Fascism in Europe, 1919–1945*, 'conservative authoritarianism proved to be both fascism's best and worst friend'.[2]

Romania

Romania had a large peasant population and a varied ethnic demography of Hungarians and Ukrainians, as well as a large Jewish population, and fascists had more success in exploiting a combination of social, racial and economic problems. After various false starts, other fascist groupuscules merged with the League for National Christian Defence (LANC) in 1925 to become the dominant ultra-nationalist organization. It was led by the fascist mystic Corneliu Zelea Codreanu, who 'believed devoutly in redemptive violence' and had been arrested for the murder of a police chief.[3] He went on to form his own Legion of the Archangel Michael, whose militia became the Iron Guard, and believed that 'violence and murder were absolutely necessary for the redemption of the nation'.[4] By 1933, the Legion had grown to twenty-eight thousand members, 'was involved in a number of vicious incidents and several deaths', and ended up being suppressed by the government, with 1,700 members arrested. They began to organize death squads 'who developed the fascist cult of

---

1   Jörg K. Hoensch, *A History of Modern Hungary: 1867–1986* (London: Longman, 1996), 129.
2   Morgan, *Fascism in Europe*, 39.
3   Payne, *A History of Fascism*, 136.
4   Ibid., 280.

violence more elaborately' and assassinated the prime minister, which led to Codreanu's arrest—although he later got away from a murder charge again.[5]

The rival fascist National Christians wore blue shirts and swastikas and their black-shirted militia were more Nazi-like and violently anti-Semitic. As with most fascist organizations, they were subject to major schisms, with many groupuscules splintering off over minor ideological disputes and major leadership ego problems. Given the vampiric associations that many have with Romania (although *Dracula* was written by an Irishman based on local myth), the initiation rituals of Codreanu's death squads sound even more grotesque: 'members of the death squad, in turn, each contributed some of their blood to a common glass, which all drank from, uniting them in life and death'.[6] The levels of political violence increased to such an extent that the government banned militias, although this did not prevent vicious inter-party rivalries in the run up to the 1937 election when the legion engaged in street fights with the LANC.

Codreanu's excesses could not be co-opted by the right-wing government, and he was eventually jailed for ten years for subversion, but 'the Guard behaved as it always had done, violently attacking Jews, officials [and] political opponents'.[7] Unable to control the violence of his followers, Codreanu was taken from jail with thirteen others and met a gruesome and bloody end: they were strangled, then shot and dumped in a lime pit on 'the night of the Vampires'.[8]

Following the demise of Codreanu, the Romanian king eventually handed over power to Antonescu, a pro-German and fascist sympathiser who demanded and got dictatorial powers. The Legion revenged themselves on Codreanu's executioners and targeted Jews and political opponents who suffered torture and murder, although like much violent anti-Semitism, it was as much to do with the appropriation of property and outright theft as it was religious intolerance. This was a policy that was carried out with extremist vigour

5   Ibid., 284.
6   Ibid., 285.
7   Morgan, *Fascism in Europe*, 89.
8   Payne, *A History of Fascism*, 289.

by the Romanian army in occupied territories against Jewish communities. After the war, Antonescu was executed as a war criminal.

Poland

Like Hungary and Romania, but to a lesser extent, Poland's fascist organizations were marginalised by an authoritarian and nationalistic government, this time under Józef Piłsudski. Later, more nationalistic incarnations proved not reluctant to utilise native anti-Semitism, and there were claims of pogroms and 'extensive accounts of Polish Jews being beaten by Polish soldiers, of contributions being extorted from the Jewish communities of several towns, and of Jewish women being stripped of their shoes'.[9] The National Democratic Party 'was strongly conservative, nationalist, anti-Semitic and anti-communist. If it were not for the fact that the National Democrats were historically anti-German the party may have become a Nazi-type organization.'[10] The Falanga, 'an unambiguously fascist youth movement',[11] whose leader christened himself *Il Duce*, broke away from the National Democrats but made little impact outside the conservative student body. More successful was the Camp of National Unity (OZN), which was 'conspicuously proto-fascist' and had two million members at its peak, but faded away.[12] The Communist Workers Party of Poland was small and under-represented, and one of the most prominent Polish militant moments was when a young anti-fascist assassinated a German bureaucrat in Paris, which led to *Kristallnacht*.

---

9   Richard M. Watt, *Bitter Glory: Poland and Its Fate, 1918–1939* (New York: Hippocene, 1998), 75.
10   Ibid., 352–353.
11   Martin Blinkhorn, *Fascism and the Far Right in Europe, 1919–1945* (Harlow: Pearson, 2000), 53.
12   Watt, *Bitter Glory*, 355.

Ireland: Blueshirts and Red Scares

> The Blueshirts were a powerful movement, but the remarkable thing
> is that they were defeated on the streets. Communists, Republicans,
> socialists and democrats got together and beat them off the streets,
> to such an extent they were non-existent as a threat.
> —Mick O'Riordan of the Connolly Column, International Brigade

For obvious reasons, much of twentieth-century Irish political history has been dominated by the Republican struggle, the 'troubles' and the subsequent peace process, not to mention the Celtic tiger's untimely extinction. However, like much of Europe, Ireland saw the emergence of a 'shirt movement' that flourished briefly before being run down by Republicans, militant anti-fascists, government pressure and assimilation into the conservative *Fine Gael*. Rather than being a full-on replication of continental fascism, the Blueshirts were more of an ultra-nationalist or ultra-conservative movement that lacked the dominant anti-Semitism of other movements, but its members wrapped themselves in paramilitary grab that was very reminiscent of continental fascists. It is important to look at the success of anti-fascist/left/Republican tactics against them and their political efficacy, as well as the other political and personal anomalies that rendered them ineffective after 1936—especially O'Duffy's disastrous attempts to drum up supporters to fight on Franco's side in Spain.

> It was the growing menace of the Communist IRA…that called forth the
> Blueshirts as inevitably as Communist anarchy called forth the black-
> shirts of Italy.
> —Professor James Hogan, advocate of Mussolini's corporate state

The Army Comrades Association (ACA) formed in 1932 to support ex-soldiers, the preservation of free speech, and opposition to the IRA and the 'communist threat.' Like other proto-fascist militias, they initially sided with the government against any possible working-class uprising. Republican newspaper *An Phoblacht* accused the ACA of being blatantly fascist and pro-imperialist. The ACA responded by calling the IRA a 'mixed grill of gangsters, neurotics and half-baked communists'.[1]

The ACA used typical 'Red Scare' tactics, conflating the IRA with communism and in 1933 publishing *Could Ireland Become Communist?* by Professor James Hogan, an advocate of Mussolini's corporate state. It also accused the prime minister, Éamon de Valera, of 'leading the country straight into Bolshevik servitude...getting daily orders from Moscow'.[2] Such politics were naturally confronted by Republicans and Communists alike, and the ACA organized a stewards group to protect meetings of both the conservative Cumann na nGaedheal as well as the more right-wing Centre Party, whose meetings had come under pressure. In October 1932, fights broke out amongst audiences, and meetings were closed following further disturbances. Several hundred opponents confronted one ACA meeting in Kilmallock, and the ACA joined with Garda as brawling intensified. Temporarily halted, the violence flared up again even more fiercely, and the ACA had to be escorted out of town by the army. This was not an infrequent occurrence, and many ACA meetings were likewise attacked or halted by left-wing and Republican opposition. This did not prevent the ACA from attracting 30,000 members at its peak.

> Party meetings were routinely protected by its members [as] the spiral of IRA violence escalated.
>
> —Mike Cronin in *The Blueshirts & Irish Politics*

The violence continued in the 1933 election campaign, with many ACA meetings attacked: one of their meetings on O'Connell Street

---

1   Maurice Manning, *The Blueshirts* (Dublin: Gill & Macmillian, 1970), 33.
2   Ibid., 44.

was 'completely wrecked and over fifty people were injured in the
police baton charges and during the clashes between members of the
ACA and their opponents'.[3] Two other meetings were wrecked on
the same day by what Manning calls 'opponents'. At one meeting in
Castlerea in 1934, 'an attack was made by the Blueshirts on men in
the crowd. The attack was made by batons previously concealed under
their coats and in some cases walking sticks or what appeared to be....
There were fights in various places over the Square and through the
town'.[4] When faced with violence and intimidation, it is understandable that anti-fascists responded likewise. Fascism is an ideology that
fetishizes physical violence, and the Blueshirts were no different in
using it to propagate their aims: 'The main targets of Blueshirt violence were the IRA, the Communists and the government officials...
and the atmosphere of violent conflict which the Blueshirt attacks
produced were aimed to heighten the state of emergency.'[5]

One Blueshirt steward recalls his role: 'It was our job to protect [the speakers] from hecklers and to preserve law and order. We
often got into fights with hecklers.... I was stewarding a Blueshirt
meeting down at Trinity Green when this young boy, young thug
actually, came up and hit me on the head with a plank of wood....
Some of my friends chased him and gave him a good hiding'.[6] It is
unsurprising that violence escalated and the Blueshirts' fascist tactics
were widely condemned by de Valera, socialists, communists and Republicans, with the *Irish Workers' Voice* demanding that 'every section
must unite against them. Form the united front of the Irish working
class against the fascist class and their anti-communist allies'.[7]

The Wearing of the Blue

In addition to stewarding right-wing party meetings, the ACA also
stood as Cumann candidates with small success: de Valera and Fianna

3   Ibid., 50.
4   Mike Cronin, *The Blueshirts and Irish Politics* (Dublin: Four Courts,
     1997), 55.
5   Ibid., 54.
6   Ibid., 131–132
7   Ibid., 57.

Fáil won the election. Electoral success not withstanding, the ACA had developed into a significant political force and continued their anti-communist rhetoric in defence of 'free speech'—that is, free speech but not for Republicans, socialists or communist party members. Early in 1933, the ACA adopted the paramilitary blue shirt and black beret, citing the promotion of comradely feeling and the prevention of 'friendly fire' incidents during disturbances. The ACA disingenuously claimed that this decision was not taken in solidarity with other European fascist groups and ignored the fact that a large group of men in uniform is also an intimidating spectacle.

The later introduction of the 'Roman salute' leaves little doubt of their dominant political mindset. Manning claims that in 1933 fascism had yet to gain the negative connotations it subsequently got—which is a narrow claim in light of widely documented Brownshirt's violence and Mussolini's much longer record of political violence in the world's media. The Blueshirts rhetoric of defending the free state with the 'strong hands and stout sticks' of members 'who will not shrink from combat' was all too reminiscent of Mosley.[8] They were certainly not equivalent to the Squadristi or the Brownshirts, despite their bravado. Political opponents accused the ACA of planning a paramilitary coup against the democratic government following their own electoral failure, but the ACA responded by saying they were there to 'prop up the democratic structure against attacks from the left'.[9]

Along with 'Red Scare' and intimidation tactics, the ACA attacked an unemployed workers meeting and a Revolutionary Workers Group meeting two days later. The next day there was a similar attack when 'there was prolonged street fighting during which thirty three people were injured'.[10] So much for propping up the democratic structure. By mid-1933, Blueshirt numbers had increased along with smashed meetings and street violence. In 1933, a change of leadership under Eoin O'Duffy, a former police commissioner who had been dismissed in 1932, heralded a name change to the National Guard. They adopted a much harder anti-working-class line and

8   Manning, *The Blueshirts*, 58.
9   Ibid., 56.
10   Ibid., 61.

aimed to 'oppose Communism and alien control and influence...
[and to] prevent strikes and lock-outs and harmoniously compose
industrial differences',[11] much like their blackshirt antecedents in the
general strike of 1926 and other examples across mainland Europe.
F.S.L. Lyons describes the National Guard as 'certainly proficient in
the use of batons and knuckledusters.'[12] Militant Republicans were
not unaware of developments of the Blueshirts in a wider context:
the Sinn Féin publication *An Phoblacht* had already accused the Blueshirts of being supporters of the Anglo-Irish treaty which limited
Irish sovereignty and supported England's policies in Ireland, and it
was not difficult to see overtones of Euro-fascist military fancy.

O'Duffy denied that his organization was a fascist one, although
he was willing to adapt fascist policies if he found suitable points.
De Valera became concerned over the Blueshirts: leading figures
had weapons confiscated as guards on government buildings were
increased. This did little to curb street violence, and in August a
Blueshirt social was attacked on O'Connell Street, leading to police attacking demonstrators. The car of one leading figure 'was assailed with flying stones, stick and hurleys, and the occupants had
to receive protection from police and Blueshirts'.[13] Following this,
O'Duffy proposed a mass parade through Dublin, in a weak version
of Mussolini's march on Rome, which was banned by the government because of 'the military character of its organization and the
symbols it has adopted are evidence that its leaders are prepared, in
favourable circumstances, to resort to violent means to attain this
end'.[14] Despite vowing that the parade would go ahead, O'Duffy was
forced to back down. Armed police were put on the streets in case
of trouble, but little happened apart from two Blueshirts being man-
handled. O'Duffy faced increasing political pressure, with meetings
being closed by police, so the Blueshirts moved closer to the Centre
Party as Cumann eventually became Fine Gael and the Blueshirts
became the Young Ireland Association.

---

11 Ibid.,74.
12 F.S.L. Lyons, *Ireland Since the Famine* (London: Fontana, 1985), 529.
13 Manning, *The Blueshirts*, 82.
14 Ibid., 85.

O'Duffy's public appearances increased throughout 1934, the crowds supplemented by bussed-in supporters from elsewhere, and the fascist salute became more obvious. Again de Valera responded by raiding offices and seizing weapons. As well as state opposition, violence against the Blueshirts continued from the IRA, the Republicans, and the left. Elsewhere, hostile opposition attacked a Blueshirt group, and shots were fired to quell the disturbances. O'Duffy took a hammer to the head in October as his meeting was smashed up and opponents bricked attendees; the police lost control as O'Duffy's car was burnt, and he was escorted away under armed guard. A hand grenade was thrown but failed to explode. At another meeting shortly after, O'Duffy accused hecklers of being part of a well-armed 'Communist anti-God cell'. Locals were unamused and two Blueshirts were abducted and beaten, one dying months later from his injuries and becoming a Blueshirt martyr. At one meeting,

> a hostile crowd of about 50 men and boys came outside the hotel where they engaged in shouting and stone throwing.... When Colonel Carew went outside the hotel he was attacked and sustained an injury to his left hand. He was also hit with a missile on the back of the neck.[15]

Cronin lists a number of 'principal outrages attributed to the Blueshirts and allies during 1934', which include numerous battles with opponents, gunshots, attacks on small groups and individuals, and murder.[16] There were a number of arson attacks on venues where Blueshirt social occasions took place: 'Their opponents burnt down their platforms and dance halls, fired shots at the venue for the dance, and engaged Blueshirts in a mutual punch up.'[17]

Despite all this, the Blueshirts maintained a political presence and meetings continued to be attacked, with one leading figure shot at and another speaker dragged off the stage as the place was wrecked. The Blueshirts were under pressure from the state over their legality

---

15   Cronin, *The Blueshirts and Irish Politics*, 174.
16   Ibid., 147–148.
17   Ibid., 188.

and could only hold meetings with a large police presence. Militant anti-fascism had curbed their political space on the streets, and it was only a matter of time before the Blueshirts collapsed.

O'Duffy faced heavy opposition wherever he tried to organize, and following the worst excesses, de Valera declared his intolerance of political violence from all sides as another Blueshirt was killed. Meetings continued to be attacked by stone-throwing youths, fist fights broke out in the audiences, police led baton-charges to quiet the disorder, gunshots were fired, and a bomb led to another fatality. Despite this, opposition to the Blueshirts still commanded support, and O'Duffy led a march half a mile long with sixty Blueshirts on horseback. The Garda could not control some of the more violent episodes and called in the army: in Drogheda, a group of Blueshirts were attacked and the military stepped in. The Blueshirts foolishly returned that night and police had to use tear gas and an armoured car to prevent further disorder. Despite, and perhaps because of, anti-fascist violence and attention from the state, the Blueshirts continued to grow in numbers, and the leadership became confident of an electoral landslide in their favour, but that failed to materialise. As usual, boots on the cobbles do not automatically translate into seats at the Dáil, despite drawing much support from the middle classes and cash-strapped farmers resentful of government policy.

O'Duffy had been in contact with the Norwegian Grey Shirts and expressed admiration for Hitler and Mussolini, which caused the milder members of Fine Gael to hesitate in backing him when it was mooted that he could be leader. He was urged to drop his overt fascist trappings, but he was far too unpredictable and volatile to be seriously considered for the role. His sudden resignation caused chaos for Fine Gael and the Blueshirts. By 1934, O'Duffy was consorting with various extremists and neo-Nazis at the International Action of Nationalisms conference, and at the International Fascist Congress whilst making plans for the National Corporate Party, which advocated the fascist idea of the corporate state. Resignations, splits and schisms followed a drop in membership as the Blueshirts rapidly declined in 1935: by 1936 it was redundant. The violent climate of 1933–1934 had changed.

O'Duffy's Debacle in Spain

Six hundred Irish blueshirts [were] under General O'Duffy, but their contribution can be ignored, as they were withdrawn after only one action in which they found themselves attacked by their own side.

—Antony Beevor in *The Battle for Spain*

In 1936, O'Duffy began organizing volunteers for a Blueshirt Brigade to aid Franco in Spain, playing on Catholic anti-Communist sentiment. Financial and logistical problems dogged his efforts: although he did manage to mobilise some volunteers, getting them to Spain proved difficult. The ship that was to take them to Spain failed to arrive. According to Lyons, only seven hundred actually made it to Spain, compared to the two- to three hundred from the IRA 'in a cause which had nothing to do with any of them'.[18] Nepotism seriously afflicted the few Blueshirts who did manage to get there as 'O'Duffy diminished the military efficacy of his brigade by giving the most responsible appointments to his own political supporters, regardless of experience'.[19] Not only that, but during the battle of Jarama, 'one of their companies was fired on by a Falangist unit which mistook them for International Brigaders and a minor skirmish ensued'.[20] O'Duffy's men, many of whom were not original Blueshirts, suffered badly on the battlefield and endured 'appalling conditions'. This dismal and demoralising lack of success saw many heading back to Ireland after a mere six months and having to rely on outside sources to get them home. Thomas Gunning, a member of O'Duffy's NCP stayed on in Spain 'and spent the war in Germany as an admirer of Hitler'.[21] It was not long after the 1936 debacle that the Blueshirts disappeared from view. Their political progress had been severely affected by militant anti-fascist activity in Ireland and Spain.

---

18   Lyons, *Ireland Since the Famine*, 533.
19   Preston, *The Spanish Civil War*, 93.
20   Ibid.
21   Cronin, *The Blueshirts and Irish Politics*, 26.

UNITED AGAINST MOSLEY

Scotland: 'Six-Hundred Reds...Led By A Jew'

And freedom's opposing forces are hidden too,
But fascism has its secret agents everywhere
In every coward's castle, shop, bank, manse and school.
—Hugh MacDiarmid, 'Third Hymn to Lenin'

The Scottish Fascisti

Whilst on strike-breaking duties during the 1926 General Strike, a Scottish member of the British Fascisti (BF) inadvertently poked his head out of a train window and was promptly decapitated. Hardly a grand start to a campaign. The BF had initially been funded by the Earl of Glasgow and had set up headquarters in Glasgow. The BF was happy to engage in anti-working-class activity, even to the point of actively assisting Special Branch and MI5. Billy Fullerton, who was the leader of the Loyalist Billy Boys' 'razor gang,' was also awarded a medal for his services in 1926. As described later, the BF was soon assimilated into Oswald Mosley's larger British Union of Fascists amidst the usual squabbling and infighting so character-istic of fascist groupuscules. Despite, or because of, Mosley's input, Scotland remained hard slog for the advancement of fascism. In imitation of their southern counterparts, the Scottish branch of the BF were diluted Mussolini copyists but just as anti-communist and anti-Semitic. The BF had pledged to support the state in 1925 in anticipation of a General Strike, although one sceptical MP stated that 'the British Fascisti...were not much use, because they always seemed to clash with the communists and had to call in the police'.[1]

---

1   Liam Turbett, 'Blackshirts in Red Scotland' (master's thesis, University of Glasgow, 2012), 7.

Scottish Anti-Fascism

Mosley had first campaigned with the New Party at a rally in Glasgow in 1931, which was subject to much heckling and abuse from political opponents, as elsewhere, but was relatively violence-free. At Glasgow Green later, anywhere between twenty- and forty thousand were said to have shown up, and he faced a hostile crowd: 'Sections of the crowd interrupted continuously. Other sections sang the "Red Flag"…several free fights were in progress simultaneously'.[2] Mosley and his bodyguards were attacked by anti-fascist demonstrators led by members of the Communist Party and Glasgow's Jewish community. After the meeting, Mosley and his supporters were pelted with missiles, 'and in the ensuing melee several people were attacked with razors'.[3] The violence was to be repeated at other Mosley meetings, which were systematically smashed by opponents, and were partly responsible for Mosley becoming 'more fascist', and also increased his determination to organize his stewards into a more disciplined fighting force.

The British Union of Fascists (BUF) continued to do poorly in Glasgow: 'a crowd of 2,000 anti-fascists lay siege to the local BUF office and 13 fascists were reportedly trapped inside'.[4] Another incident led to 'the BUF press report[ing] that a hostile crowd had broken up a fascist meeting at the Mound in Edinburgh in February 1934'.[5] Copsey reports that the BUF required a police escort to get them safely away; such was the fierce opposition.[6]

Mosley held two rallies in Edinburgh and both were subject to militant opposition. In 1934, hundreds of blackshirts had been brought in to protect the meeting, but after it closed there were violent clashes with anti-fascists, the vehicles that had bussed the blackshirts in from afar had smashed windows, and fascists were hospitalised. Again at Edinburgh, anti-fascists infiltrated a meeting aiming to heckle Mosley and drown him out. A Spanish Civil War veteran

---

2   Ibid., 15.

3   Ibid.

4   Nigel Copsey, *Anti-Fascism in Britain* (Basingstoke: Palgrave-Mac-Millan, 2000), 29

5   Ibid., 24.

6   Ibid., 62.

described disrupting the meeting: '[It was] a rush and in the rush I got a bit of a knocking about, and taken up to High Street [police station].'[7] At Lanarkshire in 1934, there was a mass mobilization of anti-fascists who stopped a BUF rally, attacked the speaker, and set up an anti-fascist meeting in its place. The BUF did manage to keep their headquarters in Glasgow and maintain some street presence, but meetings usually met with militant and organized opposition: 'At Glasgow a crowd of 3,000 tried to rush the St. Andrew's where Mosley was to speak. "Biff boys" and police fought to eject them, but enough remained in the hall to render Mosley inaudible'.[8] As the opposition to the BUF in Glasgow so was fierce they had to employ advanced hyperbole in their newspaper, claiming they were making great leaps, whilst in reality, membership remained at a staggeringly low fifty. Pressure was maintained and '200 communists could descend on them whilst selling papers at Charing Cross', whilst 'a mob of 600 Reds...led by a Jew' attacked Blackshirts leaving their HQ.[9] The Jewish-based Workers' Circle was acutely aware of fascist anti-Semitism and was engaged in militant anti-fascism: when William Joyce held an open-air meeting in Glasgow, it was smashed and the Workers Circle seized the platform.

In 1937, Aberdeen witnessed a large mobilization of the left, which was interrupted by the arrival of a fascist speaker van escorted by the police who 'batoned down defenceless workers in the interests of preparing the way for the entry of the BUF'.[10] The resultant outcry led the police to revise their tactics. The BUF also needed to rethink their public strategy as their meetings faced constant disruption. They made a decision to hold spontaneous street meetings using loudspeaker vans, but anti-fascists managed to monitor their arrivals and respond accordingly—with one attempt attracting 'a hostile mob of over 6000 people' in Torry, Aberdeenshire; they subjected the hapless fascists to a bombardment of 'burning fireworks, sticks, stones,

---

7   Turbett, 'Blackshirts in Red Scotland', 21.
8   Colin Cross, *The Fascists in Britain* (Tiptree, Essex: Barrie and Rockliff, 1961), 49.
9   Turbett, 'Blackshirts in Red Scotland', 24.
10   Ibid., 27.

and pieces of coal'.[11] The leading fascists fled in panic. Despite arrests and beatings by police, anti-fascists kept up their militant activities, causing the police to consider banning fascist meetings in order to prevent disturbances. The opposition outweighed the BUF, and the police manpower was viewed as wasteful. Militant anti-fascists outnumbered their opponents, who could not organize political space to prosper within—yet this militant approach was only part of the reason for the BUF's Scottish failure.

Sectarianism

The BUF either misread or failed to identify the strength of sectarianism in Scotland, and in particular they failed to assimilate possibly sympathetic groups such as the Scottish Protestant League, headed by Alexander Ratcliffe, or John Cormack's Protestant Action (PA). Ratcliffe had briefly been a member of the Scottish Democratic Fascist Party, was anti-Catholic and anti-Semitic, and was an admirer of Nazi Germany. Cormack had been in the Black and Tans in Ireland before becoming the little dictator of PA, and he was a strong adherent of anti-Catholic violence—not adverse to 'Squadristi' tactics, which 'look[ed] far more "fascist" than anything the BUF ever did in Scotland'.[12] He also formed the paramilitary group 'Kormack's Kaledonian Klan' to counter 'popish dictation', yet also confusingly stated, 'When I get control, I will put a ban on Fascists on the street.'[13] These two groups tended to remain localised rather than exerting any kind of national influence. Cormack was reportedly seen leading the opposition to Mosley in 1934. Despite being superficially in agreement on some matters, the hostile protestants and the fascists were ill-matched: 'Although Protestant Action shared the BUF's anti-Semitism, it attacked the BUF for pro-Catholic tendencies as well as Mosley's long-standing sympathy for Irish nationalism'.[14]

The BUF also antagonised Scottish nationalists.

---

11   Ibid., 28.
12   Ibid., 10.
13   Ibid., 11.
14   Copsey, *Anti-Fascism in Britain*, 62.

The Catholic community, many of them of Irish descent, were on the receiving end of Protestant bigotry and had a more confusing relationship with fascism as they 'were part of an institution, the Catholic Church, that vocally supported the fascists in the Spanish Civil War'.[15] The future communist MP Willie Gallagher said, 'In Scotland, the fascists were not anti-Jewish but anti-Irish.'[16] Mosley's urging of religious egalitarianism (Jews aside, obviously) alienated a potential voter base and encouraged hostility within the protestant community. If the BUF had been seen to embrace the anti-Catholic sentiments of the Protestant community they might have prospered. The BUF were also far too centred in London and around the English Mosley to successfully appeal to protestant and loyalist ideals.

Mosley attracted aristocratic Scottish backers who were fired up by his anti-Semitism, his anti-communism or both. Other fascist groups appeared in his shadow including the pro-German Right Club, which was headed by Captain Archibald Ramsay, who was later interned under the 18b Ruling at the start of the Second World War. In 1939, the pro-Nazi group The Link held its first meeting in Edinburgh, chaired by Sir Barry Domville.

Alongside the small number of fascist supporters in Scotland were ex-pat Italians who remained sympathetic to Mussolini. Branches of the pro-fascist Dante Allegheri Society were set up in Glasgow and Edinburgh, ostensibly 'safeguarding and spreading the Italian language and culture...according to the spirit of the Fascist revolution'.[17] Given the localities of the Italian diaspora in Glasgow, and given their shopkeeping and restaurant businesses, Italians' activities remained relatively without influence outside of their own small communities. But they did maintain Casa d'Italia, an expensive and well-appointed building, which had 'rooms for playing pool and for dancing...along with a restaurant'.[18] Other Italian communities were less organized: in Aberdeen, the majority of the six hundred Italians

---

15   Turbett, 'Blackshirts in Red Scotland', 3.
16   Ibid., 9.
17   Claudia Baldoli, *Exporting Fascism: Italian Fascists and Britain's Italians in the 1930s* (Oxford: Berg, 2003), 15.
18   Ibid., 148.

were shopkeepers and ice-cream makers who lacked political leadership and thus were practically non-existent. The petty-bourgeois nature of Italian fascism was preserved in Scotland, it seems. Dundee was even less coherent and the local Fascio had been for a long time in 'complete ruin'. Integration and apathy meant that any pro-fascist Italians remained marginalised and insignificant. The Italian fascists did not link up with the BUF.

Militant opposition to the BUF saw fascism struggle to make any progress in Scotland, but fascists' own misunderstanding of sectarianism hindered them further. It was anti-Catholicism not anti-Semitism that aggravated their most likely allies. The BUF's fuehrer principle and its base in London would further alienate nationalists. Fascism in 1930s Scotland remained a small and localised annoyance rather than any significant political threat.

England: 'A Bloody Good Hiding'

Early Fascist Groups

Following the Russian Revolution, English anti-Bolshevik panic manifested itself in a host of far-right groupuscules, many short-lived and suffused with typically rancorous anti-Semitism. Leadership figures such as Rotha Lintorn-Ormon, Arnold Leese and Oswald Mosley, at the head of early organizations like the Comrades of the Great War, were ultra-patriotic. The British Workers League was made up of imperialist nostalgists who emphasised 'the intrinsic unity of interest between employer and employee'— as did the British Empire Union who all prefigured the British Fascisti, Mussolini copyists who included Maxwell Knight of MI5, the Government Intelligence Service.[1] Tony Greenstein writes, 'It's difficult to put an exact date on the beginning of British fascism.... I would pinpoint the formation of the British Brothers League in 1902 as the key moment in British fascism.'[2] Rosenberg writes, '[although the BBL] described itself as "anti-alien" [it] left little doubt as to which aliens it saw as a principal target' and they organized

> the poorer local populace into angry street marches calling for an end to Jewish immigration. Hoisting 'Britain for the British' banners, flanked by Union Jacks, its supporters took part in

---

1   T.P. Linehan, *British Fascism, 1918–39: Parties, Ideology and Culture* (Manchester: Manchester University Press, 2000), 44.
2   Tony Greenstein, *The Fight Against Fascism in Brighton and the South Coast* (Brighton: Brighton History Workshop Pamphlet Series, 2011), 13.

intimidating marches through the East End more than 30 years before Sir Oswald Mosley first attempted to set foot there.[3]

According to Greenstein, 'the BBL would though be more accurately described as a proto-fascist group'.[4] The first group to openly describe themselves as fascists was the British Fascisti (BF). The BF characteristically featured multiple double-barrelled surnames amongst its ranks, as well as its own would-be Squadristi, 'the fascist shock troops who would eventually grapple with the Red revolutionaries on the streets'.[5] With its cross-class appeal, the BF also 'harboured an intense aversion to Bolshevism, radical socialism and militant direct action trade unionism', members of all of which would oppose them and the later British Union of Fascists (BUF) in violent confrontations.[6] In 1926, the BF leadership fell out over allegiance to the government during the General Strike with one faction advocating strike-breaking and the other anxious not to alienate working class support.[7] Rotha Lintorn-Ormon funded the BF and envisioned it as a militant scout outfit, pouring thousands of pounds into 'the movement' until she was cut off by her family over 'disreputable elements who lived off her...making her increasingly dependent on alcohol and drugs'.[8] Drunken orgies were also reported. Despite its paramilitarism, scabbing and other anti-labour activity, the BF eventually fizzled out.

The British Fascisti's inaugural meeting on 7th October 1923 was attacked by communist militants, as were the next two. Despite their admiration of Mussolini, the BF did not initially have the muscle to repel opponents. Confrontations with anti-fascists increased in violence and led to the formation of the pacifist People's Defence

---

3   David Rosenberg, *Battle for the East End: Jewish Responses to Fascism in the 1930s* (Nottingham: Five Leaves, 2011), 23.
4   Greenstein, *The Fight Against Fascism in Brighton*, 13.
5   Linehan, *British Fascism*, 62.
6   Ibid., 64.
7   Nigel Todd, *In Excited Times: The People Against the Blackshirts* (Tyne and Wear: Bewick Press, 1994), 6.
8   Richard Thurlow, *Fascism in Britain: A History, 1918–1985* (Oxford: Blackwell Publishing, 1987), 56.

Force. This was followed by the more pro-active National Union for Combating Fascismo (NUCF), which 'declared itself ready to "meet fascist outbreaks" and would pursue "vigorous socialist propaganda".'[9] The NUCF prefigured calls for a united front against fascism but these organizations, despite good intentions, made small impact. 'Minor skirmishes' between militants and fascists did not escalate radically, and much of the left viewed the nascent fascist movement with amused scepticism or outright dismissal. Militants in the Communist Party (CP) were more cautious and cognizant of the strike-breaking potential of BF 'volunteers', and leading communist Palme Dutt, after a bout of prevarication urged the formation of 'local defence organizations of the workers to prevent disturbance'.[10] A group called the Worker's Defence Corps was also active during the General Strike; it subsequently became the Labour League of Ex-Servicemen in 1927 but remained small.

The National Fascisti (NF), a BF splinter group, faced militant opposition at its meetings, was generally harassed by the more brawny CP members, and remained mostly London-based: 'Its activists engaged in periodic street fights with communists and socialists and broke up opponents meetings.... A fascist squad attempted to wreck a meeting in Trafalgar Square' and commit 'night-time raids on the premises of rival left-wing groups'.[11]

In 1926, the NF organized a meeting in Hyde Park that attracted about a thousand people but was attacked by anti-fascists and broken up; at a meeting in Marble Arch, the platform was rushed. In 1927, there were further confrontations when the BF attacked an International Class War Prisoners Aid meeting in Trafalgar Square. They were seen off by upwards of two hundred CP members. The NF quickly dissolved over embezzlement allegations, with one member threatening another with a gun and a sword. The NF was a more pro-Italian front that 'favoured direct action and did not shirk from using political violence against its political opponents'.[12] The NF

9   Copsey, *Anti-Fascism in Britain*, 7.
10   Ibid., 9.
11   Linehan, *British Fascism*, 126.
12   Ibid., 125.

organized its own defence groups along Squadristi lines, training at their headquarters on Edgware Road. Although tiny, they featured one of the most fascinating and bizarre figures of British fascism, Colonel Victor Barker—also known as Valeria Arkell-Smith—who bred dogs, played cricket and acted as a scout master.[13] Other fascist groupuscules formed and briefly flourished until faced with militant opposition from both left and right: 'the British United [*sic*] Fascists managed to upset Mosley's BUF because its premises were wrecked by a Mosleyite Action Squad which led to its premature extinction'.[14] Was it ever thus?

Arnold Leese, the camel expert and rampant anti-Semite, was over-eager to don the black shirt of the Squadristi. He went through several British fascist organizations until settling in the Imperial Fascist League (IFL), but he ultimately ended up in prison as a potential enemy agent under the 18b Ruling during World War II. A constant feature of fascist groupuscules and their leaders is the reservation of violence and scorn, not only for their political opponents but also for those who rival them in a small but hotly contested political space; Leese was no different.

Explosive internecine violence occurred between the IFL and the BUF: 'the IFL encountered fierce opposition from the Mosleyites during the 1930s, sometimes of an extreme "physical force" nature'.[15] According to Mosley's son, 'Leese was beaten up and General Blakeney got a black eye: this was the only fight, [Mosley] said later, in which his stewards got out of control'.[16] Arnold Leese was consumed with typical fascist paranoia and became convinced that Oswald Mosley was a state asset, 'an agent who had been planted to discredit the cause'.[17] This also indicates delusions of grandeur in that these insignificant groups that flare up and disappear so regularly are worthy of intense state surveillance.

---

13   Ibid., 126.
14   Ibid., 131.
15   Ibid., 78.
16   Nicholas Mosley, *Rules of the Game: Sir Oswald and Lady Cynthia Mosley, 1896-1933* (Aylesbury: Fontana, 1983), 229.
17   Pugh, *Hurrah for the Blackshirts!*, 130.

New Party and BUF

Mosley had a history of politically opportune shifting, moving from the Conservatives to Labour, then forming his own New Party, an unsuccessful proto-fascist outfit that later morphed into the BUF. The New Party,

> attracted audiences of several thousands: but they found they were increasingly heckled, and that sometimes their meetings were broken up by what appeared to be organized gangs of Labour militants and Communists. The communist paper *The Daily Worker* was in fact already referring to the New Party as 'fascist'.[18]

The New Party 'organized a group of young men from Oxford to protect New Party meetings: these were referred to in the press as "Mosley's Biff Boys" or "strapping young men in plus fours"'.[19] This protection squad was trained by the Jewish boxing champ Ted 'Kid' Lewis 'to combat Communist violence. Equipped with uniforms, flags and insignia, the stewards were basically a paramilitary force'.[20] Shades of squadrismo in the Youth Movement alarmed some members of the NP who 'feared that a group of young men trained in judo and boxing would grow into a proto-fascist defence force.'[21] They were right. As mentioned previously, during a riotous New Party event in Glasgow in 1931, Mosley was physically 'attacked by a communist group with razors', and then, despite his Biff Boys, 'a stone hit [him] on the head.'[22] At another rally, Mosley 'was heckled by 500 communists and his bodyguard were attacked with stones and razors'.[23] This violence would plague and hinder Mosley for most of his subsequent political career.

A meeting in Birmingham saw outbreaks of fighting, and the local paper blamed 'the presence of the Youth Movement that

18 Mosley, *Rules of the Game*, 184.
19 Ibid., 186.
20 Pugh, *Hurrah for the Blackshirts!*, 124.
21 Mosley, *Rules of the Game*, 187.
22 Ibid., 199.
23 Pugh, *Hurrah for the Blackshirts!*, 124.

immediately set up a militant feeling in the few who were out for trouble.'[24] The meeting descended into a mass brawl that saw Mosley arrested and charged with assault, although later, unsurprisingly, he was acquitted. The New Party fared badly at the ballot box, and their meetings were frequently attacked by the left—both factors which contributed to their rapid decline and the subsequent formation of the more overt BUF in October 1932.

> The British Union of Fascists was not in its origins a working class movement; it was composed mainly of lower-middle-class men who resented the inequalities and lack of opportunities under capitalism; they also feared the prospect of repression of individualism under socialism.
> —Nicholas Mosley in *Rules of the Game*

The BUF were not immune from militant anti-fascist attention either. At the Memorial Hall in Farringdon, London, in 1932, shortly after the BUF was formed, Mosley first gave voice to anti-Semitic sentiment—after which fighting broke out, people were ejected from the meeting, and the fighting continued outside. A month later left wing militants attacked the fascists with razors at St. Pancras and the street battles continued. Mosley was the public face of the BUF, advocated the corporate state, and gained working-class support through his vocal anti-Semitism. Like the NP, the BUF fared poorly at the ballot box and meetings were continually met with violent opposition. Historians variously apportion blame on the BUF and 'communist organized anti-fascist violence' for its decline.[25] According to T.P. Linehan, 'it should come as no surprise to scholars that anti-fascists organized a large amount of political violence against the BUF, given the communist and Jewish movements' memories of the brutality of fascist and Nazi violence'.[26] Widely reported violence did not translate into crosses on the ballot paper, an effective anti-fascist strategy.

To protect Mosley and meetings from continuous attack, the BUF organized the more paramilitary I Squad, whose members

24   Mosley, *Rules of the Game*, 200.
25   Ibid., 93.
26   Ibid., 115–116.

were schooled in the use of physical force. BUF stewarding was thus somewhat proactive, and hecklers at meetings were attacked with a variety of weapons as well as boots and fists. Mosley himself verbally and physically assaulted hecklers. Fascist violence was at all levels. In 1933, the BUF bought the Black House, a quasi-military-style barracks that could house up to two hundred Blackshirts. Black House was a converted training college, and the potential Squadristi were paid £1 a week whilst the elite I Squad were paid £3. Given the unemployment situation at the time, £1 a week and free accommodations was a significant attraction. And they earned it. Violence remained core to the fascist ideology and control of the streets is essential, as is intimidating political opposition. The Blackshirts were frequently armed with 'knives, knuckledusters, corrugated rubber truncheons filled with shot, potatoes stuck with razor blades and breastplates studded with pins'.[27] A meeting in Oxford in 1933, which anti-fascists managed to infiltrate, saw 'things become very disorderly with people throwing chairs and trying to mount the platform.'[28] The stewards responded aggressively. It was also fundamental to Mosley's belief that he alone could save the country: 'physical force was essential to prevent the left driving his movement off the streets and like most fascists he still believed that on some future occasion he might have to save the British state from chaos and subversion'.[29]

Organizationally, the BUF was plagued by corruption and continuous differences over ideology and strategy and its membership. Fascism has always prized quantity over quality and the BUF was no different: in 1935, three hundred members were sacked for using the Stoke headquarters as a personal drinking club. The Brixton branch of the BUF ran a brothel, funds were misappropriated, criminal behaviour and alcoholic excesses were widespread, and one member claimed 'cranks or worse' largely outnumbered 'normal' members.[30] In West Ham in 1935, Arthur Beavan, an ex-Communist and I Squad leader investigated disappearing funds and expelled a number

---

27   Pugh, *Hurrah for the Blackshirts!*, 136.
28   Ibid., 135.
29   Ibid.
30   Thurlow, *Fascism in Britain*, 128.

of wrong-doers to the detriment of the branch: 'After the two offi-cials and their boozing pals had gone, I had about a dozen [mem-bers] left', he said.[31] That year Beavan also organized a meeting in Stratford, 'where Mosley, against bitter organized opposition from anti-fascist groups, addressed his first important outdoor meeting in the east London area'.[32] Individual members were revealed to have long criminal records for violence and theft, and after being expelled from the Shoreditch branch of the BUF in 1936, one leading fascist was convicted of 'malicious wounding...with an antique Chinese sword outside a Shoreditch pub'.[33] His previous criminal record was now in the open and he was replaced by someone less popular, who was eventually badly assaulted by disaffected branch members and replaced by a convicted thief. The desire for the idealised fascist cadre was constantly undermined by the people who sought to live up to it—something that continues within contemporary British fascism to this day, with members being unable or unwilling to ad-here to mission statements or party discipline. Inter-faction rivalry is rarely far away.

In July 1933 at the Hyde Park demonstration, a squad of BF shouted abuse at the BUF, which led to violent repercussions when sixty BUF smashed their headquarters in revenge.[34] This was in spite of Mosley's claim that his squads were strictly 'defensive'. In Novem-ber of that year a mass brawl broke out at an IFL meeting between 150 BUF and IFL members. Arnold Leese ended up battered as Mosley's 'boys' ran riot with coshes, chairs and other weapons. The BUF were not exempt from internal violence, and in 1933, dissatis-fied Blackshirts smashed up their own offices in Kensington. BUF thugs also attacked the Nationalist Socialist League after William Joyce deserted the BUF in 1937. Joyce was hardly unfamiliar with violence: in 1924 he had been 'attacked in a most dastardly manner

---

31   T.P. Linehan, *East London for Mosley: The British Union of Fascists in East London and South-West Essex, 1933–40* (London: Frank Cass, 1996), 111.
32   Ibid., 112.
33   Ibid., 45.
34   Thurlow, *Fascism in Britain*, 96.

while acting as a steward...and slashed across the right cheek with a razor'.[35] A small indignity compared to the millions who suffered under the Nazi regime he defected to and for which he was hanged as a war criminal. Earlier on, Joyce along with Becket operated as Mosley's propaganda team.

Although at their peak the BUF seemed a lucrative venture with an increased membership and a large staff on the payroll to deal with them, poor organization and erratic funding led to a fluctuating membership and rendered many branches unmanageable. In 1935, after revelations of fraud and fiduciary mismanagement, the BUF sacked 70 percent of its staff, trimmed down administration, and let the I Squad dwindle into apathy.

As with today, 1930s British fascism attracted all kinds of adventurists, misfits, virulent racists, disillusioned workers, gangsters, the criminally violent and the violently criminal, all of whom are less than reliable. The ever-present threat of violence was no doubt an attraction for many in the fascist ranks, and there was always a schism between what the leadership felt and what the rank and file wanted. The anti-Semitism and aggressive politics were attractive to many; there were informal associations between fascist cadres, despite their organizations' antipathy towards each other; and thugs from the IFL and the BUF organized an anti-Semitic 'tough squad', which operated in the East End to indulge their sadism. The victim/martyr complex much paraded by many a far-right organization remained elusive to the BUF: during the large-scale and violent incidents no one was killed and subsequently martyred, despite the use of coshes, knuckledusters and razors.

Unlike in Germany or Italy, guns were used only rarely. The fascists could hardly express genuine surprise when they were attacked in well-known anti-fascist areas, and the employment of a uniformed defence force only exacerbated the situation. The BUF was not only characterised by its overt violent reputation and open anti-Semitism but also by its cultural conservatism. According to its adherents, 'modern' dancing, music, literature and sex were all symptomatic of a

---

35   Cross, *The Fascists in Britain*, 59.

decadent society and should be stamped out. They saw 'bottom wagging' jazz as 'the music of apes in rut' and were appalled by 'Jew-boys wailing jazz and gold toothed niggers disseminating the "culture" of the jungle and the swamp'.[36] Heterosexual conservatism was also a popular fascist theme—ironic given Mosley's rampant adultery—but nothing enflamed them more than 'homosexualism': blushing fascists reviled it and insisted that there should be no 'homosexualists' in their number. One fascist writer claimed that contemporary literature was dominated by the 'ravings of the onanist, nymphomaniac, drug-fiend, impotents, pederasts, homos, masochist and many other abuses'.[37] He could almost be describing his fellow fascists, for the far right is rarely selective over membership and has attracted many 'deviants', which, only on rare occasions, some fascists have acknowledged.

Anti-Fascism

Anti-fascism was a mostly reactive phenomenon and saw the left mobilise gradually. In 1927, the CP decided

> to launch quasi-military formations of workers. In South Wales a Workers Defence Corps was organized involving drilling and marching with a view to protecting meetings. The Labour League of Ex-Servicemen was also trained in the use of force to protect speakers and combat fascism.[38]

Although socialists and the CP did sporadically oppose the New Party and the fascist groupuscules, it was not until the rise of Hitler in 1933 that anti-fascism became more organized and decidedly militant. The CP urged a united front with socialists having dropped the class-against-class stance against social democrats' stance that, despite many ideological differences, had helped the Nazis more than the German left. The policy of invading meetings and drowning out the speaker led to the deployment of the fascist defence squads, which in turn required an equally robust response.

36   Linehan, *British Fascism*, 232.
37   Ibid., 231.
38   Pugh, *Hurrah for the Blackshirts!* 108.

Despite growing popularity and support from some parts of the establishment, Mosley faced large-scale opposition and a determined one at that: at one Hyde Park demonstration '3,000 fascists were surrounded by crowds estimated at being between 60,000 and 150,000.... At Hull in July 1936, the Blackshirts were eventually forced to withdraw after an hour's fighting..."bricks and other missiles were thrown and one of the party was seriously injured"'.[39] The militant Welsh mining community were equally unimpressed with Mosley and at Tonypandy two thousand anti-fascists turned up to confront him: 'the fascist platform was stoned and the meeting was brought to a swift close with 36 anti-fascists arrested.'[40] The negative press reaction that followed these incidents consolidated the general perception of the BUF as mired in violence, and this was something that anti-fascists could play on. Also, the press would often refer to general anti-fascists as 'communists' or 'Jews' when in truth there was a much broader range of opposition. Mosley was acutely aware of negative press coverage and consequently saw diminishing returns at elections, whilst the CP, who took the hardest stance against the fascists, increased in membership because of the coverage, especially in the East End of London.

By the end of 1933, the CP was successfully mobilising against the BUF and, in the short term, violent opposition 'closed off many of the BUF's propaganda outlets, thereby hindering its operational effectiveness'. However, for Linehan and others, this muscular anti-fascism led to the more conservative fascists becoming more intransigent and 'assisted them in their efforts to push the BUF in the direction of populist street campaigning and militant open anti-Semitism'. The fascist campaign moved from the spectacular rallies, electioneering and mainstream-media courting to the street level where militant anti-fascists were more than willing to meet them.[41]

In 1933, the CP distributed an anti-fascist manifesto called 'Unity Against Fascist Reaction' in Manchester, appealing to all left organizations. The Labour Party and the Trade Union Congress were

---

39   Ibid., 171.
40   Copsey, *Anti-Fascism in Britain*, 47.
41   Linehan, *British Fascism*,103.

reluctant to join with the CP, blaming them for the rise in fascism. Labour preferred to rely on state legislation and propaganda to combat fascism, but this did not mean that Labour members, the ILP, or trade unions were not involved in an individual capacity in the fight against fascism.

The increased violence attracted recruits to both sides: the security services 'argued that violent demonstrations…provided incentive for recruitment for both fascists and communists'.[42] Mosley acutely felt the pressure that militant anti-fascism could bring about and organized 'more rigorous stewarding at political meetings to prevent them from being broken up by left wing activists'.[43] Although arguably effective in the short term, their over-enthusiastic stewarding methods ultimately forced public opinion away from him. The BUF were seen as the principle antagonists. The violence also alienated 'respectable people' who could agree with the BUF's policies but not their methods.

At the BUF's Olympia rally in 1934, twelve thousand punters mixed with one thousand stewards and many anti-fascists. Hecklers, many of whom were attacked, continually harangued Mosley: 'Mosley was unable to make his speech because of the noise and the fighting between his stewards and supporters and the anti-fascists.'[44] There was also a large anti-fascist presence outside, with many fighting the police. The violent excesses, despite recruiting the more adventurist types, appalled the public and the journalists who widely reported it—notably the *Daily Mail*, which had previously been most favourable to Mosley and the BUF with its notorious 'Hurrah for the Blackshirts!' headline on 15th January 1934. (The Rothermere-owned *Daily Mirror* also featured a headline reading 'Give the Blackshirts a Helping Hand' on 22nd January 1934.)[45] In his paper 'The National Government, the British Union of Fascists and the Olympia Debate,' Martin Pugh refutes the idea that the BUF lost support after Olympia and 'that any claim that Mosley changed his methods at indoor

---

42   Thurlow, *Fascism in Britain*, 95.
43   Ibid., 92.
44   Joe Jacobs, *Out of the Ghetto* (London: Phoenix Press, 1991), 139.
45   Greenstein, *The Fight Against Fascism in Brighton*, 22.

meetings after Olympia flies in the face of the evidence'. Pugh also 'suggests that, as more collections of private papers become available, the close relations between Conservative politicians and fascist organizations have become increasingly clear. It argues that the relaxed attitude towards fascist methods is understandable in the context of long-term reliance on fascist stewarding by Tory politicians'.[46]

Mosley had always tried to appeal to the 'respectable classes', anxious that the BUF were only perceived as a lower-class and violent rabble. Olympia did little to help and, with the event shortly preceding the Hitler's Night of the Long Knives, led to a fall in support until the BUF revitalised itself with the promotion of open anti-Semitism. Given this loss of mainstream support, 'the techniques and methods of low politics leading to street conflict with political enemies were encouraged.'[47]

After Mosley's great Olympia PR disaster, anti-fascists operated in a reactive or defensive manner. The threat of the BUF seemed to have temporarily receded, although Manchester proved to be an exception, with many street confrontations between fascists and militants. In the predominantly Jewish area of Cheetham Hill, the communists mobilised aggressively against fascist encroachment, in particular the Young Communist League who were very keen on violent confrontations. And on winning.

Along with Joe Jacobs's book *Out of the Ghetto*, the Communist MP Phil Piratin's book *Our Flag Stays Red* is one of the most often cited first-person accounts of anti-fascism in the 1930s. Piratin describes anti-fascists being violently ejected from Olympia and pays tribute to the 'hundreds of courageous anti-fascist men and women [who] exposed Mosley, though they were battered and mauled by the Blackshirt thugs for the slightest interruption or protest'.[48] Like other accounts of the time, Piratin highlights police bias in not

---

46   Martin Pugh, 'The National Government, the British Union of Fascists and the Olympia Debate', *The Historical Journal* 41, no. 2 (June 1998): 529.
47   Thurlow, *Fascism in Britain*, 105.
48   Phil Piratin, *Our Flag Stays Red* (London: Lawrence and Wishart, 1980), 6–7.

arresting violent fascists but instead attacking anti-fascists with mounted police. This was not just anti-fascist propaganda, as one Tory MP wrote, 'I was appalled by the brutal conduct of the fascists...Mosley [is] a political maniac.'[49] The night at Olympia did not go completely in favour of the fascists, and Piratin notes that 'not all the police "got away with it".... Some [fascists] paid well for what they had done that night'. This was in contrast with the Labour Party, who claimed that 'the Communists, by smashing Blackshirt meetings are, as usual, aiding the fascists, and gaining public sympathy for them'—something that the Labour Party and the moderate left have repeated ever since.[50]

In September 1934, Mosley called a rally at Hyde Park and made threats towards anyone inclined to disrupt it. Anti-fascists mobilised 150,000, and 'the rally was an utter fiasco. The Fascists marched in at 6.00pm and out again at 7.00pm protected by a massive police force,' and Joe Jacobs was in the thick of it.[51] London was not the only site for anti-fascist spectaculars: for instance, 'crowds of 10,000 smashed a Mosley meeting in Plymouth'.[52]

But things did not always go well for anti-fascism. In March 1935, Mosley booked the Albert Hall for another rally. The anti-fascist march was prevented from getting near: anti-fascists, as ever, faced aggression from both the police and the fascists. An anti-fascist rally in Victoria Park in the East End was assaulted by police resulting in many injuries and arrests. At a counter-demonstration shortly after, the 'usual gang of BUF members in Blackshirts were packed round the platform with a heavy cordon of police round them.... Anyone bold enough to press forward to ask a question or heckle, was immediately set upon by the police'.[53] It quickly descended into chaos: 'there was a surge in the other direction which left a gap in the police cordon...Nat [Cohen, International Brigader] hurled himself at the platform in a kind of rugby tackle.... The platform went flying and all

49   Ibid., 7.
50   Ibid., 8.
51   Jacobs, *Out of the Ghetto*, 145.
52   Ibid., 146.
53   Ibid., 174.

hell seemed to break loose. There were police batons and Blackshirts' leather belts, with heavy buckles, going in all directions.'[54]

In 1935, the BUF in Bow had to move premises following 'a concerted Communist "physical force" campaign which threatened to cripple its political operation'. In Bethnal Green 'the fascists claimed to have won "the battle for the streets".' At a Communist Party meeting in Victoria Park, leader Harry Pollit was knocked off the platform by Blackshirts, but 'some of them got a bloody good hiding. [The CP] had meetings all over Bethnal Green after that, absolutely perfect meetings...no heckling, no nothing'.[55] In places such as Wapping and Shadwell, the BUF failed to engage 'the dockers of Irish descent with a strong Catholic background and a long history of working class struggle behind them'.[56] The BUF also polled dismally in East Ham where there was 'a physical confrontation between Communists and uniformed fascists at a BUF street meeting', and a BUF bulletin later admitted that East Ham was a 'very difficult area' for fascist organization.[57]

Mosley held another rally at the Albert Hall in March 1936 which was again surrounded by a large cordon of police who from the beginning 'were anxious to break up any large concentration of anti-fascists. This led to running clashes whenever crowds gathered'.[58] The streets were blocked with anti-fascists battling police, but despite this, many anti-fascists still managed to get into the hall where there was more fighting with fascist stewards. A counter-demonstration outside descended into further violence when the police baton-charged it. As Jacobs states, 'The BUF would have been unable to exist at all without police protection.'[59] On May Day, Mosley decided to hold a rally at Victoria Park, which was opposed by three thousand anti-fascists. Mosley addressed the crowds 'from the top of a loudspeaker van, surrounded by four to five hundred Fascists in

---

54 Ibid.
55 Linehan, *East London for Mosley*, 60.
56 Ibid., 63.
57 Ibid., 109.
58 Jacobs, *Out of the Ghetto*, 198–199.
59 Ibid., 199.

uniform.… Fights were breaking out all round the meeting wherever Fascists and anti-fascists made contact, despite police efforts to keep [them] apart'.[60] Jacobs acknowledges the pros and cons of this kind of mass anti-fascism and concludes the above account thus: 'So far as confrontation on the streets was concerned, [the answer] lay in getting really large numbers of people to turn out whenever Blackshirts decided to hold meetings. There was still the problem of Fascist assaults on individuals and small groups engaged in political activities as well as violence directed towards Jews in general.'[61]

This mass mobilization against BUF rallies proved successful: anti-fascists mobilised large numbers outside of London with three thousand turning up at a meeting in Gateshead, five thousand in Newcastle, and even more in Leicester. Trevor Grundy details some of Mosley's physical humiliations:

on 18th June 1936, Mosley had been stoned in Manchester and six of his supporters were knocked unconscious as they defended him against attackers in Hull. In September, he was assailed by a shower of missiles at Holbeck Moor, Leeds, during a meeting which attracted 30,000 people and at Carfax Assembly Rooms in Oxford, Mosley had taunted his opponents and caused a riot.[62]

The BUF did particularly badly at Holbeck Moor when the CP mobilised and up to fifty thousand gathered to oppose them:

In due course, Mosley's platform was attacked, stones were thrown and Mosley was struck in the face, sustaining a gash underneath one eye. As the Blackshirts left Holbeck Moor, they were subjected to a well-orchestrated ambush by members of the CPGB, Labour Party and perhaps the ILP, resulting in about 40 fascists receiving injuries.[63]

60   Ibid., 201.
61   Ibid.
62   Trevor Grundy, *Memoirs of a Fascist Childhood: A Boy in Mosley's Britain* (London: Arrow, 1999), 90.
63   Copsey, *Anti-Fascism in Britain*, 46.

This wasn't unexceptional, and in Birmingham 'a meeting of 15,000 people developed into a free fight'.[64]

In London, the East End, Hackney, the Balls Pond Road and Ridley Road were violently contested in the 1930s between fascists and anti-fascists, and, indeed, between the different fascist groupuscules. By 1936, anti-fascist organizations had increased and become more diverse in their opposition: there was the International Labour Defence of Britain and the communist-led National Council for Civil Liberties; the Jewish People's Council Against Fascism and Anti-Semitism (JPC); the Ex-Servicemen's Movement Against Fascism; and a Co-ordinating Defence Committee organized by the Jewish Board of Deputies. Smaller local anti-fascist groups organized along Labour or trade union initiatives: the Grayshirts were founded from trade union and Labour roots but, unlike the BUF, these anti-fascist groups did not have the advantage of being funded by Mussolini (the BUF received £86,000 in 1935). According to Copsey, the most significant anti-fascist organizations were the CPGB, the YCL and the National Unemployed Workers Union (a CP front) as well as well as the JPC, which set up in reaction to the Jewish Board of Deputies' meek stance. The Ex-Servicemen Movement Against Fascism formed in September and held a meeting that was attended by the YCL. The anti-fascist street resistance was in general led by CP members whose 'strategy [was] based on the active disruption of fascist meetings and shows of numerical strength'.[65] These organizations all combined to oppose Mosley's march through the East End in October 1936, in the Battle of Cable Street.

The Cable Street 'Myth'

According to Cross, 'British Union never actually captured the East End. There the forces of anti-fascism always remained stronger than fascism'.[66] Linehan writes that 'on 4th October, 1936, a large anti-fascist mobilization physically checked the BUF's attempt to

64   Cross, *The Fascists in Britain*, 49.
65   Copsey, *Anti-Fascism in Britain*, 54.
66   Cross, *The Fascists in Britain*, 151.

conduct a series of anniversary propaganda marches in the East End'.[67] On the day in question, the CP had called for a rally in Trafalgar Square in support of the beleaguered Spanish Republicans, but militants urged people to get to the East End to prevent Mosley marching through. It was with reluctance that the CP leadership eventually cancelled the well-publicised rally and redirected members to the East End. Hand-outs advertising the rally were printed over with the day's new instructions.

The violence that ensued at Cable Street was between the police and anti-fascists and local people but remained a propaganda victory for anti-fascism. Many anti-fascists felt that the police were on the side of the BUF, or sympathetic at least. In fairness, both fascists and anti-fascists feel similarly aggrieved even if the facts do not bear this out. At Cable Street it was a battle between anti-fascists and the police. Following mass publicity about the event, both left and right benefited in increased support and membership, but, despite its notoriety, it was only one of many BUF marches that was disrupted by militants. One negative consequence of Cable Street was the introduction of the Public Order Act in 1937, which effectively banned uniforms and paramilitary organizations. Although this dented Blackshirts' glamour for potential recruits, it also meant that any political march could be banned if the police felt that it would lead to disorder. State legislation against fascism was going to be used against the left.

On the day, organization was fevered and tensions were rising before Mosley had even got to his rendezvous point. The Association of Jewish Ex-Servicemen (AJEX) got into a confrontation early when 'a fight took place with the police for the rights of ex-servicemen to march in their own borough. Mounted police attacked'.[68] (Piratin, 1980, 22). For Colin Cross, 'the Association of Jewish Ex-Servicemen built up its own strong arm equivalent of the Blackshirts for the protection of Jewish people. The communists moved in on a big scale... an unofficial level of gang warfare developed.'[69] Mosley 'inspected his men...stones flew over the police cordon, one smashing the window

67   Linehan, *British Fascism*, 107.
68   Piratin, *Our Flag Stays Red*, 22.
69   Cross, *The Fascists in Britain*, 154.

of Mosley's car. Another striking him in the face.[70] A tram had been left standing by its anti-fascist driver. Before very long, others joined in, tipping over a lorry. The police kept trying to clear the way but 'were met with milk bottles, stones and marbles. Some of the house-wives began to drop milk bottles from the rooftops. A number of po-lice surrendered'.[71] It was a victory for anti-fascists against the police as well as a humiliation for the BUF. Anti-fascists had succeeded in defending the East End, and this kind of militant anti-fascism at-tracted many to the ranks of the CP to further the fight. Despite the physical, moral and, more importantly, propaganda victory of Cable Street, the BUF continued their meetings and anti-Semitic intimid-ation on the streets. A week later, Mosley tried to regain the initiative by marching through Liverpool. The march was blocked by a large an-ti-fascist demonstration, and Mosley had to drive to the rallying point after being attacked by an anti-fascist disguised as a tramp. The police attacked the anti-fascists as missiles were thrown at the besieged BUF.

In 1937, the BUF intensified their outdoor propaganda meetings (having been denied meeting spaces in certain London boroughs) as well as provocative marches and rallies that often ended in 'high pub-licity physical confrontations with anti-fascist groups'.[72] In Plaistow and Silvertown, 'Mosleyites were physically prevented from estab-lishing a regular open-air presence…[and] particularly violent con-frontations occurred'.[73] In July, the BUF organized a march to Trafal-gar Square and anti-fascists mobilised, albeit more clandestinely due to the Public Order Act, and Mosley was noticeably more cautious over inciting violence with his aggressive rhetoric.

On the day anti-fascists attacked Mosley's car, clashes broke out inevitably and led to twenty-seven arrests. Although certainly not at-tracting the massive numbers that were at Cable Street, groups of an-ti-fascists harangued the march along the route whilst five thousand occupied the Square, disrupting the speeches. Ultimately, the march was not stopped, despite the presence on the day of eight thousand

---

70   Ibid., 160.
71   Piratin, *Our Flag Stays Red*, 23.
72   Linehan, *East London for Mosley*, 127
73   Ibid., 130.

anti-fascists. The BUF marched again in London in October, which led to violent disorder. Working-class organizations mobilised and adopted a more militant approach the following summer when up to fifty thousand anti-fascists assembled near Borough station (near London Bridge) and built barricades to stop the BUF from marching. Violent incidents occurred between the mass of anti-fascists and the police who were outnumbered and who desperately tried to clear the route, to no avail; they were forced to redirect the BUF, and Mosley gave a brief speech surrounded by his police protectors, who were in turn surrounded by anti-fascists as others occupied the original rallying point. The following year, Mosley managed to march again, relatively unopposed, but by this time fascist numbers were much depleted after previous humiliations, the very real prospect of war and the fact that Mosley had been identified as pro-German. BUF membership was down to 5,800. In addition to militant opposition on the streets, the BUF lacked significant media backing and could not book meeting halls in many cities, so recruiting rallies were limited to agitating and 'Jew baiting'—and even then only in a select few places.

In Liverpool in 1937, 'Mosley had been knocked down by a brick while speaking…with his usual courage he had insisted on climbing on top of the van to speak although the air was full of brickbats. He uttered two or three sentences before he fell unconscious and was rushed to hospital'.[74] Shortly after this, A.K. Chesterton, a veteran alcoholic Jew-baiter, resigned, citing Mosley's lack of imagination, timidity and initiative and that in BUF propaganda '"flops" are written up as triumphs…[to] give the impression of strength where there is weakness, growth where there is decline, of influence where there is only indifference'.[75] The anti-fascist strategy of mass opposition, political organization, and media influence had severely inhibited the BUF's political progress and morale.

Anti-Fascism in the North East

Pre-war anti-fascism was often based in London, as this was where the far right tended to congregate given its size and relative

74   Cross, *The Fascists in Britain*, 185.
75   Ibid., 161.

anonymity, but Nigel Todd gives a spirited account of anti-fascism in the North East and documents the paltry fortunes of local fascist groups. In 1933, Newcastle's *The Journal* reported that the town 'has achieved the unfortunate distinction of becoming one of the storm centres of aggressive Fascism in Great Britain', and documented over a dozen street brawls in little over a month.[76] In 1933, a BUF street meeting was disrupted and the speakers chased off. At the rather misleadingly named Race Week, 'five Blackshirts arrived with a lorry for platform...the crowd noticed that the fascist speaker "bore a striking resemblance to Herr Hitler" and reacted by overturning the lorry and hounding the Blackshirts continually'.[77]

Subsequently, the North East Anti-Fascist Committee was set up, which included CP, Labour and ILP members, and youth organizations. The fascists organized a physical force outfit who were '"taught boxing and physical training" to assist the BUF'.[78] Mosley had also sent ex-miner and boxer Tommy Moran up to the North East to train and recruit amongst workers. His campaign was somewhat hindered by his off-putting and provocative gatherings and concerted anti-fascist efforts. Street meetings attracted disorder and were often closed by the police fearing violence, which Moran blamed on communists and Jews. One meeting was attacked by 'a shower of whelk and winkle shells', and forty fascists were seriously injured in little over a month.[79] In retaliation, the strong-arm fascist squads were soon attacking socialist meetings and attempting to raise their flags on municipal buildings. The Blackshirts were humiliated in Sunderland in September 1933, when the 'corps' failed to protect Collier, their speaker, who was chased out of town with anti-fascists 'eventually besieging Collier inside the railway station where he was protected by the police and an exceptionally large Blackshirt'.[80] Collier's bad luck continued when a few days later five hundred anti-fascists attacked and overturned his platform in Newcastle. Around the

---

76 Todd, *In Excited Times*, 34.
77 Ibid., 11.
78 Ibid., 13.
79 Ibid., 39.
80 Ibid., 14.

same time a United Front of socialists, communists, the unemployed and trade unionists was formed; although the Labour leadership resisted militant commitment as usual, not all the rank and file members proved so pliant and were active in the anti-fascist groups. Later events in Spain created further difficulties between ILP and CP members organizing at home.

In 1934, Mosley held a meeting in Town Moor again and the recently formed Anti-Fascist League (AFL) mobilised support to confront it. The police informed Mosley that his safety could not be guaranteed so he 'postponed' the rally and rescheduled it. Aware of local weaknesses, the BUF bussed in extra muscle on the day, which did little good: 'Mosley was severely heckled and met "by a volley of small stones and an old dinner fork".'[81] The anti-fascists celebrated yet another victory as the BUF slunk back home. At his Newcastle City Hall rally, Mosley's speech lasted fifteen minutes—such was the vociferous opposition—and, as usual, he had to withdraw with full police protection. A later meeting in 1935, aimed at reviving the BUF, 'disintegrated when "pandemonium broke loose" as Blackshirts tried to remove anti-fascists'.[82]

The Anti-Fascist League had formed in 1934, pledging to 'provide uniformed protection for speakers at socialist meetings. The league...also [swore] to encourage and give hospitality to refugees from Fascism in other countries and, as far as is possible, to prevent Jewish pogroms'.[83] The league militants would patrol the streets on the lookout for fascist meetings and wore grey shirts, in part to help identify each other in meetings and confrontations. The AFL organized physical training for members and was determined to stamp out the fascist threat. After a fascist attack on an ILP May Day meeting was prevented, rather than operating in a strictly defensive capacity, the AFL tactic 'now changed to one of completely breaking the BUF...[which led] to some of the largest political confrontations of the 1930s'.[84]

---

81   Ibid., 71.
82   Ibid., 82.
83   Ibid., 54.
84   Ibid., 55–56.

The fascists responded by organizing a meeting two weeks later, which saw several thousand anti-fascists turn up to disrupt it, and the meeting descended into chaos: 'The police believed that the AFL, whose members were present but not wearing their grey shirts, was behind the anti-fascist demonstration, and they told Becket and Moran to abandon the meeting'.[85] The police escorted the BUF back to their headquarters, which was besieged and the windows were put through as the fascists hid inside. A squad of Blackshirts attempted to attack the crowd but failed and two BUF were arrested. Undeterred, the BUF held a meeting the next day in Gateshead, which was opposed by thousands. It came to a premature end and the police once again escorted them back to headquarters (which was later trashed, allegedly by the AFL). The BUF did not attempt anything like it again in the North East. The AFL and anti-fascist militancy had such an effect on the local BUF that Mosley made a flying visit to assess the damage. He found an 'abject disgrace'.[86] Physical support for the BUF was weak and Todd states that they regularly bussed in extras from around the country, something that fascist organizations in the UK still do to this day when they expect large local opposition.

As elsewhere, in the North East the BUF attracted criminal elements, 'bruisers' and 'a lot of villains'.[87] Militant anti-fascism proved an effective remedy to fascist poison: in Hebburn, the Trades Council reported that the 'crowd attacked the speaker and badly mauled him since when no further attempt has been made'; and in Jarrow aggressive heckling ended a meeting prematurely.[88] The membership of the local BUF were mainly unemployed and 'possibly attracted by Mosley's ability to pay Blackshirts for part-time work'.[89] Their quality speakers were few and subject to much misfortune: one was 'felled' with a broken bottle when anti-fascists attacked a meeting. Todd points out that although anti-fascist opposition was multiple and varied, it was not co-ordinated: numbers matter on the streets,

---

85   Ibid., 56.
86   Ibid., 58.
87   Ibid., 38.
88   Ibid., 40.
89   Ibid., 34.

but anti-fascists need to be organized and focussed, however many there are.

The BUF were determined to continue with their street meetings but were constantly met with militant opposition: 'There was a kind of charge, and the platform was overwhelmed, the banners got kicked around the square, and the Blackshirts fled in little groups back to the station'.[90] Another meeting saw

> the speaker pulled down off his platform, and his bodyguard were in complete disarray...the superior numbers of anti-fascists coupled with their obvious united fury and determination, proved too much...and the Police were forced temporarily to retreat, and the Blackshirts were chased out of sight![91]

In South Shields, one 'meeting commenced, with "thousands of people" outside the cinema, "the uproar was terrific." Fights broke out between Blackshirts and hecklers.... The Blackshirts soon beat a retreat, some being chased away and others in buses "subjected to a shower of stones".'[92] It was not long after, that the BUF sensibly adopted the strategy of giving up completely. According to Todd, the AFL was wound down in 1935 in recognition of their successful campaign against the North East fascists; local CP and socialist militants had responded on their own initiatives as and when required, all of which prevented the BUF from making headway in the North East.

18b

The eve of war signalled a major change in the BUF's fortunes: many branches had become moribund, although some managed to pull themselves out of the slump to engage in an eventually fruitless peace campaign. Opposition was still prevalent and a 'number of the BUF's East End meetings were closed following crowd disorder during the first week of the war.... The BUF prematurely abandoned its

90   Ibid., 73.
91   Ibid., 83.
92   Ibid., 94.

open-air platform at John Campbell Road, Dalston following crowd disorder'.[93] However, global politics affected opposition too when 'the Nazi-Soviet pact temporarily immobilised local Communist anti-fascism', leaving CP members in a somewhat confused situation.[94] There was also the matter of conscription and a change in law.

The BUF was proscribed under the 18b Ruling as a pro-German outfit, and many leading fascists were interned for duration of hostilities. The ruling 18b was intended to prevent any pro-Nazi fifth column from forming and many fascists including Mosley were rounded up and detained—although accounts vary as to the thoroughness and consistency of applying the act, as many disappeared to avoid arrest. Far be it from anti-fascists to rely on the state to deal with fascism; the internment of many prominent fascists under the 18b Ruling must have signified quieter and less violent weekends for many militants. Leading fascist William Joyce fled to Germany where he broadcast pro-Nazi propaganda as 'Lord Haw-Haw' on the wireless. He was later hanged as a traitor at Nuremberg.

A potent mix of militant anti-fascism, political and community organization, and negative media seriously impeded Mosley's progress. This was perceived by the BUF as 'Jewish opposition' and led to them ramping up their anti-Semitism, but by 1940 most of the prominent fascists had been interned and the movement fell into obscurity for the moment. When Mosley was released in 1943, public animosity remained high with a mass demonstration in London and a strike threat by Glamorgan miners. Still, Mosley's post-war career was to prove as violent as his pre-war one.

---

93   Linehan, *East London for Mosley*, 164.
94   Ibid., 165.

PART II

43 Group and 62 Group: 'It Is Not Possible to Legislate Fascism Out of Existence'

After the war, Mosley looked increasingly like an ageing failure with waning charisma and diminished oratorical skills. Several former acolytes continued to keep British fascism alive with limited success: Arnold Leese and Jeffrey Hamm had both been subject to robust discussions with militant anti-fascists but were determined to reinvigorate Nazi doctrine. They actively denied the Holocaust—the dominant opinion that has hindered the attempts to recuperate UK Nazism ever since—and propagated anti-Zionist conspiracy theories, but organizationally they remained small with other followers distributed through various groupuscules. These tiny fascist groups formed and fragmented with their usual acrimony: the far right was, as ever, their own worst enemies as tiny fuehrers waged internecine warfare for control over a diminishing number of party faithful.

The Union Movement

Post-war, Mosley's re-emergence with the Union Movement (UM) was a poor do as he tried to reinvent himself yet again, this time as a pan-European anti-Semite determined to preserve the Empire. Other pre-war fascists continued to support his lost cause, mainly because they were ill-equipped to do anything else. Roger Eatwell writes that Hamm 'was a brave street speaker, often facing physical opposition from Jewish and left wing groups which inevitably emerged to counter a revival of fascism and its provocative activities'.[1] We are, perhaps, more reserved in our judgments. Hamm's meetings were characterised by fierce rhetoric but were frequently attacked by

---

1   Eatwell, *Fascism: A History*, 260.

anti-fascists, the most physical and organized being the 43 Group whose members had gone through the war opposed to fascism only to find it flourishing on street corners back home, particularly in the East End of London.

The one time Jeffrey Hamm visited Liverpool in 1947, under the aegis of the British League of Ex-Servicemen, the fascists were unprotected by the police and, when he took to the platform, a large, aggressive crowd gathered and he was 'bundled off the rostrum by a number of young men.... The rostrum was then smashed'.[2] The meeting was closed down and they never returned. He did just as badly in Sheffield as one anti-fascist recalled: 'Hamm mounted a platform they brought and was surrounded by 10 or a dozen local fascists. A couple of policemen stood by.... Then suddenly [militant anti-fascist] Bill Ronskley asked us quietly to let him through. He made a dash, broke through the platform and knocked Hamm clean off the platform.'[3]

Having grown up with fascist parents who knew Hamm personally, Trevor Grundy gives an insider's account of the post-war 'movement' in his autobiography *Memoirs of a Fascist Childhood*. Hamm lived in London after he was released from the Isle of Man under 18b and 'was extremely tall and thin and always wore the same jacket of trousers.... He lived with his wife, Lily, in a single room and shared an outside lavatory'.[4] Even Grundy's diehard father, an abusive drunk and ex-18b, felt that Hamm was misguided and 'wasting his life if he ever thought there would be a Mosley revival'.[5] His father also warned Grundy to be careful when canvassing 'because the Jews would be out in force and they had formed a vicious razor gang called the 43 Group. We had to watch out for them all the time', Grundy writes.[6] Grundy attended many outdoor meetings that ended in violence, often addressed by Victor Burgess, a leading fascist, who 'had

2   Dave Renton, *Fascism, Anti-Fascism, and Britain in the 1940s* (Basingstoke: MacMillan, 2000), 119.
3   Ibid., 173.
4   Grundy, *Memoirs of a Fascist Childhood*, 22.
5   Ibid.
6   Ibid., 34.

been razored by the 43 Group of militant Jewish anti-fascists'.[7] The 43 Group also drove Grundy, Sr. off his photography pitch at Hampton Court. He said, 'If I go back I'll get razored. They knew me from Speakers' Corner and Ridley Road.'[8]

Like every other fascist party, the Union Movement was populated by 'colourful characters' who seemed to contradict doctrine somewhat, one being Alf Flockhart, 'who had been convicted of "interfering" with a man in a public lavatory. My mother said he had been framed by Jews, but it was his second offence,' Grundy writes.[9] Another character was Freddie Shepherd whose male 'girlfriend' was beaten badly at Blackshirt headquarters for allegedly stealing money.

The renewed Union Movement dropped the overt fascist trappings and attempted to capitalise on the conflict in Palestine, where Jewish groups like the Irgun and the Stern Gang were fighting against the British. The UM used the killing of British soldiers as anti-Semitic propaganda. Following events in Palestine, the Union Movement experienced a temporary upsurge in support as well as a simultaneous growth in militant opposition. Although the National Council of Civil Liberties (NCCL), Communist Party (CPGB), Socialist Party (SPGB) and Revolutionary Communist Party (RCP) all contributed to the anti-fascist struggle with their own methods, it was the 43 Group who organized a continuous and violent opposition to the fascists.

The 43 Group

> We unhinged the fascists.... They never believed we would out-violence them.
>
> —Len Solnick, 43 Group member

It seems incredible that British fascism could re-emerge following the war, the blitz and the horrors of the concentration camps that were broadcast around the world, but according to Morris Beckman, 'by February 1946, fourteen identifiable fascist groups were operating

7 Ibid., 40.
8 Ibid., 69.
9 Ibid., 112–113.

on the streets and inside schools and halls in London alone', [10]along with a slew of inky scandal sheets that revamped the new fascist vision. There was early resistance to this new form of fascism in late 1945 when the Association of Jewish Ex-Servicemen (AJEX) initiated a series of speakers in counter-propaganda measures. AJEX was not averse to occasional militant action either, and in the East End in 1945 they took over a fascist speaker's pitch. Undeterred, the fascists set up another one close by: 'Trouble soon began; heckling, abuse, and then fighting. The police closed down both meetings and made two arrests. This was the first physical clash of fascists and anti-fascists since the war's end'.[11]

AJEX was originally the Jewish Ex-Servicemen's Legion and led by Lionel Rose who organized to counter anti-Semitic and fascist propaganda in street meetings. One AJEX member recalled observing fascist meetings, taking notes, then passing the information on to anti-fascists to use: 'The idea was to find out what the hell they were talking about…so we could evaluate their propaganda so that we could then counter it with our own leaflets.'[12] AJEX unsuccessfully called for a state ban, and their speakers programme was not viewed positively by some 43 Group members who felt that reasoning with fascists was never going to work and that they only understood the language of violence, or the threat of it. The Board of Deputies of British Jews (BoD) was alarmed by the militancy of the 43 Group and tried on several occasions to curb their enthusiasm with little success. The Board at the time preferred the 'heads down' compliant approach whilst not wanting to encourage anti-Semitism given the situation in Palestine. AJEX had worked with the conservative Board but now began to step up their game when they occupied fascist pitches to prevent them from speaking. Undeterred by the Board of Deputies, many Jewish ex-servicemen were outraged by fascist developments and gravitated towards the 43 Group.

---

10   Morris Beckman, *The 43 Group: The Untold Story of Their Fight Against Fascism* (London: Centreprise, 1993), 14.
11   Ibid., 16.
12   Dave Renton, *This Rough Game: Fascism and Anti-Fascism* (Gloucester: Sutton Publishers, 2001), 177.

The 43 Group had formed in early 1946 after a violent confrontation between four Jewish ex-servicemen and the fascist British League of Ex-Servicemen on Hampstead Heath: Hamm ended
up on the floor and his stewards were routed. Although predominantly Jewish, it also contained many socialists, communists and trade
unionists who were committed to the renewed anti-fascist struggle
which few would have predicted after Victory in Europe (VE) Day.
The 43 Group, like many anti-fascists who followed them, realised
that the 'hard men' of the right could be found wanting, and to successfully defeat fascism a move from the defensive to the offensive
was necessary: 'We had shown the way ahead: the fascists could and
had to be attacked, but in an organized and disciplined manner.'[13]

In 1946, the Britons' Vigilante Action Group held an ambitious
rally at the Albert Hall which severely lacked the BUF's pre-war
Rothermere pomp, flags and big numbers. The 43 Group decided
to infiltrate. Also in the crowd were members of the CP intent on
disrupting the usual speeches on the Jewish-Communist conspiracy. The first speaker was hardly into his opening words when the
heckling started with one fascist steward panicking, saying, 'Christ—
here come the fucking Communists!'[14] Although not pre-planned,
the various anti-fascists outnumbered the fascists and the stewards,
whose bravado crumbled with their reputations as they exited swiftly,
and it was over after barely half an hour. For Morris Beckman, 'This
was the first time the Communists and 43 Group members had ever
encountered each other.'[15] In light of this 'joint operation,' and perhaps aware of the competition, the CP organized their own militant
V Corps, a relatively undocumented group.

Anti-fascist numbers of whatever affiliation were needed in
1946 as fascist street meetings in the East End increased in both
number and size. Militant opposition from the 43 Group, CP and
AJEX had to increase accordingly if the spread of fascism was to
be curtailed. The Group were attacking a dozen meetings a week,
speakers' platforms were overturned and stewards were battered, or

---

13   Beckman, *The 43 Group*, 24.
14   Ibid., 29.
15   Ibid., 30.

the police closed down meetings in fear of further violence. The militants quickly developed effective tactics in order to further inhibit fascist street presence. They realised that heckling was not enough, so they formed 'wedges' of about a dozen men who moved through the crowd, disabled the stewards, and knocked over the platform. Anti-fascist teams would confiscate propaganda from Mosleyite street vendors who were battered if they refused to comply. Realising that physical force was only one tactic, the 43 Group used the much riskier tactic of infiltrating fascist groups to gather intelligence: 'Information gleaned by Group spies was passed onto other anti-fascist bodies such as the JDC, AJEX, sympathetic MPs, the press and even the police'.[16] This strategy of inside information, street level militancy, community organization, negative media coverage and political pressure combined to successfully counter fascist activity.

The militant anti-fascists found themselves in a 'three-cornered fight' against both fascists and the police, many of whom were anti-Semitic themselves; one 43 Group member recalled 'a first class anti-Semite who would have done a good job at Belsen'.[17] According to Renton, anti-fascists were statistically three times more likely to be arrested than fascists. The police justified this by interpreting anti-fascist activity as aggressive and thus, wittingly or not, acted as stewards for fascist meetings to 'preserve the peace'—hence more anti-fascist arrests.[18]

In June 1947, Mosley organized a secret rally where he would speak for the first time since his internment. Anti-fascists were curious and naturally tried to find out the location and infiltrate it. The meeting at the Memorial Hall, Farringdon, was well protected and the ticketless were spurned. After an hour, groups of anti-fascists converged and stormed the entrance. Fierce fighting broke out at the door and the police tried to intervene. The anti-fascists attacked again and, as more police arrived, 'others threw bricks and stones at the doors and windows. Mosley's supporters raced to the fourth floor of the building and retaliated by dropping missiles from the

---

16   Ibid., 37.
17   Renton, *This Rough Game*, 174.
18   Copsey, *Anti-Fascism in Britain*, 90.

windows.'[19] The meeting continued and Mosley was greeted with the 'Heil Hitler' salute as he announced the official formation of the UM. He was later seen escaping in a fast sports car with bodyguards at his side. His other supporters, it is assumed, made less dignified and pedestrian exits.

The 43 Group set up headquarters near Hyde Park in London to cope with increased membership. Three hundred members were prepared to operate at the physical end of things, whilst 'the next largest section was intelligence'.[20] Unlike Mosley who retained his own fortune and had the covert backing of anti-Semitic and anti-Communist establishment figures, the 43 Group operated on a minimal budget. Mosley attempted to increase his influence across the social strata by forming more 'respectable' book clubs, for the bourgeois members alienated or terrified by the violence, whilst keeping in touch with his aristocratic acquaintances. These groups were sometimes infiltrated by 43 Group members in order to gain information. This could be a very stressful and dangerous business and could backfire: the unlucky 43 Group member Wendy Turner 'was caught and then very badly beaten up by members of the Union Movement'.[21] Mosley also built up a group of experienced orators who were protected by stewards to prevent, usually unsuccessfully, anti-fascist interruptions.

As ever, the British fascists' main problem was themselves: far right disunity and tiny groupuscules vying over who was leader proved counter-productive to their progress. There was the British Action Party, the Union of British Freedom, the Gentile Christian Front, the British League of Ex-Servicemen and Women, and the British Workers Party for National Unity all competing for a small, potential membership. Mosley's meeting programme began to attract more supporters: 'Despite the street fighting, perhaps because of it, the fascists were still drawing recruits in considerable numbers. They were talking now of organizing rallies of up to 5,000'.[22] The 43 Group mobilised accordingly and, by the time 1946 had ended, things had

19   Beckman, The 43 Group, 86.
20   Ibid., 46.
21   Renton, This Rough Game, 176.
22   Beckman, The 43 Group, 53

escalated, with the Mosleyites now seeing the 43 Group as a formidable enemy who forced them on the defensive. As one leading character said, 'If we don't find a way to finish off those bastards, they'll do for us.'[23]

In London in 1947, there were dozens of violent confrontations on the streets between fascists and anti-fascists. By this time the British League of Ex-Servicemen were attracting crowds of up to three thousand, facing large anti-fascist opposition, and becoming almost a local attraction. As confrontations increased so, too, did the level of violence: 'knuckledusters, socks tightly packed with wet sand, coshes, steel-capped boots and knives…[and] razor blades stitched to protrude beyond the edge of a cap peak' were taken from fascists, but it is unlikely that the anti-fascists faced with these weapons were not above carrying such things either.[24]

The fascists counter-attacked in the East End in August 1947, and '3,000 anti-fascists defended a meeting on Ridley Road'.[25] A few weeks later, anti-fascists took the initiative and rushed the Mosleyite platform. There were numerous other incidents. Ridley Road in Hackney again became the site of many confrontations, and up to three thousand regularly attended: on one day 'there were "huge crowds" of Jews and Socialists offering a "violent opposition" to the fascist speakers "followed by disturbances and violence"'.[26]

As street meetings and brawls increased, arson attacks on Jewish shops, homes, and synagogues were stepped up, causing the 43 Group to organize patrols: 'when they did catch the culprits they beat them up badly to make them think twice before taking part in such activity again'.[27] Group members in a taxi apprehended some midnight fascist fly-posters and enthusiastically piled out to confront them causing them to flee. Being better funded than the anti-fascists, the UM started using loud-speaker vans for their larger meetings, which were well protected by stewards. Group members would form

23   Ibid., 55.
24   Ibid., 57.
25   Renton, *Fascism, Anti-Fascism, and Britain in the 1940s*, 137.
26   Ibid., 138.
27   Beckman, *The 43 Group*, 59.

themselves into several wedges and successively run into the meetings, scattering the stewards and forcing the meeting to a close. In this period, Beckman claims that two-thirds of the meetings were halted. However, these figures have been difficult to quantify, and Copsey expresses scepticism over their accuracy, stating that 'no records of operations were kept', something that would be no surprise to many active anti-fascists.[28]

Many of these confrontations occurred on Ridley Road where AJEX, the CP and religious fanatics, as well as the fascist organizations, all gathered to speak. Beckman describes a typical encounter: after holding the pitch overnight, the fascists would start speaking surrounded by a large number of stewards as well as uniformed and plain clothes police. The Group would arrive in small numbers, with friendly taxis and cars waiting nearby for swift getaways, as well as two doctors to deal with any casualties. As the speakers increased their anti-Semitic vitriol, Beckman writes,

> I glimpsed the wedge on our side drive through the fascist stewards. Fists were flying and I heard shouts that were a mix of fear and rage. The people in front of us were pushing back with alarm, panicking to get away from the fighting around the platform. Police in uniform were tearing into the melee trying to separate the combatants.... Then [the speaker] disappeared from sight. The platform with its two Union Jacks swayed to and fro and up and down, and then it was gone.[29]

Savage brawling continued, and as the police struggled to gain control, the anti-fascists left the scene.

Indoor fascist meetings were also attacked. The tiny but grandiosely titled British People's Party (founded by the Duke of Bedford) held a meeting, which was raided, during which their film projector was disabled. These smaller groups tended to fragment and merge with each other over time, but it was Mosley who remained the figurehead of post-war British fascism. Increased pressure from the 43

28   Copsey, *Anti-Fascism in Britain*, 93.
29   Beckman, *The 43 Group*, 77–78.

Group, AJEX, trade unions, socialists and communists was exerted as Mosley gathered the willing fascist groupuscules under the banner of the Union Movement. Mosley focussed on fewer but larger meetings, and the 43 Group needed to co-operate with other anti-fascists on a broader scale, not just to out-violence them, but to outnumber them.

For anti-fascists, London has always been the main 'theatre of war', so those outside of the capital saw anti-fascism as secondary to their other political activities: 'Fascism, they believed, was a London problem'.[30] Perhaps due to its proximity to London, the coastal town of Brighton has many seen fascist incursions, which have usually come off badly despite their best efforts. In June 1948, the UM decided to hold a 'secret' march there, but 43 Group intelligence learnt of this and, together with AJEX, Group militants went to confront it. The UM gathered at the train station, led by a marching band and flags and followed by a speaker van and a phalanx of two hundred fascists with the inevitably large police escort flanking them. As they got halfway towards the seafront, a hostile mass of anti-fascists lined the street with some heckling and others throwing bricks, causing confusion amongst the UM. The police started to lose control as anti-fascists began attacking the march; flags were snatched, and the speaker van was hammered. It descended into chaos as the march closed in on its destination and more joined the brawl. A group of fascists were attacked by local ex-servicemen who had turned out in large numbers. The fighting continued for over an hour until the police could evacuate the fascists and their van. Some 43 Group members came across Jeffrey Hamm and some UM members—both of whom were hospitalised shortly after. The UM were humiliated and escorted out of town by the police. Beckman reports that not only did the UM never return to Brighton, but the incident signalled the end of the movement.

Anti-fascist organizations were active elsewhere. The Manchester Union of Jewish Ex-Servicemen (MUJEX) broke up a fascist meeting by attacking it with bricks. They also linked up with the 43 Group and worked alongside local communist militants in order to break up

30   Renton, *This Rough Game*, 178.

fascist gatherings. In Leeds, the Jewish Ex-Servicemen's Association also contained CP members, and together they forced a fascist meeting to a close.[31]

The violence continued in 1948 culminating in Mosley's attempt to march from Highbury Corner to Camden: 'Around 1,000 anti-fascists came into conflict with at least that many fascists and up to 1,000 police officers. Along the route of the march there was continual fighting'.[32] The march was finally halted at Holloway prison, signifying Mosley's failure to organize a rational and coherent political party, and his destiny to remain 'mired in the realm of fascist street violence'.[33] Copsey also attributes Mosley's waning potency as an orator, alongside ageing, which led to disillusion amongst his supporters.

In the face of well-organized and coordinated anti-fascist action, propaganda, political pressure and physical confrontation, Mosley was heading for obscurity. One Mosleyite defector set up the Anti-Fascist League in 1948 to propagate the message that 'militant anti-fascism worked, especially in areas where fascism was already weak and said "I believe a united and bitter opposition amongst the audience is effective…provided such opposition is sustained"'.[34]

Lacking funds and facing political oblivion, Mosley tried to rally again in 1949 in Kensington Town Hall, but it was not to be:

> The rally was disrupted by large numbers of anti-fascists.… Six divisions of London police were used to keep the anti-fascists from storming the meeting but anti-fascists did get in, setting off tear gas canisters which affected up to 100 fascists and brought the meeting to a premature end.[35]

Violence between fascists, police and anti-fascists continued outside. Later that year Mosley led the UM through Tottenham on another doomed march, and

---

31 Copsey, *Anti-Fascism in Britain*, 98.
32 Renton, *Fascism, Anti-Fascism, and Britain in the 1940s*, 139.
33 Ibid., 140.
34 Ibid., 141.
35 Ibid., 142.

5,000 anti-fascists and left wingers turned out to oppose the fascists. The protesters threw stones at the fascists, buses were stopped and their tyres let down. For the first time anti-fascists went further and openly attacked the police. They used ball-bearings and marbles to stop police horses from charging.[36]

Mosley tried to address Ridley Road again but was shouted down, pelted with rubbish and bricks, and the police closed the meeting. He retired from the front line soon after.

Fascist stalwarts like Jeffrey Hamm and Raven Thompson may have been deluded and paranoid, but they were more resilient than Mosley. Despite the humiliation of the UM on the streets, the constant assaults and smashed meetings, they continued to promote the fascist cause. For the 43 Group things continued as before under the directive 'Don't ease up—keep at them!'[37] In 1948, the 43 Group learnt of fascist plans to hold a meeting in Brixton, so they occupied the pitch with local anti-fascists, forcing the fascists to move elsewhere. After one speaker gave the fascist salute and shouted, 'Heil Mosley!' the police closed it down and dispersed the fascists, taking some to Victoria station where the 43 Group was waiting for the predictable chaos and violence. The salute was an inflammatory device: standing on top of a speaker van, Hamm saluted at an East End street meeting, fighting broke out, and he was hit on the head with a brick.

By early 1949, 'it dawned on the group that the fascists were beaten' and Mosley was over.[38] For now. Group members started to ignore the much diminished meetings by the UM and the cranks of the newer Imperial Fascist League. Many of the stewards had retired from the fray and, without Mosley's charisma and leadership, the threat of fascism had significantly receded. In the summer, in a desperate last move, the UM started to become both more vitriolic and anti-Semitic in their meetings and more violent on the streets, attacking anti-fascists and trades council meetings: 'Its speakers had

36   Ibid.
37   Beckman, *The 43 Group*, 149.
38   Ibid., 177.

never been so openly splenetic, and the fighting took on a desperate, almost crazed, edge. Every fascist had his length of lead piping and metal toe-caps to his boots'.[39]

Mosley had handed over leadership to the more rabid Hamm and Raven Thompson. Blackshirt gangs started to attack Jewish areas of London and the 43 Group escalated patrols: several of the marauding Blackshirts were apprehended and severely dealt with. Despite this last flurry of activity, the 43 Group realised that the fascist movement had been successfully broken and it was wound down.

Mosley's decline was not solely caused by the 43 Group and other anti-fascist organizations, but by a number of factors such as post-war repulsion over Nazi atrocities and fascism in general, and the economy becoming much stronger than in the 1930s. However, the 43 Group contributed magnificently to the demise of Mosley and the UM. Their fervent opposition to Mosley's meetings meant he had to book them under false names. When the Group found out the venue they would inform the owners. If the meetings were not cancelled, they were threatened and attacked. Leaflets would be distributed around the area to increase local opposition and then Group members would storm the meeting. These incidents attracted much negative media attention and Mosley's name once more became synonymous with violence. The 43 Group also produced their own propaganda such as the monthly *On Guard* paper. Other papers reported on the violence associated with the UM, such as the *Daily Mail* story on the Bethnal Green UM meeting, which was faced with much anti-fascist opposition, and 'a fierce battle raged with batons and knuckledusters being brought into use'.[40]

The militant approach was certainly successful, but the 43 Group, according to Beckman, hoped 'that one day the government would ban them', which was a mistake.[41] Militants can never rely on the state to defeat fascism, as the methods the state uses against the fascists—such as banning meetings, marches and propaganda—will

39   Ibid., 186.
40   Ibid., 98.
41   Ibid., 108.

always be used against anti-fascists. The state, as ever, is as repelled by hard-line anti-fascism as it is by fascism itself.

The Communists and Anti-Fascism

Renton notes that the CP 'had a reputation for anti-fascist work going back to Cable Street and the campaign against Mosley's release in 1943.... The party made a point of obtaining information on the various fascist groups.'[42] The CP's militancy had been a successful recruiting tool in the 1930s and when the fascists re-emerged again after the war, attacking meetings in Liverpool and Manchester (the latter with AJEX), as well as when they confronted the UM in Derby, Leeds, Hampstead and Ridley Road in Hackney. But by 1947 the CP had de-escalated their militant anti-fascism in favour of calling for a state ban. For Copsey this was also to avoid damaging their links with the Labour Party. The CP now preferred a Popular Front approach to militant activities and made moves to court the Trades Councils and unions, local parliamentarians and moderate Jewish organizations. Although the CP officially withdrew from the streets, they still operated a cell within the 43 Group. The CP also had an eye on electoral respectability, unlike the 43 Group and AJEX who were not in the business of catching votes and anyway embraced members of differing political persuasions.

The Revolutionary Communist Party (RCP), a Trotskyite faction, urged a united front with the CP, which was rejected: one member said that 'the leaders of the Communist Party discouraged their members' from militancy, although 'many rank and file members of the CP and YCL continued at Ridley Road together with members of the Revolutionary Communist Party and other organizations in a united front of protest'.[43] Copsey points out that the RCP, like the CP, urged a state ban, arguing that it could be effective if 'backed by determined organized activity on the part of the workers'—although they qualified this by admitting that 'it is not possible to legislate fascism out of existence'.[44] The RCP was also active in Manchester: one

42 Renton, *Fascism, Anti-Fascism, and Britain in the 1940s*, 80.
43 Copsey, *Anti-Fascism in Britain*, 91.
44 Ibid.

member stated that when Mosley turned up, 'it was the RCP that stopped him, the RCP first, and the Communist Party second.... We just chased them off, just a few hundred of us'.[45]

Mosley's Last, Last Stand (Parts 1 and 2)

During the 1950s, Mosley and the UM augmented their anti-Semitism with agitation against the arrival of workers from the Caribbean. In 1951, the Mosleyites had begun to complain about the 'coloured work-shy, dope peddlers, [the] molestation of white women and black crime' and propagated the myth that many of them ate pet food.[46] These same arguments have been applied by racists to Jews, Afro-Caribbeans, Muslims and asylum seekers over the last hundred years; urban myths of preferential treatment remain largely unsubstantiated, as are those of 'strange eating habits'—be they Gentile blood in Jewish bread or Chinese takeaways serving cat, all rarely, if at all, confirmed by evidence. There is also a strong sexual aspect to the myths of 'race mixers', 'foreign pimps and white women' and 'grooming'.

In 1958, populist racist sentiment against Caribbean workers in Notting Hill and Brixton in London led to gangs of teddy boys venting their frustration on what they considered a passive and alien community. Marauding teds attacked Caribbean men and women in an unprovoked and random manner. The teds were also receptive to the sexual mythologising of Caribbean men, resentful that 'West Indians were making quick money and riding in flashy cars, and their money came from immoral earnings of white and coloured prostitution'.[47] Mosley attempted to capitalise on this racist violence, but although the gangs may have been fired up by Mosleyite rhetoric, they were hardly fascist converts: the tedious political work of canvassing and leafleting was nowhere near as exciting as a razor gang rumble or Bill Haley. Violent confrontations in the streets of West London escalated over several days and the Caribbean community was forced

45   Renton, *This Rough Game*, 179.
46   Thurlow, *Fascism in Britain*, 246.
47   T.R. Fyvel, *The Insecure Offenders: Rebellious Youth in the Welfare State* (Harmondsworth: Penguin, 1963), 101.

to respond. Trevor and Mike Phillips have since described the notion of a 'fightback' as a retrospective re-evaluation that bears small relation to actual events. They claim that members of the Caribbean community organized informally in the face of violent attacks and abuse in the streets, and eventually the violence subsided.

Afro-Caribbean servicemen had been stationed near Nottingham during the war and, after it was all over, naturally gravitated back to a place with which they were familiar. Local recession, poor housing conditions and casual racist scapegoating had led to violence in 1958: 'Around St. Ann's black men were, more or less, legitimate targets in the constant interplay of gang fighting'.[48] One person claimed that teddy boys who were 'armed with daggers…issued fascist directions to coloured people. They shouted "Don't walk in groups or you will be attacked".'[49]

Whilst it is unclear whether these teds were actual fascists, their actions were intimidating in the extreme and, with a complacent local constabulary unwilling to intervene or who simply put it down to 'local gang fights', Afro-Caribbeans felt seriously threatened. This led to an absence of non-white faces on the streets after dark until one night teds attacked a lone man. Black residents 'went out the following week to see if they could find Teddy Boys to hit back, but nothing happened. And then, gradually, an incident took place at a pub. And the fighting started'.[50] Several people were badly injured during the violence, but the Afro-Caribbean group left before the police arrived. Shortly after, 1,500 people were on the scene scouting for black people to attack until the incident de-escalated. The following week, hoping for a more direct confrontation, a large crowd again arrived at the same place but, lacking black people to fight, ended up brawling with themselves.

Serious assaults were not uncommon in West London around Notting Hill where Caribbean migrants mixed with poor white working-class folk and other exiles. Illicit drinking and gambling

48   Trevor Phillips and Mike Phillips, *Windrush: The Irresistible Rise of Multi-Racial Britain* (London: Harper Collins, 1999), 166.
49   Ibid., 167.
50   Ibid., 168.

dens, prostitution and gang fights were common, and like in Nottingham, shabby accommodations was an issue with the recent arrivals at
the bottom of the housing list. A small number of Mosleyites were
also active in the area holding provocative street meetings, which
'provided an idiom, a vocabulary and a programme of action which
shaped the resentments of inarticulate and disgruntled people at
various levels of society'.[51] These social conditions and inflammatory
political language combined with the usual sexual paranoia. Like in
Nottingham, there were sections of the black community who were
not prepared to be passive in the face of such racism, and when gangs
and locals amassed they confronted them. One witness reported that
she: 'looked through the fifth floor window where I was, and there
was a battle between black men, policemen and white yobbos and
Teddy Boys.... Black men used to come from surrounding areas....
They would come in solidarity, to fight'.[52]

The disorder lasted three days, eventually burning itself out. The
riots did not recur following the unsolved racist murder of Kelso
Cochrane several months later, which began to mobilise anti-racists
and anti-fascists in the area. Although hardly classifiable as militant
anti-fascist activity in the classic sense, the riots at Nottingham and
Notting Hill indicate the racial and political climate of Mosley's final grab. His return was a failure but he still had one last, last stand
before he quit street politics for good.

The most significant fascist groupuscule following the UM's
decline was the League of Empire Loyalists (LEL) led by A.K.
Chesterton, who combined vicious anti-Semitism with animosity
towards the break up of the Empire. The LEL had formed in 1957
and, according to Thurlow, was made up of 'retired military gentle-
men, ex-colonial administrators, anti-communist and anti-Semitic
Roman Catholics, alienated scions of the Conservative establishment
and energetic upper-middle-class ladies'.[53] This was hardly the calibre
of opponents that many militant anti-fascists would concern themselves with. The LEL was funded in part by a wealthy ex-pat, and

51   Ibid., 172.
52   Ibid., 175.
53   Thurlow, *Fascism in Britain*, 249.

specialised in publicity stunts such as gate-crashing Tory conferences or disrupting meetings whilst dressed outlandishly. The LEL were not a group disposed to violence or militancy, and they maintained a minimal street presence. Although not specifically 'Nazi', the LEL is more significant for having contained John Tyndall, John Bean, Martin Webster and Colin Jordan, who all fell out with Chesterton but emerged at the head of the National Front and the British Movement in the 1970s. The clownish antics of the League of Empire Loyalists and their seemingly desperate publicity stunts hardly represented any kind of political threat. The terminal UM was vying with the usual far-right alphabetti-spaghetti of groupuscules like the National Front (NF), National Labour Party (NLP), White Defence League (WDL), British National Party (BNP), National Party (NP), National Socialist Movement (NSM) and so on.

> When the White Defence League held a meeting in Trafalgar Square the Sunday after Cochrane's murder the speakers were mocked with Nazi salutes and shouts of 'Sieg Heil', and students chanted 'No Colour Bar in Britain' and 'Who killed Kelso Cochrane?'
>
> —Trevor and Mike Phillips in *Windrush*

The White Defence League (WDL) was formed by Colin Jordan, who was far more openly Nazi, in 1956 after leaving the LEL. The stance of the WDL was articulated by one member saying, 'I loathe Blacks. We are fighting a war to get them out of Britain. They spread disease and vice.' They also propagated typical sexual fears: 'material rewards are given to enable semi-savages to mate with women of one of the leading civilised nations in the world.' Through the 1960s, the WDL soon merged with John Bean and John Tyndall's NLP to form the BNP, which eventually merged into the NF with sundry other groupuscules and individuals.[54]

Following the disbanding of the 43 Group, anti-fascism became sidelined for many on the left. The post-war political situation had changed with the rise of anti-imperialism across the globe, CND, the cold war and the declining fortunes of the Communist Party

---

54   David S. Lewis, *Illusions of Grandeur: Mosley, Fascism and British Society 1931–81* (Manchester: Manchester University Press, 1987), 244.

who had played such a prominent role in the anti-fascist struggle. Through the 1950s, migration to other parts of London caused the decline in Jewish support in the traditional Communist stronghold of the East End. Khrushchev's revelation of anti-Semitic activities carried out under Stalin and the brutal suppression of the Hungarian uprising alienated many members, Jewish or otherwise, by the end of 1956. The left in the 1950s and early 1960s was focussed on anti-colonialist movements in Africa and elsewhere, which attracted fascist interest. In 1960, the UM and members of the newly formed BNP attended a demonstration against the Sharpeville Massacre in Trafalgar Square to hand out leaflets and heckle, but they were rebuffed by stewards from the Movement for Colonial Freedom (MCF) and the Anti-Apartheid Movement (AAM), and fighting broke out. The *News Chronicle* reported 'a mile-long running battle, involving thousands of people', where

> Union Movement men headed by Sir Oswald Mosley had gathered in the forecourt of Charing Cross station…Then members of the Young Communist League who were selling their official journals, moved in to the attack. Within a few moments about 50 people were exchanging blows. I saw a dozen police officers and four men sprawled on the ground. Two other men were knocked down and kicked by the crowd.[55]

This was not an infrequent event: fascists attacked MCF meetings but faced physical resistance, which was reciprocated by anti-fascists heckling Jordan and the BNP in Trafalgar Square later that year. But in general, fascist activities were along the lines of the LEL-style buffoonery and bitter infighting over severely depleted ranks.

In 1961, the BNP's magazine *Combat* reported 'a story of a white lady coming back from work, pursued as ever by sex-crazed Indians. Looking up, she even saw a naked immigrant in a tree'.[56] In 1963, they also reported on

---

55   Anti-Fascist Action, *Heroes or Villains* (London: AFA, 1992), 25.
56   Paul Foot, *The Rise of Enoch Powell* (Harmondsworth: Penguin, 1969), 114.

Indians blocking drains with stagnant refuse, threatening [white residents] when they protested, urinating and excreting in the streets, living in garden sheds, entertaining prostitutes, accosting local white women, fighting amongst themselves and with West Indians—[and] driving out sitting white tenants.[57]

Combat also claimed that immigrants were 'breeding three times as fast as our own people'.[58] All the phobias over sex, hygiene and violence were prevalent. In 1965, Jordan's National Socialist magazine reported that non-white residents were in cahoots with landlords to evict white tenants by making 'deliberate, continual noise at all hours, systematic insults, threats and violence and actual assaults, calculated humiliation and obscenities'.[59]

The rabidly anti-Semitic and unapologetic Nazi Colin Jordan held a 'Free Britain from Jewish Control' meeting in Trafalgar Square on 1st July 1962 with the NSM. Several thousand anti-fascists turned up to welcome him and bombarded the stage with various projectiles for twenty minutes as Jordan and Tyndall attempted to speak. One 43 Group veteran recalled the following:

I had been in the 43 Group and had opposed the decision to close down their operations nine years earlier. Each year I saw more and more people turning up to listen to Nazi and fascist speakers in Trafalgar Square and marching in torchlight parades in Deptford and Islington. When I heard that a new group openly calling itself the National Socialist Movement was calling a rally in Trafalgar Square...I started to ring round a few mates.[60]

With predictable results: 'Then it went off. Fights were breaking out all over Trafalgar Square...and when we got our hands on the Nazis we really laid into them, but it was disorganized'.[61] Another

57　Ibid.
58　Ibid., 120.
59　Ibid., 115.
60　Steve Silver, 'The Fighting Sixties', *Searchlight* (July 2002): 15.
61　Ibid., 5.

anti-fascist recalled slightly excitedly that 'some bright spark in the crowd had lassoed the loudspeakers and dragged them into the crowd. The placards and Mosleyites followed in quick succession'.[62] The subsequent publicity and trial of the NSM members 'led to the revival of militant anti-fascist activity in the early 1960s. As the NSM lost its leadership as a result of the jail sentences it was the Mosleyites who bore the brunt of new anti-fascist anger'.[63]

Several weeks later in the same place, Mosley held a rally that was greatly outnumbered by anti-fascists, including one thousand who were wearing yellow stars. These were worn to show support of the Yellow Star Movement, an informal and peaceful group protesting against anti-Semitism and centred around the pacifist Reverend Bill Sargeant. Other militant anti-fascists had gathered then broke through the police lines surrounding Mosley, and a general brawl developed, which ended the meeting and saw many arrests. Mosley blamed the YSM for some of the violence. Long gone were the days of the I Squad heavies and ranks of Blackshirt stewards protecting the leader, and he was assaulted at several other meetings. The YSM membership divided over tactics, with the more militant anti-fascists tending towards outright confrontation rather than peaceful protest. As the UM withdrew from the scene, the YSM, like many other reactive anti-fascist organizations, radically contracted.

The 62 Group

Militant anti-fascists came together under the aegis of the 62 Group to pursue a more rigorous approach towards the emergent fascists gathered around the likes of Jordan. Harry Green, a member of AJEX, had joined up with Sargent and the Yellow Star Movement but realised that a broader, more physical approach to anti-fascism was required: the 62 Group realised that passive resistance and petitions were hardly deterrents to hard-core Nazis, and militants were soon joined by 43 Group members. Green gravitated towards the militants whilst Sargeant moved towards the more moderate London Anti-Fascist Committee. The 62 Group quickly established

---

62   Ibid., 15.
63   Thurlow, *Fascism in Britain*, 267–268.

itself as a small but busy and effective force with activities mainly centred on the East End of London. In September 1962, the BNP were attacked on the Balls Pond Road:

> The Field Commander of the 62 Group, Cyril Paskin, told us that in ten minutes we would split into three attack groups and get the Nazis who would be in the Balls Pond Road.... Around 400 anti-fascists led by the 62 Group leaders mounted a running attack at the Nazis. It was all over within five minutes. Nearly every Nazi present needed hospital treatment, including some of their professional boxers from Leeds.[64]

Anti-fascists regrouped at Victoria Park to confront a Mosley meeting where 'only a huge police presence saved the Mosleyites from getting the same treatment as the BNP but the fighting was very fierce. The fascists were chased out, there were many arrests on both sides, but [the anti-fascists] had prevailed'.[65] Mosley himself was attacked and injured there, and this would not be the last time he would receive a drubbing. In 1962, the *Hackney Gazette* reported that

> about 1,500 people had gathered at the corner of Ridley Road. Immediately he appeared, the crowd pressed in on Sir Oswald. He was pulled to the ground, punched and kicked. Fierce fighting broke then out, combined with shouts of 'Down with Mosley, Down with Germany'. Mosley disappeared under a group of struggling, punching men and women, only to reappear and start hitting, fighting his way to a loudspeaker lorry.... Coins and tomatoes were thrown at the lorry, and Sir Oswald fought his way to a green car, just as the police stopped the meeting.[66]

He performed just as well in Manchester where he 'was knocked down three times, there were 47 arrests, and the meeting was called

---

64   Silver, 'The Fighting Sixties', 17.
65   Ibid.
66   Anti-Fascist Action, *Heroes or Villains*, 25.

off after seven minutes before a hostile crowd of 5000 people'.[67] Walker reports that afterward '40 BNP members were beaten up by the now militant Yellow Star Movement. No Nationalist meeting could now take place without opposition'.[68] At what turned out to be Mosley's last stand in Dalston, one of the 62 Group members told how they

> managed to cram 17 Group members into the back [of a van] and as it swung in front of the Mosleyites the back doors burst open and we all charged into a very surprised mob of them. My Irish mate was hit in the head by one of them with a large spanner, he shook his head, got up and belted seven bells out of him.[69]

West London, where the Notting Hill riots had taken place, also saw violent confrontations between anti-fascists and the BNP: one fascist named Lelieve

> tried to club a young anti-fascist with a wooden club, the victim was pushed aside and Lelieve was felled by a booted karate kick to the side of his head. He spent two months in hospital. People were fighting all over the place. As [the anti-fascist] turned, the street lights bounced off something in John Bean's hand. It was a knuckle duster which caught me down the side of my head and face.[70]

As well as large-scale successes like the ones in the East End, between 1962 and 1964 fascist meetings, paper sales and rallies were targeted by the 62 Group who one day captured Mosely's headquarters causing a fascist march that day to be cancelled. In 1965, the grandiosely titled 'Great Britain Movement' held a meeting on Ridley Road, which turned extremely violent as both the 62 Group and the police were attacked with various weapons. Repercussions against the fascists was swift as 'later that night GBM members [were] attacked

---

67   Martin Walker, *The National Front* (Glasgow: Fontana, 1977), 42.
68   Ibid., 43.
69   Silver, 'The Fighting Sixties', 17.
70   Ibid.

at their Norwood headquarters.'[71] Once again, the fascists were their own worst enemy: just as Jordan and Tyndall readied themselves to dominate the tiny far-right platform, they were imprisoned in 1962 for paramilitary activities. This sounds a lot more ominous than it actually was: it amounted to dressing up in costumes and running around the country with decrepit weaponry. Tyndall was to be arrested and jailed several times and received many beatings from anti-fascists right to the end of his unimpressive political career. British fascism was about to enter a state of transformation: as Mosley went into noticeable decline the most significant changes amongst the fascist groupuscules was the increasingly gradual side-lining of their overt anti-Semitic rhetoric, or the decentralisation of it at least, in favour of anti-Black and increasingly anti-Asian propaganda. Whilst some fascists to this day perpetuate the 'Zionists conspiracy', others see it as obscure and potentially alienating to supporters. There are always new targets after all.

In 1965, a group of fascists including Jordan attacked a Labour by-election meeting in Leytonstone where the 62 Group were stewarding. They swiftly apprehended and battered the fuehrer then kicked out the remaining Nazis. Other more covert and dangerous anti-fascist activities took place: a printing press owned by Jordan was destroyed, then a couple of weeks later two 62 Group members were arrested trying to burn Tyndall's print shop down. The subsequent trial was an exposure of Tyndall's racism. Following a series of arson attacks on synagogues and Jewish property, 'Paul Dukes, a teenage Nazi, [gave] himself up to the 62 Group and turn[ed] Queen's Evidence against 12 fellow Nazi arsonists, responsible for 34 attacks on Jewish buildings in London'. These 'fellow Nazis' were members of the NSM.[72] To avoid attacks on meetings by the 62 Group, the Union Movement started to hold 'snap meetings', to which militants responded both by attacking individual fascists on sight and organizing a 'hot line' through which supporters could alert anti-fascists about spontaneous street gatherings. They would infiltrate the crowd to disrupt it by heckling, or run in and attack the platform; both

71   Ibid., 15.
72   Ibid.

tactics proved successful. A first-person account of the 62 Group's activity appeared in an open letter to Anti-Fascist Action's journal, *Fighting Talk*, in 1993, which gives a good insight into the time:

> Mosley's Union Movement started holding snap unannounced meetings in Ridley Road. Out of the blue 30–40 fascists, accompanied by their minders from Dalston police station, would suddenly appear in multi-racial Ridley Road. Once the fascists had 'captured' the venue, anti-fascists were arrested if they tried to hold a counter-meeting. With the cooperation of Ridley Road stall holders and shop owners acting as informants, a fast call-out scheme was organized, so that within 30–45 minutes 80–100 young men (almost exclusively men as I remember) arrived, prepared to remove the Nazis from the streets by any means which with few exceptions they did. Tactics varied from (1) quietly infiltrating the fascist supporters until we had enough there— then do them, to (2) meet ¼ mile away until we had sufficient numbers, then a running wedge straight in, and do them.[73]

Sometimes the 62 Group caught the fascists without police protection as they gathered up:

> The predictable carnage meant that the broken and bleeding fascists had to seek the assistance of the Metropolitan Casualty Hospital. To their horror and outrage the duty doctor turned out to be black and naturally they refused treatment, carried their injured onto the street where they were further encouraged (by us) to leave the neighbourhood (never to return). The result of many such clashes on street level and otherwise meant the fascists and their supporters could not and would not hold public and street meetings in East and North East London.[74]

By 1963, the UM was utterly demoralised and finally withdrew from street politics. Copsey cites the lack of political space both on the

73   Anti-Fascist Action, *Fighting Talk* 5: 16.
74   Ibid.

streets and in municipal buildings as significantly hindering Mosley; many councils feared violent disturbances and wrecked property so they refused to rent rooms to fascist groups. This and a combination of militant anti-fascism, peaceful protest, negative publicity, age, and exhaustion finally saw Mosley give it up. A broad anti-fascist front of communists, anarchists, socialists, AJEX and 43 Group members, the 62 Group, CND members, YSM members, trades council and trades union members, and labour activists, amongst many others unaligned, played their part in fighting off a fascist revival. Mosley retired to Paris ruminating on the crisis that never came (again), whilst the remaining fascist groupuscules—Jordan's NSM, Tyndall's GBM and the BNP formed by John Bean and Andrew Fountaine, along with remaining Mosleyites—offered meagre portions of racist gruel to a diminished and demoralised few.

After Mosley

Despite Mosley withdrawing from active politics, fascist groups, though small, were still active, and the 62 Group did not withdraw entirely from the streets. The fascist organizations varied in their tactics: the GBM under Tyndall was always going to be more provocative and openly Nazi, whereas the BNP under Bean and Fountaine began to waver under pressure. According to Silver, Tyndall's

> street sellers at the Notting Hill tube station had been hammered after attacking what they thought was a smaller group of Jews. Tyndall scurried off to the police to complain, whereupon the police found his battle wagon full of improvised weapons and promptly arrested him on the spot.

When Tyndall tried to organize in East London, 'a pitched battle was fought around their lorry and they were forced out', whilst anti-fascists fought with police after the 62 Group had taken over the fascist speaking pitch.[75] The GBM were later ambushed by anti-fascists as they escaped from the fray. Keen to save face after

---

75   Silver, 'The Fighting Sixties', 19.

his recent humiliations, Tyndall organized another East London meeting in October 1964, and the scene was set for another routing for the fascists:

> We knew that the police would block both ends of the street to defend Tyndall and his thugs. We did not want to fight the police but needed to have enough people within running distance to go through their lines and hit the GBM. We hid them on the other side of the local railway track and poured them in over a narrow foot bridge on our command.[76]

There was considerable mayhem as the meeting was disrupted, the police lines broken, and the speaker assaulted. Martin Webster, later of the NF, took yet another beating and there were many arrests. After this, the far right went through a period of reshuffling and, despite all their usual fallouts and bitterness, managed to unite as the much more effective National Front, who became a serious problem for anti-fascists in the 1970s.

---

76   Ibid.

The National Front: 'Under Heavy Manners'

And the only real kick we get out of life is when we go out on a
march, when marching with people of our own kind who feel the
same way as we do, who think the same as we do—even though we
get missiles and bricks and bottles and God knows what thrown at
us from the other side.

—National Front member

Call me a racialist because that is exactly what I am. As a racialist
I want to see the last coloured immigrants take the boat out of
this country. When we get to power our opponents will be swept
aside like flies.

—Wishful thinking of John Tyndall

'Political Violence Was to Be a Catalyst for Recruitment'

The National Front formed out of multiple Nazi groupuscules and
bought together the geriatric LEL, the BNP and the Racial Preservation Society, who were less a fascist group and more of an ultra-conservative, anti-immigration pressure group. The rump of the Union
Movement and Jordan's NSM preferred a lonelier route. It was Tyndall who was to benefit most from this merger and, despite early ex-
clusion, he managed to amalgamate his GBM and gradually assume
control. Tyndall realised that the tiny factions were getting nowhere
and that only a unified body could have any hope of gaining political respectability: with the Mosleyites forever tainted by association
with violence and 'the leader', and Jordan too tied up in Nazi fantasy,
Tyndall managed to secure his role on the fuehrer principle—that is,
he and he alone would be wearing the jackboots in this relationship.

The usual anti-Semites, Nazi fetishists and disgruntled racists stood alongside extreme Tories, disaffected Labour supporters and the football hooligan fraternity that the UK far right still draws from.

Although the leadership tried to present an electorally worthy façade, this was undermined time and again by outbreaks of violence, arrests for explosives or weapons, or the sexual crimes of fascism's thuggish followers, which caused the far right much upset. Some leadership figures failed to disguise their ill will towards the 'foot soldiers', or 'cannon fodder', who were most active on the streets. Tyndall was one of the three most successful far-right leaders to gain a political foothold in the UK—not quite a Mosley, nor as electorally successful as Nick Griffin. Tyndall had already been arrested and imprisoned for weapons offences and organizing the Spearhead Nazi camping trip, and he was frequently embroiled in the political violence that would hamper his career and simultaneously attract and alienate supporters. Thurlow comments: 'As in the 1930s, political violence was to be a catalyst for recruitment and with a much greater public antipathy towards immigration in the 1960s than in the 1930s even the more eccentric nature of the new form of fascism was given greater credibility.'[1]

Fallouts are endemic in the far right and unsurprising given the extremism of their politics and their frail, vain and dysfunctional personalities. Thurlow further identifies

> mutual back-biting, suspicion and paranoia…personal incompatibility, mutual recriminations about inefficient administration and authoritarian behaviour, disputes about jurisdiction on disciplinary powers within the movement, and ideological differences.[2]

Was it ever thus? With the different extremes of members in the NF, unity appeared to be unlikely, and it remains elusive to this day. As usual, the British far-right in the 1960s was characterised by multiple splits and splinter groups. It is often difficult to keep track of

1   Thurlow, *Fascism in Britain*, 265–266.
2   Ibid., 279.

who was leading whom and in which party, as the tiny leadership lead their cliques off in a huff to invent a new acronym. This has an even worse effect on voters when two or more far-right candidates stand in same constituency, squabbling over the small amount of votes therein. Many fascists held dual membership of organizations and often flitted from group to group depending on the clique leaders' fancy and their own attempts to get on in 'the movement'. Tyndall had been in the NLP, BNP, NSM and GBM before joining the NF. Jordan had been in the WDL, BNP and NSM, becoming more extreme and ultimately setting up the street-based British Movement—a skinhead-orientated mob that eschewed the electoral process in favour of street confrontation. Tyndall meanwhile toned down the fuehrer bit as he gradually dominated the NF, though not without the usual internal rivalries, which contested his political direction and leadership qualities. Although characterised by a typically anti-Semitic and racist political programme, there were differences about the overt Nazism and swastika-isms of Jordan and the more 'British' nationalism of Tyndall: the Union Jack proved to be the more politically successful.

1966

When fascist organizations regroup and begin to make their presence felt on the streets, anti-fascists organize in response. When the NF held its first meeting in Westminster in December 1966, the Anti-Apartheid Movement was meeting simultaneously upstairs. Predictably, chaos prevailed:

> Within minutes hundreds of anti-fascists, all claiming they were going to the AAM meeting, were trying to push through a large police presence inside the building into the NF meeting. Many were turned back. Threats of mass arrests cut no ice with the anti-fascists and confusion reigned as fascists were caught outside and anti-fascists were ejected from inside it.... Outside, a fascist heavy mob armed with bottles assaulted anti-fascists while the police looked on.[3]

---

3   Silver, 'The Fighting Sixties', 22.

Scenes like these would characterise the NF's attempts to mobil-ise throughout their violent history.

Early Travails

In October 1967, the NF held their first annual conference, which nat-urally became a focus of anti-fascist zeal. The NF members were given

> instructions from the stage about leaving the hall in groups, to which guards would be assigned to protect members against the left-wing demonstrators who were waiting outside.... [Those] who laughed at these precautions were chastened when they did face a running skirmish as they left the Hall. One BNP member had his arm broken at a nearby tube station.[4]

Like the LEL, the early NF engaged in silly publicity stunts, and in late 1968,

> the NF invaded a London Weekend TV show, gaining publicity but also a reputation for rowdiness that appalled Chesterton [NF Chairman], when he heard of it. His return to London in the spring of 1969 came shortly after the most militant of all the NF demos, when two Labour Ministers, Denis Healy and Arthur Bottomley, were assaulted in a general brawl at a public meeting. It had begun with flour bags being thrown (an old LEL tactic), continued with chants of 'NF...NF...NF' (and Chesterton abhorred chanting), and ended with Bottomley being kneed in the groin and Healy clambering to his rescue.[5]

Chesterton was old-school and must have realised that a new gen-eration of fascists had arrived on the scene with ambitions of their own, however questionable of calibre. Anti-fascists continued to mobilise:

> In May 1969, the office of its Croydon organizer was raided, documents were stolen and the Union Jack was burnt. The

4   Walker, *The National Front*, 85.
5   Ibid., 89.

following month, a stolen lorry was reversed into the Nationalist Centre at Tulse Hill.... The NF annual conference of 1969 had to be switched to another hall when two men sneaked into the Caxton Hall's switch room and smashed the electrical gear with axes.[6]

The NF organized their next demonstration in Cardiff to support the South African rugby team, which was being subjected to anti-apartheid protests, and managed to get a few vans full from London and elsewhere. This was not a great success: Martin Webster was attacked and beaten up, which did little to change his reputation for cowardice; in 1971, Chesterton described him as 'the fat (and fatuous) Boy of Peckham'.[7] Webster was an easy target for anti-fascists to identify: portly, pompous and hardly representative of the *Ubermensch* they so fetishized. He was ousted from the NF for 'homosexualism' and, although still floating on the fascist periphery, retained few followers. One militant, TC, says,

I recollect NF paper sales in Croydon in the early eighties. It was almost always youngsters who were up front holding the papers. It used to be a bit of a squabble as to who got to give them a few digs. This was not by organized lefties but a few anarchists, locals lads, generally outraged passersby. The NF gave up the regular papers sales not long after their bookshop got fucked off by the Council. I got a proper beating off of some NF types from the bookshop in about 1981/2. This was revenge for me splodging chips on Martin Webster's head and then wearing him out by running round and round in circles as he chased me, then kicking him up the bum when he was puffed out.[8]

The NF's counter-measures against such opposition varied: one member had infiltrated an anti-fascist group in South London but was exposed after six months. This hapless character was also

6   Ibid., 92.
7   Ibid., 98.
8   Personal correspondence.

attacked by two NF members whilst 'undercover' on an anti-fascist counter-demonstration. He was also a 'grass' and had been forwarding information on militants to the police. A later 'infiltrator' was immediately identified at an International Socialists meeting at a later date: '[I] wasn't wearing a pin badge or anything but somehow they just knew I was NF, they just picked me out.'[9] An NF meeting with German neo-Nazis in Brighton ended dismally: a small group of anti-fascists attacked the meeting, which was attended by the delightfully named Horst Bongers. In revenge, a female journalist from the *Jewish Chronicle* was attacked and left unconscious in the street.

Enoch Powell and the NF

Mr. Powell has nothing to do with racialism.

—Edward Heath, MP

In thirty years we could be a coffee-coloured nation.

—John Cordle, MP, in 1967

In 1968, Enoch Powell's 'Rivers of Blood' speech against immigration, particularly the recent influx of Kenyan Asians, was given in Birmingham and gave the NF a welcome boost. Powell fulminated about the 'tragic and intractable phenomenon which we watch with horror on the other side of the Atlantic', which for Douglas E. Schoen articulated the racist feelings 'of the pubs and clubs, the bingo halls and the football terraces. The bitter anecdotes of a thousand Coronation Streets poured forth'.[10] Quite. The Tories 'opposed racialism and discrimination', and leader Edward Heath criticised the speech for being 'racialist in content and liable to exacerbate racial tension'.[11] The Tories were quick to distance themselves to a certain extent from the outspoken Powell. The speech, with its disparaging urban myths about an old lady and 'wide eyed, grinning picaninnies', encapsulated

---

9   Nigel Fielding, *The National Front* (London: Routledge, 1981), 181.
10   Douglas E. Schoen, *Enoch Powell and the Powellites* (New York: St. Martin's Press, 1977), 33.
11   Ibid., 34.

the NF's twin sentiments of victimization and xenophobia.[12] Powell may have lost his previous standing within the Tory party but he did not automatically move over to the far right despite the far right being willing to assimilate his rhetoric and political momentum. In this notorious speech, Powell, being a model of establishment politics, had legitimised racism in contemporary discourse, and Chesterton stated that Powell's vision was the same as the NF's. Not only that but 'the Huddersfield branch of the National Front was built almost entirely on the strength of support for Powell's speeches'.[13] Tyndall celebrated in Spearhead that 'Mr Enoch Powell has now spoken out [and it] is to be welcomed', whilst simultaneously implying that fascists like Mosley and Jordan had thought of all this first.[14]

The reaction and support for Powell's speech has been somewhat mythologised. Paul Foot reports that 'meat porters from Smithfield, led by a supporter of Sir Oswald Mosley, and dockers from Tilbury marched to Parliament in support of Powell—though a dockers' one-day strike and march the following week attracted only a small minority'.[15] Martin Walker reports, 'Not all the dockers felt strongly enough to join the demonstration. There were 4400 strikers (leaving 25 ships idle) but only 800 on the march...[and] the dockers refused to march against the Ugandan Asians in 1972.'[16] A lesser acknowledged fact was that 'on the same day as the dockers and porters marched, representatives from over fifty organizations... came together at Leamington Spa to form a national body, the Black People's Alliance (BPA), "a militant front for Black Consciousness and against racialism"'.[17]

Powell's 'Rivers of Blood' speech was hardly a first, and his use of racist and inflammatory images were well established in previous outbursts: 'Can we afford to let our race problem explode?' he asked in the *Sunday Express* in 1967. He called for repatriation and fretted

12   Foot, *The Rise of Enoch Powell*, 116.
13   Ibid., 126.
14   Ibid., 127.
15   Ibid., 117.
16   Walker, *The National Front*, 110.
17   A. Sivanandan, *A Different Hunger: Writings on Black Resistance* (London: Pluto, 1982), 25.

that 'the breeding of millions of half-caste children would merely produce a generation of misfits and create national tensions'.[18] The subtext of sexual fear is fairly obvious. As well as the 'swamping fears' (something that Thatcher would pick up on over ten years later), 'there was an inflow of over 10,000 from the West Indies and the Indian subcontinent alone.... Such a rate of inflow is still far too high to be acceptable'.[19] We must also not 'lose sight of achieving a steady flow of voluntary repatriation for the elements which are proving unsuccessful or unassimilable'.[20] It is noticeable that the vocabulary of populist racism has little changed, only those subject to it.

The 1970s

The publicity surrounding the violence at NF gatherings established them in the popular consciousness, either as articulating populist racism and resentment over the economic and political climate of Britain, or as a violent ultra-nationalist outfit made up of thugs and hooligans. The NF had been under pressure from militant anti-fascists since its inception, with members attacked, meetings smashed up and marches disrupted—so the NF began to organize an Honour Guard, like Mosley's I Squad, ostensibly to protect marches and meetings, but also to attack or intimidate anti-fascists and anyone else they didn't like the look of. A solid phalanx of streetwise fascists, according to Webster, was determined 'to turn and smash our enemies into a pulp'. Which it didn't.[21] This move, pushed by Tyndall and Webster, disgruntled the more 'moderate' wing of the NF who were seeking political legitimacy rather than street brawls and negative publicity. Despite this, NF's returns at the ballot box were increasing both locally and nationally.

It was not only militant anti-fascists who were concerned over the growth of the NF; establishment parties and trade unions also began to take notice. In 1974, the leaders of the TGWU called on Labour and the TUC 'to mount a campaign to expose the NF as a

---

18   Foot, *The Rise of Enoch Powell*, 102.
19   Ibid., 90.
20   Ibid.
21   Walker, *The National Front*, 177.

Fascist organization, pointing out the disastrous effects of Fascism and racialism in the 1930s in Europe which could be repeated in this country now'.[22] The National Union of Students (NUS) also launched a No Platform initiative. The NF found it difficult to gain positive media coverage and also failed to make an impact via television. Like with Mosley earlier, Labour councils started to deny access to municipal buildings, and NF meetings were booked under false names—although even these were usually discovered and the proprietors duly informed.

'Expect Aggro!'

In March 1974, the NF marched in Islington surrounded by six hundred police: 'they marched past 4,000 counter-demonstrators who jeered and booed the NF's Union-Jack-bedecked parade, almost hidden by the blue uniforms of the police'.[23] The NF had been warning that there were 'Reds mobilising from all parts to "smash" its meeting. Counter-mobilization...[is] required to defend free speech'.[24] There was fighting between anti-fascists, the NF and the police, and the International Socialists (IS) defended their activities on the day, saying that the 'only way to deal with bully boys is to actually physically prevent them organizing.'[25] In Oxford shortly after, an NF meeting was blockaded by five hundred demonstrators who attacked the police lines and blocked the streets whilst fighting with the NF's Honour Guard. According to AFA's *Fighting Talk* journal, 'Within minutes of its opening, thirty members of the Oxford Anti-Fascist Committee burst in. They tore down the Front's Union Jack emblem, overturned the speakers table and threw [Ian] Anderson out on his arse.'[26]

The Honour Guard was apparently out on the streets later, 'armed with a vicious assortment of offensive weapons', and attacked two black men at a London hotel meeting where one of the targets was beaten with bicycle chains, which caused an NF official to resign in

22   Ibid., 157.
23   Ibid., 181.
24   Fielding, *The National Front*, 174.
25   Ibid., 175.
26   Anti-Fascist Action, *Heroes or Villains*, 33.

disgust. Anti-fascists attacked an NF meeting in Canterbury, which ended with ten arrests.[27] Nigel Fielding, who was observing, was told that they should 'expect aggro' and came to the conclusion that if the NF wanted to avoid trouble, they could.[28]

An anti-EEC NF event in Glasgow in May ended in a riot, with nearly seventy arrests and the police being criticised for heavy-handedness. By the time the meeting got going, twelve people were in attendance. In Newham, NF members tried picketing an IS meeting in response, so the NF's subsequent meeting was occupied by the IS. This descended into a brawl, with IS members blocking the NF in with tables, and the NF claiming a victory. At an NF meeting in Hastings, anti-fascists fought with police and 'demonstrators linked arms to bar entrance to the meeting.... When six NF stewards took up positions outside the main door in front of the demonstrators police told them to get inside or they would be arrested for "provoking the demonstrators"'. Three anti-fascists were jailed.[29]

Red Lion Square: 15ᵗʰ June 1974

As political pressure increased so did militancy on the streets, with the biggest anti-fascist mobilization at Red Lion Square on 15ᵗʰ June 1974. The day was most memorable for the death of an anti-fascist protester named Kevin Gately, who, along with Blair Peach, was one of the very few people to have died in the violent conflict between far right, police and anti-fascists in the UK. Like Cable Street, Red Lion Square is seen as a seminal moment in post-war British anti-fascism, and like Cable Street it has also been misinterpreted: it was a pitched battle between anti-fascists and police, not between fascists and their political opponents.

The NF was to march via Downing Street and then hold a meeting against immigration in Conway Hall near Holborn where they had met several times before. There had been one minor disturbance the previous year when anti-fascists picketed the NF meeting then fought with police, which led to a number of injuries and arrests.

27   Fielding, *The National Front*, 165.
28   Ibid., 162.
29   Ibid., 163.

This time the anti-fascists were to march and then stage a counter-demonstration. Liberation, a CP/broad-left front that was previously known as the Movement for Colonial Freedom, was also to hold a meeting in Conway Hall. Lord Justice Scarman later described this, in panicky rhetoric, as 'a mischievous ploy'.[30] The NUS worried over possible violence and urged Liberation to cancel. The police allowed both marches to go ahead, although with different routes and different assembly points. The NF expected trouble and planned accordingly: they marched behind the drums and flags and arrived at the hall along with a pair of protective squads numbering about a hundred each: 'Scouts were sent forward to identify side-streets from which counter-demonstrators might emerge to attack the column, and members of the defence parties were ready to move forward to man the exits from these side-streets'.[31]

The two demonstrations converged on the area at the same time although separated by the police. The counter-demonstration, a massed anti-fascist front that included the International Marxist Group (IMG), IS, CP, anarchists and trade union members, had grown to a considerable size. The IMG 'linked arms and charged the cordon. This charge took the police by surprise and the cordon almost gave way'.[32] They responded with force, on foot, on horseback and with the notorious Special Patrol Group (who were later discredited and disbanded) as they tried to clear the counter-demonstrators out of the immediate area. Lord Scarman called the IMG move 'unexpected, unprovoked and viciously violent'.[33] The police wanted to clear the streets to avoid disorder, and anti-fascists regrouped to block the NF march. One NF member broke ranks and began threatening the opposition when 'a small, squat figure emerged.... He carried a chunk of wood from a broken banner. No fucking about with formal introductions, he dashed straight up and struck the ranting bonehead directly on the noggin'.[34]

---

30   Richard Clutterbuck, *Britain in Agony: The Growth of Political Violence* (London: Faber and Faber, 1978), 155.
31   Ibid., 157.
32   Ibid., 157.
33   Ibid., 161.
34   Martin Lux, *Anti-Fascist* (London: Phoenix, 2006), 25.

The police managed to keep the two groups apart in the main by forcing the anti-fascists away from the scene with horses. This led to a violent response from the anti-fascists who attacked the police with wooden poles, then regrouped again, and there was more fighting with the police, as Lux says: 'Soon we found ourselves being pushed back into a corner of Red Lion Square with about a hundred other anti-fascists, brawling all the way.'[35]

The police overreacted with violence that left many injured and Gately dead: fifty-one were arrested and forty-six police were injured. In addition to the death of Kevin Gately, the left was widely represented as instigators of the violence in the press and on TV, and the NF's reputation remained relatively untarnished for the day. Following the violence at Red Lion Square, it was impossible for the NF to mobilise en masse without police protection, as they faced such large-scale opposition—although the sight of police surrounding fascists for their own protection was hardly a new sight.

Leicester, 1974

In August 1974, Asian workers at Imperial Typewriters in Leicester called a strike over bias towards white workers:

> Besides the usual grievances of low pay and poor conditions, the strikers found that the company had been cheating on its bonus payments for over a year. Yet the local TGWU staff refused to make the strike official. In a wave of racist feeling many of the white workers broke the strike. The National Front stirred up the situation and only the urgent intervention of senior TGWU officials and a backing down by management prevented a massive confrontation between the black workers on the one hand and the white workers and management on the other.[36]

So much for the TGWU 'pointing out the disastrous effects of Fascism and racialism'. A statement by the strike committee criticised

35 Ibid.
36 *Crisis: Special Report* (London: CIS, 1978), 21.

the unions for 'functioning as a white man's union and this must be challenged.'[37]

Fifteen hundred NF marched through Leicester in support of the white workers, guarded by twelve hundred police and confronted by six thousand anti-fascists. Webster was attacked again, claiming rather meekly that 'two men tried to rough me up. They went for my sex life, but fortunately they missed'.[38] Two anti-fascists were jailed for ten months. The NF meeting finally took place in a school completely surrounded by police. Ray Hill reports that

> when the NF marched through Leicester [they] precipitated some of the worst political violence in British election history. Outraged anti-fascists ended up fighting a pitched battle with police to prevent the Front from rallying and many were arrested. Police dogs were turned loose on the crowds.[39]

Fraser rewatched the footage much later and wrote the following:

> The NF marchers appeared to have been bussed in but I reminded myself that in three of the city's ten wards they had won over 20 percent of the vote the previous year. They carried Union Jacks and crude cheap banners. Most of them appeared to be old and angry, their faces marked by many years of bad diet.[40]

The ensuing riot gained vital coverage for the NF, playing up their 'victimization' by violent anti-fascists and the local Asian community. Fraser met up with a journalist from the time who said, 'The National Front people weren't terribly intelligent people.... They wanted to scare people, but...old ladies didn't like the big boots and skinhead clothes.' Fraser characterises the NF rather harshly as 'a collection of crackpots: white Imperialists, gun runners, halitosis-ridden

---

37 Ibid., 22.
38 Fielding, *The National Front*, 169.
39 Ray Hill, *The Other Face of Terror: Inside Europe's Neo-Nazi Network* (London: Grafton, 1988), 159.
40 Fraser, *The Voice of Modern Hatred*, 172–73.

child molesters, purple-veined vestiges from the sad past of Oswald Mosley and his not so merry men'.[41]

In September 1974, the NF march in support of Ulster Loyalists had to be redirected when seven thousand anti-fascists occupied their rallying point in Hyde Park. The march had been previously hindered when 'four hundred demonstrators were delayed by police searching for weapons'.[42] As usual, the NF boasted of their physical stamina and claimed that 'it's time to turn our young men loose on the Reds'.[43] The NF infiltrated an anti-fascist meeting in Brighton in September 1974 but walked out 'after failing to disrupt it'.[44] In nearby Horsham, an NF meeting was picketed and fighting broke out, with one anti-fascist being hit by a hammer: 'There was blood all over the place. All chaos broke out. They were kicking and hitting right, left and centre.'[45]

Later, in a pub, there was a fight between anti-fascists and an NF steward. The NF and far right, who had long seen the Irish Republican struggle as anathema to imperialist aims, were variously seeking support in the loyalist communities of Northern Ireland and Scotland, and frequently mobilised against pro-Republican marches. Following the riot at Red Lion Square, the NF organized a 'Smash the IRA' march in London, fully realizing that it was a provocation to many on the left who tended to support the Republican struggle (though not necessarily the IRA). About two thousand anti-fascists and Republicans counter-demonstrated and, at the end of the rally, listened to speeches 'from a platform ringed by youths wearing crash helmets'. The rally soon turned into brawling with police. The NF, which was about a thousand strong, had since been diverted from their original route by the police, although 'there were a number of minor clashes on the way, and NF supporters were photographed wielding clubs'. Several people were arrested.[46]

---

41   Ibid., 174.
42   Fielding, *The National Front*, 158.
43   Walker, *The National Front*, 163.
44   Fielding, *The National Front*, 159.
45   Ibid., 164.
46   Ibid., 168.

In 1975 at Preston, anti-fascists attacked NF leafletters, confiscating their literature, 'and a girl was hit to the ground and kicked on the chin'.[47] In revenge, the NF, led by carpet-salesman John Kingsley-Read, ambushed the anti-fascists the following week, an attack that *Spearhead*, Tyndall's magazine, gloated over. In 1975, the NF marched through Bradford, which was 'the biggest ever outside London, with 1,000 marchers, a pipe band and flag column'.[48] Numbers vary depending on sources: Walker claims fifteen hundred NF. Whatever the actual figures, the NF were seriously outnumbered by opponents and needed police protection. This incited local youths who attacked both fascists and police in a running battle.

Martin Lux describes Bradford as a 'near riot' where

> police were attacked as they tried to escort the Front through Lumb Lane, and police vehicles were overturned. Human barricades linked arms across the road preventing the Front from taking their intended route. I recognised some anarchos with black flags up in the front of the photographs.[49]

In 1975, Paul Rose MP, claimed that there had been a thousand cases of far-right violence, with

> people being beaten up, windows being broken, posters being defaced. There have been far more serious incidents where people have been razor-slashed when they've been by themselves coming out of anti-fascist meetings, where squatters in one case in Camden were fired upon by shotguns and also that one far-right member had been sentenced for 10 years imprisonment for gun-running in connection with the UDA.[50]

This does not even touch upon the casual and not-so-casual racist violence meted out by NF members that went unreported by victims

47   Ibid., 170.
48   Ibid., 159.
49   Lux, *Anti-Fascist*, 42.
50   Fielding, *The National Front*, 177–78.

from ethnic minorities. Later, *Crisis* alleged that the Honour Guard was 'breaking up other organizations' meetings and beating up individual opponents at their own meetings'.[51]

In 1975, Tyndall was ousted from his much coveted leadership role by a more 'moderate' faction, and replaced by solicitor John Kingsley-Read, which Tyndall dragged into court to contest. At the meeting that led to Tyndall's removal, the Trades Council picketed outside, and the IS ended up in confrontation as the NF fragmented and fell out with itself. Tyndall was resigned to raging in *Spearhead* about 'misfits, inadequates [and] failures' that inhabited 'the movement' as a new splinter group, the National Party, emerged in 1976. The electoral progress of the NF had been improving, but the NP was in danger of splitting the far-right vote. Muhammed Anwar reports in *Race and Politics* that, in 1974, the NF stood ninety candidates and received a 3.1 percent average, whereas by 1979 their 303 candidates polled 1.4 percent average. The split was only one of the factors. As Thurlow notes, most of the legal cases that subsequently surrounded the NF were 'increasingly bitter disputes…petty squabbles or arcane disputes about control of property and legal costs'.[52]

When two hundred members of the NF attempted to march through Birmingham in 1976, a thousand anti-fascists clashed with police, and twenty-eight were arrested after violent disorder: 'five hundred police were involved, and demonstrators threw bricks, stones and bottles as they tried to break police cordons'.[53] The police station was attacked, and looting occurred in the melee that followed. The ante was being upped: the SWP was determined 'to physically oppose the Front on the streets. At the same time the Front began a policy of marching into strongly immigrant areas'.[54] Asian communities had begun organizing 'a continuous, disciplined self-defence organization which could effectively stop white gangs, National Front hooligans, or anyone else, from picking on Asian individuals and on Asian homes.'[55]

---

51   *Crisis: Special Report*, 37.
52   Thurlow, *Fascism in Britain*, 284.
53   Fielding, *The National Front*, 175.
54   Ibid.
55   *Crisis: Special Reports*, 39.

Wood Green

The Front and their police protectors were faced with much more numerous, better organized and determined opposition armed with smoke bombs, flares, bricks, bottles, and planned ambushes. At Duckett's Corner...there was a spontaneous move to block the road and physically attack the Front...[and] a squad of black kids accurately hurling training shoes borrowed from Freeman, Hardy and Willis.
—David Widgery in Andy Beckett's *When the Lights Went Out*

In April 1977, the National Front marched through the north London district of Wood Green, leading to a large-scale confrontation. The *Hornsey Journal* reported the following:

Violence erupted in Wood Green on Saturday when a racist march by National Front protesters provoked a massive protest and wrought havoc in the High Street. Fifty people including some marchers were arrested and 13 others injured by flying bottles, stones and smoke bombs. At several points along the route the heavy police cordon broke and there were bitter clashes between the National Front and objectors.[56]

The Met's notorious Special Patrol Group (SPG) was much in evidence and clearly anticipated a violent response from anti-fascists. Martin Lux noted sardonically that 'the Front were gathering, affording spectators the usual contrast between the impressive forest of flags and the shabby lowlife gathered beneath'.[57] As the fascists set-off they faced much opposition from local Greek, Turkish and black youth who attacked the march alongside militant anti-fascists: 'A little way along Wood Green High Road the march was attacked. Red smoke bombs filled the air and a battle was soon under way. Everything that could be thrown was thrown at the fascists in an attempt to stop the march'.[58] Anti-fascists showered

56   Anti-Fascist Action, *Heroes or Villains*, 34.
57   Lux, *Anti-Fascist*, 54.
58   Dave Renton, *When We Touched the Sky: The Anti-Nazi League*,

the NF with eggs, flour and tomatoes (which could actually have made a nice quiche) whilst the police were attempting to clear the counter-demonstrators from the sides of the road as the march advanced: 'We all struggled forward, kicking, punching, into police lines. Helmets flew, bottles smashed. The fighting raged as the head of the Nazi column reached the crossroads'. The march was 'protected by even more cops...[and] buckled but didn't break thanks to the large reinforcements of SPG'.[59] There were eighty-one arrests, seventy-four of them anti-fascists.

The violence continued away from the march on public transport with the British Movement 'Leader Guard' making a belated appearance. Renton writes that

> At first they did a lot of damage, but as the train journey away from Wood Green continued they were cut down and down until finally a handful of them remained battered and bleeding and they made their escape.[60]

Many anti-fascists became radicalised by such experiences: one SWP member recalled that after infiltrating an NF meeting where he was roughly forced out, 'any illusions I may have had about non-violent means of opposing them were destroyed in that school'.[61] Dave Renton records that 'the Wood Green mobilization had been a victory: reducing the NF to "an ill organized and bedraggled queue"'.[62] Lux writes that 'the Front certainly wouldn't be coming back here in a hurry'.[63] When they did return to nearby Hoxton two weeks later, five hundred anti-fascists showed up to greet them, whilst in Brick Lane black defence patrols were called for.[64] The violent anti-fascist struggle continued.

1977–1981 (London: New Clarion, 2006), 52.

59   Lux, *Anti-Fascist*, 54–55.
60   Renton, *When We Touched the Sky*, 53.
61   Ibid.
62   Ibid., 51.
63   Lux, *Anti-Fascist*, 56.
64   Renton, *When We Touched the Sky*, 53.

Lewisham

> We broke the march just behind the 'Honour Guard'. There followed a few minutes of vicious fighting, the fascists were left battered and bruised, many were clearly terrified of what had just taken place. The march disintegrated, with fascists running round in blind panic. Most ran away, a few stood their ground and got overwhelmed by the sheer weight of anti-fascists.
>
> —Anti-Fascist Action in *Heroes or Villains*

It is clear that the riot in Lewisham was the pivotal point in 1970s militant anti-fascism and the moment when many on the left united with the single purpose of smashing the NF off the streets. And it was the realization for many that the only way to combat increasing fascist and racist violence was physically. On the day, militants fought side by side with members of the local black community who were resentful of the provocative fascist march but also of prejudicial police activity in the area that targeted black British youth on a daily basis. According to Ambalavaner Sivanandan, in 1975 in Lewisham, 'the SPG stopped 14,000 people on the streets and made 400 arrests'.[65] Under heavy manners indeed. This 'cracking down' on suspected street crime by local black youth involved dawn raids and many arrests. A defence campaign was started to highlight the situation, and public meetings were held, something the local fascists saw as legitimate targets:

> Very soon members and supporters of the National Front were subjecting these meetings to organized attacks…a number of organized retaliatory raids were carried out upon the Front members involved, and large scale stewarding operations were organized to protect Defence Campaign meetings and demonstrations.[66]

The NF decided to hold their march to propagate their 'March Against Muggers' campaign, which claimed that the majority of

65   Sivanandan, *A Different Hunger*, 34.
66   Birchall, *Beating the Fascists*, 33.

muggers were black and the majority of victims were white—with disastrous results. Lewisham, like other parts of South London, has long been home to many of the black British community and the choice of route was bound to cause trouble. Which is what it intended to do. Unemployment was 14 percent in the area, and in 1976, the NF and NP gained 44 percent of the vote between them in Deptford. The NF, still on the election path, was keen to generate positive publicity in the media, and after Red Lion Square they realised that many on the left could be provoked into violence by the police. If the fascists maintained 'good order' then the NF would be shown in a good light whilst exposing the left as the aggressors. For the fevered 'extremist of the centre' Richard Clutterbuck, the SWP were equally as canny: 'the true aim was to discredit the police, first, by casting them in the role of protectors of the racist NF and secondly by obtaining reports and pictures of policemen using force to arrest legitimate, liberally minded and, in many cases, coloured protesters'.[67] However, Clutterbuck had an almost pathological disposition towards the SWP, so this should be taken with liberal buckets of Saxo. He hopelessly misreads the situation and claims it backfired on the SWP when, in fact, it was the catalyst for the SWP's most successful venture, the Anti-Nazi League.

As the NF was in the vote-catching business, it was deemed necessary to present a form of 'reasonable fascism' whilst exposing the 'long haired lefties' as the instigators of (usually anti-police) violence. Black youth and many militants were not pursuing the electoral path, so did not particularly care how they were represented in the media as long as the NF was confronted and taken off the streets.

On Saturday, 13th August 1977, over six thousand anti-fascists congregated near New Cross station where eight hundred fascists assembled, surrounded by what would prove to be an inadequate number of police. There was to be an 'official' anti-racist march organized by All Lewisham Campaign Against Racism and Fascism (ALCARAF), a liberal protest that the police actually routed near to the NF; then there was to be a more 'lively' secondary protest which

---

67   Clutterbuck, *Britain in Agony*, 62.

was comprised of anarchist and left-wing militants, including the SWP. Lux was, naturally, in the thick of it and writes, 'The demo was poorly policed—they obviously hadn't expected trouble from this quarter—whilst stewards were virtually non-existent. An ideal scenario.'[68] The police tried to prevent the more militant anti-fascists from getting near the march, but they were outnumbered and the anti-fascists easily evaded them to block the NF's route; it was clear that the police were losing control. The anti-fascists, buoyed by their numbers and increasingly aggressive, moved towards the police engaging in hand to hand combat with 'stout clubs made of chair legs, broken banner poles, bits of fencing, bottles, the odd half brick or two. It was the revival of a great British tradition, all the implements of a Saturday afternoon riot.'[69]

The Metropolitan police, supplemented by the City police, employed horses to try to force the anti-fascists away, unsuccessfully, and the anti-fascists broke through police lines towards the NF: 'Bricks and bottles raining all around, it was bloody, no holds barred, hand to hand fighting.... Flying kicks, punches and the clashing of improvised weaponry filled the space around me,' Lux writes.[70] 'The attempt by police to clear the anti-fascists had failed and, after several minutes of close-quarter brawling, they redirected some of the NF towards Lewisham not knowing that many anti-fascists had already gathered there intent on further confrontation. 'We charged down the hill against the police cordon', Renton writes. 'The rows of demonstrators in front of me broke under the strain of the pushing, but by the time our line came to the front, the police cordon weakened sufficiently and we broke through into the middle of the march.'[71]

The march had been cut in half and the anti-fascists were in amongst the NF, who received a terrible beating and their banners were confiscated and destroyed. Although many anti-fascists went in pursuit of the NF, locals and militants continued to fight with

---

68   Lux, *Anti-Fascist*, 60.
69   Ibid., 61.
70   Ibid., 62.
71   Renton, *When We Touched the Sky*, 63–64.

police, feelings being somewhat hyped by recent events. The police tried to contain the more enthusiastic elements who had broken free from the main body of counter-demonstrators and were moving out of the area towards Lewisham—which by now had been completely taken over by anti-fascists. Counter-demonstrators also attacked the police station in Lewisham and many police were injured during the day. The police did eventually manage to escort the NF to an empty car park in Blackheath away from the chaos, where Tyndall gave a 'triumphant' speech then left the area utterly defeated.

Racist Murders

Lewisham was significant for several reasons: the NF was shocked that they could be so violently and successfully routed on the capital's streets; and anti-fascists and the local community realised that fascist marches could not only be stopped but they could be smashed, and the so-called 'hard men' of the far right could be defeated physically. Lewisham also made the NF leadership think twice about venturing into areas like Lewisham ever again, and many members quit 'active service' altogether out of humiliation. The violence associated with fascism appalled a lot of 'normal' and middle-class supporters who pulled away from the NF; but those who preferred violent alterca-tions to reasonable debate remained. The successful routing of the NF in Lewisham did not decrease racist and fascist violence: the murder of Gurdip Singh Chaggar in 1976 was followed by the murders of Altab Ali, Ishaque Ali, Michael Ferreria, and Akhtar Ali Baig.[72]

Militant anti-fascism at Wood Green and Lewisham had been both large scale and successful but remained uncoordinated to a great extent, and it was only now that people began thinking about a broader political response to fascist provocation and organization:

> While large anti-fascist mobilizations during 1976 marked an important watershed in the anti-fascist struggle, it was the events at Lewisham that really brought matters to a head. Soon afterwards. On the back of this successful event, the Anti-Nazi

72   Sivanandan, *A Different Hunger*, 40.

League (ANL) was launched.[73]

Ladywood

> We intend to crush the National Front. We will intimidate them off the
> streets. Of course there will be violence. And to achieve our object we
> will have to condone the use of every weapon that was wielded on
> Saturday [in Lewisham].
>
> —SWP member

Two days after their Lewisham humiliation, the NF held an election
meeting in Ladywood in Birmingham, which had a 40 percent non-
white population. The venue was surrounded by hundreds of police
who were, yet again, surrounded by hundreds of anti-fascists. John
Tyndall had to sneak into the venue via the back entrance, as his
'honour guard' were apparently unable to protect him. The hopeful
candidate was Anthony Reed-Herbert. Lux notes that so soon after
Lewisham the NF was in for a rough ride: 'It came as no great surprise when the good citizens of Brum took a leaf out of our book,
pelting the police protection with bricks and bottles.'[74]

According to Clutterbuck, whose bias is on the harsher end of
obvious, 'a crowd of SWP supporters attacked the police cordon...
[using] the same kind of weapons as at Lewisham. Of the 400 police
on duty, fifty eight (one in seven) were injured.' The SWP was, un-
usually, also standing a candidate: Kim Gordon, who was arrested at
the riot. He was quoted by the *Daily Mail* as saying, 'I can understand
youngsters carrying weapons. They are not afraid. They are just more
militant.' As the far right became increasingly more violent, they also
needed to be.[75]

---

73   Birchall, *Beating the Fascists*, 34.
74   Lux, *Anti-Fascist*, 69.
75   Clutterbuck, *Britain in Agony*, 219.

Anti-Nazi League and Rock
Against Racism: Mass Mobilisation

We are against the NF.

—Joe Strummer, The Clash.

It was Lewisham that brought one of the most successful examples of broad-based anti-fascism into existence in the UK. The SWP was instrumental in organizing the Anti-Nazi League (ANL), which gained considerable support from parliamentarians, community groups, trade unions, leftist groups and general anti-fascists. ANL activities ranged from street-level confrontation against the far right on a more clandestine level, to mass coverage of highly successful anti-racist carnivals in London, Leeds and Manchester. Crucially, several influential punk musicians aligned themselves against the NF and with the ANL, including Sex Pistols singer John Lydon (a big reggae fan), who famously said, 'How can anyone vote for something so ridiculously inhumane?' Many punks supported Rock Against Racism (RAR)/ANL simply because their favourite bands expressed sympathy, and it was often through the ANL that they became politicised. It also caused many bands to think through their politics and reject the nihilism of early punk.

Rock Against Racism

> There was terrible violence...pitched battles between students and British Movement members on the University campus. We could see the struggle between the SWP and the BM capturing the straying youth. We were sympathetic to the SWP, we had done some benefits [for them].
> —Andy Gill, Gang of Four

Those who don't want to see an RAR gig go on will use the issue
of security as a 'risk' factor—damage to venue, etc. So try and get
your own local heavies organized. Have at least one by the door
as people come and go and make sure they are around in case of
trouble.

—Temporary Hoarding fanzine

Rock Against Racism (RAR) was started by a group of SWP af-
filiates dismayed over the right-wing racist overtones in the proc-
lamations of rich rock stars like David Bowie or Eric Clapton. It
gained momentum amongst musicians and supporters, and the
SWP put considerable means at RAR's disposal: 'The SWP print
shop became the powerhouse for RAR propaganda'.[1] RAR used
a distinctive star in a circle symbol with the DIY/cut-and-paste
graphics of early punk and presented a fresh, exciting aesthetic,
immediately appealing to young music lovers, students and punks.
Under the RAR banner, gigs were organized around the country,
which spread the word. In April 1978, RAR and ANL organized
a demo in Trafalgar Square and then marched through East London to a gig in Victoria Park (symbolic for its connection with anti-fascist battles with Mosley). The gig was headlined by The Clash
(with frontman Joe Strummer in a Red Brigades T-shirt), which
was at the time the principal punk band, following the demise of
the Sex Pistols on their American tour. Estimates put the number
of punters at anywhere between 50,000 and 100,000, but whatever
the number, it was the biggest anti-fascist mobilization since the
1930s. As the march proceeded to the park, Lux and a like-minded
'gang of malcontents [he] hung around with, all chafing at the bit...
[went] down to Brick Lane where the Nazis were gathering. Sure
enough, a couple of hundred of England's finest idled'.[2] The NF,
amply protected by the police, were suitably chastened by the size
of the march, although not 'engaged'.

Although the carnival was a success, the NF marched completely

---

1   Andy Beckett, *When the Lights Went Out: Britain in the Seventies* (London: Faber, 2009), 450.
2   Lux, *Anti-Fascist*, 70.

unopposed from Portland Place to Hoxton the following day. Hackney Committee Against Racialism, a local anti-fascist group

> had pressed the Anti-Nazi League to mobilize opposition from the platform at the Carnival but ANL organizers insisted they had become aware of the Front's intentions too late to organize mass opposition to the NF march…this failing indicated a shift in priorities whereby the Anti-Nazi League was diverting anti-fascist protest off the streets and into the parks, so avoiding direct confrontation with the National Front.[3]

The ANL's turning a blind eye to blatant fascist provocation in the East End was to happen again at a later date.

Carnival II

ANL/RAR organized more carnivals in Leeds and Manchester, and held Carnival II at Brockwell Park in South London in July 1978. Sham 69, who was headlining, had had a short but eventful career with many NF and BM supporters turning up at gigs to cause trouble. Sham was ambivalent about these boneheads, who would often target other members of the audience and eventually cause the band to split: at an RAR gig, according to Andy Beckett, 'we had to hold the [anti-racist] dockers back from attacking the skinhead Sham fans with pickaxes.'[4] Carnival II was even larger than the first one, but as anti-fascists were punking it up in the South London sun, the NF called a march through Brick Lane at the same time. Again, with an eye on potential respectability and their parliamentary friends, the ANL leadership refused to mobilize anti-fascists and get them over to prevent the NF from marching. To not confront this march with so many anti-fascists on hand was an embarrassment, risked a possible PR victory for the NF and begs the question: what is the point of dancing to 'anti-racist music' whilst violent racists march a couple of miles away unhindered? Luckily, there were militant anti-fascists who were not inclined to

3   Copsey, *Anti-Fascism in Britain*, 138.
4   Beckett, *When the Lights Went Out*, 451.

listen to The Members or The Ruts and managed to make their presence felt in the East End, despite police efforts to prevent them. Typically, Lux made the argument less delicately: 'Come down to the East End. Meet up in Brick Lane, and let's batter the nazis.'[5] Despite militants avoiding police blocking tactics, and despite hooking up with local Asian youth, a major fracas did not occur. Some ANL supporters realised that the leadership was less keen on confrontation than they were:

> Militants were pouring from the exits. Most were pissed off as the ANL had withheld information about doings around the Lane.... Talk was of a more bitter future. Guerrilla actions, hit and run against nazi hangouts. Without the blessed sanction of the Party, a handful had been sporadically doing this form of action for a while already.[6]

This 'handful' would go on to play a vital part in militant anti-fascism in the 1980s and 1990s.

The ANL/SWP leadership was fully cognizant of the NF march. Renton quotes one militant as saying, 'Lots of us were trying to make sure Brick Lane was covered. The ANL wanted to keep an eye on just one thing, the carnival. They didn't think we could spare people but we could.'[7] Out of 100,000 attendees, surely a couple hundred experienced anti-fascists could make their presence felt at Brick Lane. One SWP figure stated that the carnival 'was more important than any stunt the NF pulled. Even if we had sent more numbers to Brick Lane, it couldn't have been enough. The police already had it covered.'[8] The small number of militants who did get over to Brick Lane met up with another group arriving late, but the police effectively controlled the area and were in no mood for compromise. The leadership of the SWP later admitted they had made a blunder by making sure the carnival was 'peaceful'

5   Lux, *Anti-Fascist*, 73.
6   Ibid., 74.
7   Renton, *When We Touched the Sky*, 133.
8   Ibid.

200

whilst neglecting to confront fascists in the East End. Birchall is more critical than Renton of the SWP's decisions, which had more long-term effects on the anti-fascist struggle: ever since 'the leadership refused to deploy stewards from the second ANL carnival to help supplement a counter-demonstration against an NF march on the area of Brick Lane, there had been growing tensions between the political priorities and perspectives of the working class rank and file and a largely upper middle class leadership.'[9]

As Nigel Copsey points out, the SWP now tried to shake off the 'throw a brick' reputation (which many punks and others found to be the most attractive aspect) after they 'realised that its tactics were alienating it from more moderate opposition groups'.[10] Leading figures of the SWP had joined up with Labour Party members and celebrities to launch the ANL in 1977 at the House of Commons as a broad anti-fascist front. As 1978 progressed, more Labour MPs were becoming worried over the NF taking their votes, and they began to express support for the ANL, which could save them from deselection.[11] At its peak, the ANL counted fifty thousand members: there were branches and activities around the UK and the ANL dominated street politics for that year, drawing people in to wider campaigns against unemployment and sexual inequality. ANL's principle success was to unite people in the face of the NF's increasing vote count and political progress. It was a single-issue organization whose wide appeal and huge roster of supporters presented a cultural opposition to fascism from many previously disconnected quarters: school kids and teachers, religious leaders and trade unionists, punks and rastas, poets and political hacks. The ANL was to bring anti-racism and anti-fascism into mainstream discourse through propaganda leaflets; posters; badges and T-shirts; the support of musicians and fans at gigs and carnivals; and large-scale, well publicised demonstrations against the NF. Propaganda showed the NF as a fascist/Nazi front and exposed the anti-Semitism and racism of the leadership cliques.

---

9   Birchall, *Beating the Fascists*, 55.
10   Copsey, *Anti-Fascism in Britain*, 130.
11   Ibid., 133.

Faced with such cross-cultural opposition, and finding it increasingly difficult to organize or maintain a physical presence on the streets, the NF also suffered electorally when the leader of the Conservative Party, Margaret Thatcher, began echoing NF sentiments with her statement on TV in 1978 that many were 'really rather afraid that this country might be rather swamped by people with a different culture'.[12]

Leicester, 1979

> Following attempts by the ANL to waylay the Front, there were confrontations between counter-demonstrators and police, with television pictures later showing police dogs chasing anti-fascists onto Leicester University campus.
>
> —Nigel Copsey in *Anti-Fascism in Britain*

Following Lewisham and their complete failure to control the anti-fascist attacks on the NF, the police had been working on their tactics, as evidenced in Leicester, and later in Southall. Political violence was not about to dissipate as the anti-fascist movement grew rapidly between 1977 and 1979 with elements becoming increasingly militant. The NF decided to hold another march in Leicester, knowing full well how provocative this would be, especially after violence in 1974 during the Imperial Typewriters' dispute. Lux reports that on arrival 'things didn't look too good. Thousands of police had been deployed, making it impossible to get anywhere near the Front'.[13] Confrontation was inevitable: as the police protected the NF contingent, anti-fascists roamed the streets, heading towards the university to force a way over to the fascists. As the police formed up, they were attacked by anti-fascists, many 'armed with rocks, bottles and other ammo'.[14] The police fought back, eventually releasing their dogs and then charging in to clear the anti-fascists from the campus. According to Lux, some militants did manage to get through to the NF and inflict some damage, and on the train back to London several militants

12   Ibid., 135.
13   Lux, *Anti-Fascist*, 83.
14   Ibid.

reported contact and, as Lux writes, 'I noticed a couple of battered Nazis.'[15]

Southall

We are fed up with old men talking politics, if the police won't protect us, we can defend ourselves.

—Southall youth

The West London area of Southall was to see two serious outbreaks of violence within a couple of years and much aggression against anti-fascists by the police. On 23rd April 1979, the NF held an election meeting that ended in violence, which guaranteed pages of free publicity. Escalating racist attacks meant that many from the local community had become concerned and organized, with the Southall Youth Movement (SYM) especially more militant than the previous generations, who often declined to respond to such provocations. The SYM 'often fought against the fascists and they gave us a hope that we had reached a turning point in our struggles against fascism', reported one local IS member.[16] The SYM had formed after the racist murder of Gurdip Chaggar to defend their area from the racists of the NF. However, according to one sceptical local critic, the SYM 'was essentially formed out of a coalition of street gangs' and consisted of 'school drop-outs, delinquents, unemployed,' and they faced organizational difficulties.[17] Anti-fascists picketed the meeting and the SYM gathered 'to ensure no NF supporters could gain access to the hall before the demonstration'.[18] All around the area fights broke out with the police, resulting in many injuries and the death of Blair Peach:

Missiles were thrown at the police from the anti-fascist side, including flares, smoke-bombs and a petrol bomb, which was hurled

---

15   Ibid., 84.
16   Renton, *When We Touched the Sky*, 140.
17   Philip Cohen and Harwant S. Bains, *MultiRacist Britain* (London: MacMillan, 1988), 37.
18   Copsey, *Anti-Fascism in Britain*, 148.

at a police coach. The police also contributed to the disorder, first by making peaceful protest impossible, and then by attempting to disperse the crowd with aggressive tactics, such as 'snatch squads', charging with riot shields, truncheons and horses and even driving vans into the crowd.[19]

The area was flooded with over two thousand police in the morning, despite the NF's meeting not going ahead until 7.30pm: it was clearly an intimidatory move towards a community that was already mistrustful of the Met. The police, in particular the SPG, were accused of being heavy handed against locals and anti-fascists, and in at least one instance a police bus was driven at demonstrators. Windows were smashed, cars were damaged, and the police were pelted with bricks and bottles; they responded by charging at the anti-fascists. The police attacked the Peoples Unite building so badly it had to be demolished. Lux reports that 'people had been beaten up by the police, and subjected to racial abuse, arbitrary arrests, even buildings had been trashed by the uniforms. Seems there had been nothing short of a police riot that afternoon.'[20] Renton describes it as 'a full police riot against the left and the Asian community.'[21] Another activist simply stated, 'They wanted revenge for Lewisham.'[22] During one police charge, Blair Peach received the head injuries that caused his death. One witness reported, 'They were hitting people, pulling hair, pushing with their shields.... There were two policemen, one with a shield, one without. As they ran after people, Blair fell; I think he was pushed with the shield, as he was overbalancing the other hit him on the head.'[23]

Whilst six policemen were suspended, the Department of Public Prosecutions decided that there was not enough evidence to press charges. A search of the SPG's lockers found multiple items such as a pickaxe handle, sledgehammer, knives, a whip and various

19   Ibid., 149.
20   Lux, *Anti-Fascist*, 85.
21   Renton, *When We Touched the Sky*, 139.
22   Ibid., 146.
23   National Council for Civil Liberties (London: NCCL: 1980), 15.

modified truncheons. Also the not very P.C. Grenville Bint was found in possession of Nazi uniforms and various other weapons. In response to this police violence, anti-fascists and local community organizations held a commemorative march for Blair Peach, and when the funeral finally took place, ten thousand people turned out in solidarity. Paul Foot, writing about the injustice, delays and failure to convict anyone over Blair Peach's death, said, 'I wonder what the reaction would have been if a policeman, not a demonstrator, had been killed at Southall?'[24]

Anti-Fascist Victory!

By the time the May 1979 general election had gone, the NF seemed to have lost its will to battle. The concerted forces of anti-fascism had seriously damaged its members' confidence and ability to organize from 1976 onwards: of significance were mass opposition to fascist marches; the NF coming off second best in smaller street skirmishes; the influence of RAR/ANL on a whole new generation; RAR managing to combine popular anti-racism within the punk discourse; and the NF's generally negative and violent media image. The ANL had created a broad front of MPs, church groups, trades unions and celebrities, as well as gaining the support of an energetic youth culture, having a strong media presence and organizing physical opposition. It was one of the biggest and most successful anti-fascist movements in the UK.

The common orthodoxy is that Thatcher had simply divested the NF of its appeal, adopting and adapting their xenophobic rhetoric, but this seriously undermines the success of the anti-fascist movement—as indeed it is meant to by certain writers in certain quarters. Thatcher's contribution was to attempt to legitimise casual racism in contemporary discourse. The NF, which was in danger of becoming the third largest party in the UK, had become marginalised as a single-issue party and exposed as being a fascist/pro-Nazi front by the efforts of the anti-fascist movement. The NF had also split into the NF, the New NF (NNF) and the National Party (NP). In the

---

24   Renton, *When We Touched the Sky*, 153.

general election, the NF eventually polled 1.3 percent of the overall vote, Thatcher came to power, and political activity and social upheaval converged to make the 1980s one of the most violent decades since the 1970s. The far right's political space had been compromised on the streets, in popular culture, in the media, at the ballot box and amongst the rank and file in the workplace (the NF's attempts at union influence was far from successful and the creation of pro-NF unions was microscopic). This marginalization led the NF and other fascist groups like the BM to become more violent and more extreme now that the electoral route seemed closed. The success of the anti-fascist movement did not make the fascists go away, but it made them operate more clandestinely; many skinheads supported the openly nazi BM, which was still making their presence felt at football matches, at punk gigs and on the streets, something that the members of the SWP's 'squads' and other more militant anti-fascists continued to deal with throughout the 1980s.

FIGHTING TALK

Red Action and AFA: 'The Day's Action Might Be Rough'

> To be fair, a great deal of the credit for the militant anti-fascism in the 1980s and 90s deserves to go to Red Action. Thanks to a Red Action initiative Anti-Fascist Action (AFA) was formed in 1985 which bought together the Direct Action Movement (DAM), Workers Power, and various other groups and individuals.
> —K. Bullstreet in *Bash the Fash*

> I'd already been on a more nodding acquaintance with some of these tasty characters over the years, where it counts; at the sharp end of things.... More importantly, they'd steam in.
> —Martin Lux in *Anti-Fascist*

Although anti-fascism is in no way exempt from factional squabbles, fallouts or schisms, few militant anti-fascists would disagree with the above quotes, both written by anarchists, regarding Red Action and their highly effective war against the NF, BM, BNP and any other fascist groupuscule that tried to organize in London. Members of Red Action can rightly be credited for showing that 'fascism would not only be fought, but that the hard men of the Right could be beaten'.[1] The history of the 'squadists', why they were expelled from the SWP, and how they went on to form Red Action and then AFA is extensively documented in the 'We Are Red Action' pamphlet and *Beating the Fascists* book by Sean Birchall, so we will only highlight certain points.

Briefly, the squads were set up by the SWP to protect meetings and also to steward left-wing events should there be a fascist threat.

---

1   Birchall, *Beating the Fascists*, 36.

However, the Central Committee (CC) became increasingly concerned about the squads' autonomy and was critical of their pursuit of a fascist threat that the CC felt had subsided. Red Action members had been in the SWP squads and already gained a reputation for uncompromising opposition to fascism. As the SWP wound down the ANL, the street-based activists 'warned against the extent of the NF's demise. Whilst it was certainly true that they had been disappointed with their election results, they were by no means finished and there were disturbing signs that the far more overtly Nazi British Movement were beginning to make headway'.[2]

Red Action also wrote, 'There were quite a few Asian families with smashed up and burnt out houses that could have testified to this'.[3] Red Action thought that 'instead of being wound up, it was more pragmatic to wind it down to a level appropriate to the nature of the challenge now being offered by the Far Right'.[4] That is, mobilising an appropriate response as and when needed.

Following the expulsions and resignations from the SWP, several squad members went on to form Red Action in January 1982 and spent the next twelve years violently confronting fascists until, finally, the BNP withdrew from the streets. Anti-Fascist Action (AFA) was wound down and Red Action went on to form the Independent Working Class Association (IWCA). By the end of the 1990s, many RA members had been arrested, jailed, and harassed by both state and fascists, and had been through countless battles, many of which they won. Neither the NF, BM, BNP or Combat 18 ever recorded any decisive victory against RA or indeed AFA.

[Jim] White's worst words were left for Red Action, who always came up in BNP conversation. 'The worst of the lot, total scum. When you bump into them, you know it's a fight for survival; some of them are even skinheads!'

—Tim Hepple in *At War with Society*

2   Red Action, *We Are Red Action* (London, 1982), 17.
3   Ibid., 20.
4   Birchall, *Beating the Fascists*, 88.

Red Action was not a single-issue organization; it was comprised of militant socialists and pro-Irish Republicans, and they continued to steward, as individuals and as Red Action, many left-wing events that were threatened by the far right. Part of their success was that they refused to engage in the usual obsessive recruitment and paper-selling drives of other leftist groups, they held few public meetings, and they built a strong relationship with each other over the years of militant action. The areas of principle operations were London, Manchester and Glasgow, which severely limited infiltration by the state or fascists. Red Action was also never 'off duty', and neither were the fascists, as Birchall recalls: 'All involved knew they were just as likely to be attacked out shopping as when hawking *National Front News*.'[5] When holding paper sales, the NF never knew when to expect a visit, and 'by simply not knowing what might happen, and what they might have to cater for, [RA] could see was wearing them out.'[6] A typical example of this was reported in the Red Action paper:

> A Red Action laddie was returning from work one day when he saw this pathetic little git (Patrick Harrington, NF student organizer) selling NF papers with some mates at Hammersmith. He informed young Patrick and company that he'd be back in a minute…him and his mates were kicked all over the place by a nice little anti-nazi team.[7]

Red Action also reported the following in their usual style:

> Three swaggering boneheads who demanded to know where the commies were, to their dismay actually found some in the shape of 4 Red Action supporters. After an intense discussion one of the skinheads lost all sympathy from the motorists of West Kensington by lying in the middle of the road, blocking all traffic and generally making a perfect nuisance of himself.[8]

5   Ibid., 77.
6   Ibid., 83.
7   Anti-Fascist Action, *Heroes or Villains*, 39.
8   Ibid.

Chapel Market

The market in Islington, just round the corner from the Angel tube, was the site of left-wing paper sales, and an area which the NF sought to contest, so there were numerous and vicious confrontations. Although Islington became a somewhat fashionable and liberal place during the 1990s, partly due to Tony Blair and 'New Labourites' being resident, it was not always so. In the less salubrious 1980s, the local NF was augmented by 'a violent criminal faction', and the large post office on Upper Street was reputed to be an NF stronghold.[9] There was also a considerable range of anti-fascist support with the SWP, Militant members, Communists, anarchists and Labour supporters in the area. The NF still maintained a presence and this would take up some considerable time, as Red Action explains in *The Making of Red Action*:

> It was in Chapel Market in North London where the National Front had a particularly strong branch (with the ability to call on numbers between 60 and 100 for street confrontations) that our efforts were largely concentrated. It commanded all our attention, and was in fact at the time, the sole reason for our political existence. The 'Battle' for Chapel Market had been going on for seven years. First of all between local SWP branches and their NF counter-parts and later between the Anti-Nazi League and the National Front.[10]

Birchall writes that once Red Action had consolidated itself, the Islington anti-fascist campaign 'took just forty-nine weeks…for the former squadists, now in the shape of Red Action, to register their first triumph, when a stunned NF were driven off their prestigious sales pitch at Chapel Market.'[11]

Red Action's attentions became so intense that the NF, and the short-lived National Action Party, put out a contract on some of the leading militants, which was met with no success whatsoever. The

9   Birchall, *Beating the Fascists*, 58.
10   Red Action, *The Making of Red Action* (London, 1986), 1.
11   Birchall, *Beating the Fascists*, 72.

'hit and run' techniques against the NF unnerved the far right and undermined their ability to maintain a continuous street presence: 'Here then was anti-fascism stripped down to the tactic of violence as a first resort. It was an outlook the NF locally were clearly struggling to come to terms with'.[12] The conflict also spilled over into the local area with pubs being declared fascist and anti-fascist strongholds, and street battles a regular occurrence.

Redskins

One of Red Action's early informal operations was at a Greater London Council (GLC) festival in 1984, which was attacked by BM skinheads and, although the skins managed to invade the stage to attack two of the bands, they soon found their positions reversed. The festival took place during the miners' strike in protest over rising unemployment and Tory cutbacks in public spending. As the crowd sat in the sun listening to the music, a large gang of skinheads, led by fascist 'face' Nicky Crane, tore through the crowd, jumped on the stage, and attacked the Redskins, a punk/soul outfit that had adopted skinhead clothing and was aligned with the SWP. The audience was slow to react, and by the time militants had gathered themselves the skins had disappeared. Had they stayed disappeared they may have been able to chalk up a significant victory against a large left-wing gathering in the middle of town. However, elated with their earlier success, the NF came back for seconds to attack the Hank Wangford Band, in a personal recollection LiamO recalls:

> Suddenly a smaller group of Nazi's, emboldened by their previous victory, attacked this stage too. One particularly graphic memory was the bass guitarist being butted and his 'Axe' being swung by a bonehead straight into the face of the lead singer. This time, the 'distilled' crowd were better prepared and nearly all the Fash were captured and set upon by irate punters. There were some brutal kickings being handed out, and well deserved too. At one stage two coppers had managed to drag two of the beleaguered

---

12   Ibid., 77.

Boneheads from the mob, and were holding back the crowd using a couple of chairs (a bit like lion-tamers). At this point we were being screamed at by various pacifist types 'Stop it! Stop it! You're as bad as they are.' I recall PC was offended by this and replied, 'No we're not—we're fackin worse'—in between encouraging others to keep up the pace.

By this time, LiamO wrote, that Crane had gone to ground, shielding himself with a woman he had grabbed: 'I recall two miners (family blokes in their mid-forties, bare-chested and dressed in just shorts and trainers) just missed capturing him and one missed the back of Crane's head with an almighty swing of a cider bottle by millimetres. But Crane escaped.'

The Nazi skinheads received a serious battering and many ended up in St. Thomas's hospital nearby. This was no safe haven as Red Action found out where they were and headed over to further 'discuss' the day's proceedings. Hubris over strategy had undone the fascist attack, and they faced the violent consequences. After the festival, Red Action went up to Islington to the skinhead hangout. LiamO continues,

Later PC, who was just out of jail and whose face would have been not too well known to the fash in the Agricultural [pub, Islington], volunteered to go and check it out whilst the rest of us hid in a pub round the corner. He was sipping a glass of lager when in came this shaven-head bone, whom they all called 'Nicky'. He was proudly showing off his black and blue torso to the assembled boneheads. Crane was told he was lucky to be alive and replied, 'I know. All I could hear was some cunt shouting, "Kill him, kill him".' Little did he know that the same 'cunt' was five yards away half-chuckling, but also half choking, into his drink. Anyways, PC returned with his report and an ambush on some passing bones was followed by a 'show of strength' walk by the Agricultural—which of course descended into a pitched battle in jig-time.

Later, the *Red Action* paper reported, '[We were] cursing ourselves for our reasonableness and moderation.'[13]

Anti-Fascist Action

Despite their successful and militant anti-fascism, Red Action realised that they were at risk of being outnumbered by the far right. They were also increasingly isolated from the far left due to their previous bad relations with the SWP and the unwillingness of other leftists to engage in violent anti-fascist activity. The logical thing would be to find allies who, although differing on the larger political principles, were just as willing to take on the NF and the BM on the streets. In July 1985, AFA was launched at Conway Hall with a statement that determined 'the need to oppose racism and fascism, physically and ideologically'. Amongst the early members were the anarchist groups Direct Action Movement (DAM) and Class War, as well as 'elements drawn from anti-racist groups who, in the main, identified with the liberal left-wing of the Labour Party'.[14] After the meeting, members of Hatfield Red Action headed back to King's Cross accompanied by what would become the AFA stewards group only to be met by a 'welcoming committee' of fascists. As AFA members emerged from the tube station, they were confronted by a group of BNP members, one of whom was armed with a potentially lethal flare gun. Ex-fascist Bernard O'Mahoney gives an account of the evening from his side of the barriers, which is remarkable for a couple of serious inaccuracies: firstly, he refers to RA as the Red Army Faction and as 'students' and 'spoilt members of the bourgeoisie'; he also claims that fascist spotters were in contact via mobile phones—which at the time were not only enormous but expensive and the preserve of 'yuppies'.[15] The 'bourgeois students' of RA swiftly overwhelmed the fascists, and several were caught and battered—something which the BNP and the NF factions were getting used to.

13   Birchall, *Beating the Fascists*, 98.
14   Ibid.,107.
15   Bernard O'Mahoney, *Hateland* (London: Mainstream Publishing, 2006), 97.

Up North

London was not the only place where this was happening. In July 1984, the Bradford *Telegraph and Argus* reported the following:

Members of the National Front in Bradford were driven from their newspaper pitch by members of Workers Against Racism. About 30 WAR supporters approached NF paper sellers on Broadway and told them to move on. When they refused, a brawl developed, during which NF papers were seized and destroyed. Local WAR organizer Eileen McEvoy said her group was prepared to take the law into its own hands to keep the NF and the BNP off the city's streets.[16]

Several members of the Manchester squad were now operating under the RA and AFA mantle following their expulsion or resignation from the SWP, some whilst in prison for anti-fascist activities, and they now continued their previous tactics unfettered by party criticism. In 1986, the NF tried to hold a march in Stockport, which met with considerable anti-fascist opposition, especially when NF members were trapped in the train station. The SWP and other less militantly inclined opponents were gathered near the town hall behind the police whilst militant activists remained uncontained on the surrounding streets. AFA later reported that as the NF was walking 'past waving banners two vans travelling in opposite directions pull alongside the Nazis, whereupon anti-fascists emerge from the rear and engage in meaningful dialogue with them'.[17] As the group of NF split, AFA gave chase and the terrified fascists fled to the train station for shelter, where luckily they could lock themselves in. After attempting entry, the militants dispersed then came across more NF members, on foot and in vehicles, and these were likewise attacked, particularly four fascists in a new Saab, which was wrecked and had a flare and smoke bomb thrown inside it.

AFA was also acting on intelligence, and a number of attempted fascist attacks were prevented: 'On one occasion, St. George's Day, a

16   Anti-Fascist Action, *Heroes or Villains*, 39.
17   Ibid., 40.

protest by "English Nationalists" did not materialise after anti-fascists chanced upon the same pub they were meeting in. (We weren't tipped off, honestly.)'[18] Around this time many anti-fascists from Manchester and the North West were involved in the Viraj Mendis campaign. Mendis was a Sri Lankan political refugee and a member of the Revolutionary Communist Group whom the government wanted to deport, despite the fact that he claimed that he would face dire repercussions if he went back home. Mendes sought sanctuary in a church in Hulme, and the RCG campaign lasted some time as many anti-fascists rallied round the cause. One year, an anarchist conference was held at the church as some far-right football hooligans had threatened to 'get that Paki' and drag him out of the sanctuary. Needless to say, despite a nervous day, they failed to materialise. Although the defence campaign was long running, Mendes was eventually arrested and deported in 1989 but luckily remains alive.

Liverpool

Throughout the 1980s, Liverpool was a left-wing stronghold with the Militant council, a large SWP group, and the anarchists who set up the Mutual Aid Centre. With limited political space or support within the community, the small NF contingent focussed their ire on easy targets like the radical bookshop News from Nowhere, run by a women's collective. Over the decade, the shop suffered burglary attempts, broken windows, fascist wrecking crews and arson. That fascists would seek to burn books should come as no surprise to anyone. The NF would try and sell their papers on nearby Church Street and then, either before or after a heavy drinking session, head for the shop for routine intimidation. Anti-fascist groups warded off several attacks, and in one incident a DAM comrade of some repute ended up in a protracted brawl with an NF member and punched a tooth out of his head before one of them left seeking a dentist. Progressive Books, another radical shop, was the focus of several would-be book-burners: two local fascists were caught at the back of the shop by a kicked-in door and charged with burglary. The Trades Council

---

18   Anti-Fascist Action, *Fighting Talk* 7: 17.

building in the Wirral was defenestrated, and the Mutual Aid Centre became subject to the far right's random attentions, usually when there were very few people around so they could launch surprise attacks on individuals leaving the building before running away.

In April 1984, the BNP tried to hold a St. George's Day rally in Liverpool and, after a change of venue forced by anti-fascists, they ended up at the Adelphi Hotel (where in 1936 a large brawl between the BUF and anti-fascists had taken place). It was inevitable that anti-fascists, local groups and members of the local black community would mobilize en masse. John Tyndall was to address the meeting and soon found the venue besieged. After a brawl in the foyer, the manager told the BNP to leave, but they were reluctant to engage an increasingly large and hostile mob. The police arrived to cordon off the hotel so the BNP could carry on with their meeting, but after a short while they were escorted through a side entrance to their coaches by the police who were desperate to avoid a confrontation, as the 1981 Toxteth riots were still in recent memory.

By 1986, AFA had become a national organization with branches in London, the North West, Yorkshire, the North East and Scotland. National mobilisations became increasingly larger, co-ordination better, and success continuous. Despite mobilisations that did not make contact with 'the enemy', such as at Liverpool in 1986, an impressive number of anti-fascists could convene and work together successfully on many occasions. At times there were conflicting expectations of what was required: Militant activist John Penney was involved in preparing for the Liverpool NF demo and 'rushing around Merseyside for AFA whipping up counter demo numbers for an announced fascist demo in Liverpool.... AFA wasn't just going to wave placards but wanted numbers of people willing to confront 'em hard—and so warned that the AFA bit of the days action might be rough.'

In June 1986, the NF applied to march but was refused permission by the council. The BNP and NF turned up anyway but realised that anti-fascists had mobilised and an anti-racist march was heading through the city. Needless to say the NF kept a very low profile, avoiding the large roving mob of 250 who were in no mood for a quiet debate. Later in the day, Militant supporters spotted and attacked a small group of fascists who were then arrested. When one of them came out of the station later, several anti-fascists were waiting for him, causing him to run back inside. By then the police had removed the remaining fascists from town and put them on a train for their own safety. Both sides agreed that the NF 'march' had been a disaster.

Liverpool AFA was mainly anarchist, with DAM and Class War members and others who were affiliated to the Liverpool Anarchist Group, which organized in 1987. Liverpool became part of the AFA Northern Network with North West and Yorkshire groups, responding to local and national callouts. In 1988, Liverpool AFA organized a coach and minibus up to confront a BNP rally in York but were stopped by police and forced back home. As usual, militants organized gigs and meetings and distributed information whilst being involved in Poll Tax protests and the campaign to support the locked-out dockers. Liverpool AFA proved effective militants:

> Within a year or so, the Liverpool BNP went from boasting about how the 'reds' were always beaten in Liverpool when they tried to force the BNP off the streets (according to confiscated copies of the *British Nationalist*), to the effective collapse of the group. Years later, the BNP admitted in the *Liverpool Echo* that 'they were driven underground by left wing extremists in the mid-80s.[19]

As we have seen, not much happened in the way of direct confrontation in Liverpool, as the NF kept hidden. Anarchist groups like DAM, Class War and Green Anarchist, hunt saboteurs, Red Action, 'off-duty' SWP members, Young Socialists, Revolutionary Communists and Militant members all contributed to these national mobilisations in varying numbers where ideological differences had to be put aside for the 'greater good' (although were frequently discussed in the

19   Ex-Liverpool AFA Member, *Anti-Fascist Action: An Anarchist Perspective* (London: Kate Sharpley Library, 2007), 5.

van on the way back).

In 1986, the broad alliance of AFA #1 began to break up: anti-fascist organization Searchlight accused Class War of having far-right connections, something which proved to be completely untrue and caused further divisions (although some anarchists and members of Class War and RA had been in far-right groups before). It was clear there were elements of political careerists and 'professional anti-fascists' in AFA who were keen to distance themselves from the more excitable anarchist factions. It was also clear that AFA was divided, with a militant wing and a more formal, less-aggressive faction that was quite prepared to work with the state and police. The accusations against Class War were found to be completely unsubstantiated, and the incident created mistrust by militants who claimed that *Searchlight* was passing on information to the authorities about the far left as well as the far right. Many in AFA, particularly the militants, took the view that the state is no fan of extremists from whatever end of the political spectrum they happen to come from, and are just as interested in anti-fascists as they are in fascists. Despite this, AFA's relationship with *Searchlight* continued albeit on a more cautious level seeing as they had access to useful inside information on the far right, especially from disenfranchised fascists.

Bury St. Edmunds

One of our strongest [NF] units of all was Bury St. Edmunds, that was the place where we finally realised that marches were a counter-productive waste of space because we had this tremendous march and ruck with the reds and so on. We had great fun.
—Nick Griffin's spin on a disastrous day for the NF

After the Stockport rout, the NF decided to march in Bury St. Edmunds but was met with another AFA national mobilization. The NF was not the only one to make tactical blunders that day:

NF supporters were attacked before, during and after the march.

At one stage a Red Action led ambush from a building site in a narrow side street caused largely inexperienced police to rush forward, leaving the back of the march unprotected. The resulting free-for-all lasted a couple of minutes during which time the NF lost a banner, and a lot of their composure.[20]

After the march, there were several confrontations, one notably outside a chip shop.[21] Red Action reported that 'from the point of view of the fascists the whole thing was a disaster with the "race warriors" taking second prize in a number of skirmishes'.[22] Several sources report that as some anti-fascists were leaving the scene in a van, they passed Nick Griffin with a group of supporters and

> to the utter astonishment of the local plod, one of the political soldiers was felled by a cheeky denim-clad arm swinging a blunt instrument. The motorised cudgel-carrier then sped off, hotly pursued by an outraged Old Bill leaving NF chairman Nick Griffin holding his hands in the air as if appealing for divine intervention.[23]

K. Bullstreet recalls it was Nicky Crane, the notoriously violent fascist who led the attack on the GLC festival, who was thus humiliated after 'shouting abuse and doing cocky "V" signs, blissfully unaware that another minibus was approaching him from behind'.[24] Crane was also at Glastonbury festival one year working security when

> Carole caught up with Crane, and his minder, and started battering him about the head. Crane and his pal legged it up the path towards the security compound with Carole and Sean in

---

20   Birchall, *Beating the Fascists*, 119.
21   See K. Bullstreet, *Bash the Fash: Anti-Fascist Recollections, 1984–1993* (London: Kate Sharpley, 2001).
22   Anti-Fascist Action, *Heroes or Villains*, 41.
23   Ibid.
24   Bullstreet, *Bash the Fash*, 10.

hot pursuit shouting 'fucking Nazi' at Crane. Two Rastas leapt out of a darkened tent and one them floored Crane with a right rural haymaker![25]

Shortly after the embarrassing rout in Bury St. Edmunds, the NF split yet again, with Griffin going on to form the ill-fated 'political soldier' groupuscule, whilst the main body of the NF struggled into obscurity for a while. Griffin later wrote despairingly of this time that 'all the politics of the punch-up had achieved in twenty years was to allow Red Action's influence to grow on the streets'.[26] Strange praise indeed.

Remembrance Days

In 1985, AFA took over the fascist assembly point with 100 people, causing the NF much embarrassment at not being able to remove us and they had to form up elsewhere. In 1986, AFA organized the biggest anti-fascist demonstration since the 1970s when 2,000 people marched to the Cenotaph and laid wreaths on behalf of victims past and present of fascism.

—London Anti-Fascist Action

AFA was able to draw on willing militants from different organizations and they could mobilize in more ambitious ways. Despite being pro-Nazi, the far right had always celebrated Remembrance Day in London (and still does) for the fallen soldiers of the first and second World Wars. Contradiction is available in unlimited amounts on the far right, it seems. In November 1985, AFA occupied the NF's assembly point in Victoria. As the fascists advanced on them, AFA 'stood firm' and the NF began to slow down to a complete stop once they realised that the anti-fascists were of a different calibre than the ANL and other less violent opponents they were used to. The following year, rather than disrupt the NF, AFA organized its own two-thousand-strong

---

25   Ian Bone, *Bash the Rich: True Life Confessions of an Anarchist in the UK* (Bath: Tangent, 2006), 228.
26   Birchall, *Beating the Fascists*, 120.

demonstration and laid a wreath at the Cenotaph to commemorate the victims of fascism. Despite an impressive turnout and subsequent front-page coverage, a number of more inexperienced anti-fascists came unstuck after heading off to Trafalgar Square for something more exciting than a minute's silence. There they met a gang of fascists and came out a poor second. Later, members of RA and the stewards group, smarting over the fascists claiming an easy victory in Trafalgar Square, came across a group of the NF's colour party, replete with flags, at King's Cross, who quickly sought sanctuary in a fast food restaurant. This proved to be a costly mistake as the anti-fascists entered via both doors, cutting off any hope of escape, and for several minutes the fascists felt the wrath of the frustrated militants. The demonstration was a success, despite the small group splitting off it. The action in the restaurant may seem unnecessary, but as one RA member said, it had a knock-on effect for far-right morale:

Each and every one of them [NF] would know a dozen or more people intimately. So within hours, hundreds would probably know of their humiliation. Then there are the personal and political recriminations that would inevitably follow...and all so corrosive to the discipline and good comradeship fascism set so much store by.[27]

In 1987, AFA organized another Remembrance Day march but had also learnt from previous experience. On these days it was common practice for fascists to leave the NF march and attack the twenty-four-hour anti-apartheid picket at South Africa house, something that AFA was preparing to curtail. As AFA gathered in Trafalgar Square at midday, a gang of football hooligans from the Chelsea Headhunters, who had broken away from the NF meeting point, headed towards them, briefly attacking the end of the march, causing many to flee before stewards could restore order. This further exacerbated the split between militants and liberal anti-fascists.

AFA militants had clearly taken on board the events of the

27   Ibid., 124.

221

previous year when in 1988 the march went ahead but ended nearer Trafalgar Square to be closer to any potential trouble from the NF leaving their rally. As expected, the Headhunters arrived seeking another easy victory but instead were frightened off by the sudden appearance of a large mob of AFA members. The football hooligans were later introduced to militant anti-fascism in the Underground, another mob was chased off near Leicester Square, and sporadic clashes broke out all night with one particularly unfortunate fascist being spied on a bus and then beaten up. The far right had clearly gotten an inkling of things to come and now acknowledged the persistence and tenacity of AFA.

AFA #2

The relaunch of London AFA in 1989 was around the following strategy: to set up a democratic structure that can involve the growing numbers of militant anti-fascists supporting our activities; to make our activities as effective as possible; to involve ourselves in the fight against racist attacks; and to operate from a (working) class based opposition.

—London Anti-Fascist Action

By the end of the 1980s, despite considerable success in taking the initiative in the struggle for the streets, several changes affected AFA's progress. The most significant was based on political differences. AFA had been a single-issue, broad front with the more 'respectable' members working alongside militant RA and anarchist factions. However, it was not just differences over tactics but also over ideology and how AFA should be organized in the future, so the split between militants and liberal anti-fascists widened. In 1986, when *Searchlight* moved to expel Class War, John Penney was charged with investigating the charges and found them to be 'groundless, simply a *Searchlight* smear campaign.' His recollections give a flavour of the conflict: 'I was shocked at the glee with which so many on the Left sniped and badmouthed Class War...[then] other Lefties tried to expel Red Action.'[28] East London DAM also condemned the attempt to smear Class War and the whole scenario disrupted the relationship between *Searchlight* and the anarchists as RA, DAM and other militants sided with Class War. The relationship between AFA and Searchlight did not completely end, and information about the far right was passed on. LiamO captures the atmosphere of mistrust between the factions at the time:

> There was much residual (and mutual) suspicion between Red Action (and their fellow-travellers) and the semi-state sector (Newham Monitoring Project and various 'right-on' lefties) from previous history—but it was a political and operational imperative that a way to work together was found. In fairness to those centred around the NMP, there were some very capable, principled, hard-working activists among them, but there were fundamental political, tactical, strategic and social differences between them and us—and there were also some of (what we saw as) the worst examples of hysterical, white middle-class, lifestyle lefties.

The militants had by now determined that fascism was a class problem and that the state and respectable liberalism could not be relied on to keep it in check. RA stated somewhat militarily that 'the job for AFA is not to be content with merely confronting the organized fascist gangs, but to cut off their supply line of renegade recruits at source: on the terraces, at the gigs, in the working-class communities. We must bring the war home to the fascists'.[29]

AFA #2, launched in 1989, was now stripped of some of the 'careerist' and moderate tendencies; these people had gone their own way. The DAM, Trotskyite Workers Power, and other anarchists and left-wingers lined up with Red Action, emphasized the class-based analysis of fascism, and continued to confront the far-right on the streets and elsewhere. The Remembrance Day marches had begun to dwindle in importance for the militants, fascist numbers had

28　See Appendix 1.
29　Birchall, *Beating the Fascists*, 167.

diminished over the last couple of marches and the militants felt that energies could be spent better elsewhere. After the AFA relaunch, Searchlight pushed for another march to the Cenotaph, so five hundred anti-fascists turned up at Victoria station to occupy the fascists' traditional rendezvous point, disabling them from forming up for their march for several hours. A number of fascists received harsh treatment from the newly organized AFA.

NF/BNP

Throughout the 1980s, the NF had suffered from the usual splits and schisms, as the ousted Tyndall went on to form the BNP, which began to rise to prominence as the NF languished in apathy and mistrust. The far right had suffered many demoralizing setbacks throughout the 1980s and the NF's marches and meetings were continually smashed. Support for fascist groups fluctuated with the increasing activities of militant anti-fascism around the UK. By 1989, the BNP had become the main fascist group to feel the wrath of AFA. The BNP launched their 'Rights for Whites' campaign, following the murders of two young white men in London in 1990, and were running in local elections, gaining a significant percentage of the white working-class vote. The BNP was keen to take back the streets from anti-fascism and adopted the 'march and grow' tactic, hoping for a show of strength to impress potential voters and members, and began organizing meetings in the East End.

The Weavers Fields School Incident

As a result of thorough reconnaissance and planning we were able to infiltrate a large group of fascists approaching the meeting and before they went inside managed to inflict some considerable damage on them. Unfortunately we suffered a number of arrests and others had to leave the area being chased by the police. So when a group of fascists, their main 'firm', about 40 strong arrived our numbers were considerably weakened.... The fascists attacked but we stood our ground and somewhat fortunately the fascists 'bottled' it.

—London Anti-Fascist Action

In political confrontations, AFA was getting increasingly confident and the far right was being pushed further onto the defensive. AFA distributed thousands of anti-fascist leaflets and was also busy consolidating its presence in the East End. In April 1990, a sixty-strong team of AFA stewards arrived at a BNP meeting in Weavers Fields School, and the police, confusing them for BNP, shepherded them over to join the waiting fascists who became increasingly apprehensive (this identity mix-up was to be repeated by the police several times). The BNP contingent began abusing the passive anti-fascist counter-demonstration opposite the school until they realized just who their 'fellow travellers' actually were. The AFA members took the initiative and confusion hit the BNP ranks. Several BNP members took to the floor as others began to scatter before the police realized what was happening. After several minutes of chaos, the police managed to get the BNP into the school whilst others pursued AFA members suspected of mischievousness. Meanwhile, the remaining AFA members, now considerably depleted, faced a second angry wave of BNP members whose bravado luckily ebbed away the closer they got until they slowed to a stop. Both AFA and Copsey recognize this moment as indicative of a significant schism in anti-fascist tactics. As AFA was considerably more experienced and physically able to take advantage of confusion, other groups like the SWP preferred the safety of police protection. The meeting was successfully 'disrupted by AFA militants whilst in a park next to the school, a public demonstration against the BNP had been held by a variety of organizations'.[30] Around this time, the far right began to consider more effective defensive tactics:

> It was following a violent clash in early 1991 at a BNP by-election rally at Weavers Field school—where they had to fight off a concerted anti-fascist onslaught—that a group of younger activists began to form themselves into a small mob.... At first their targets were 'Red mobs' but they also made random attacks on blacks and Asians in the area.[31]

30 Copsey, *Anti-Fascism in Britain*, 165.
31 Nick Lowles, *White Riot: The Rise and Fall of Combat 18* (London:

Brick Lane

> The East End of London is a critically important area in the struggle against fascism in London and in Britain as a whole. It is the area which the nazi British National Party has singled out as a national priority.... Central to all their efforts is the weekly paper sale at Brick Lane market in Bethnal Green. Each Sunday they stand there alongside their fellow nazis of the National Front (Flag Group) at the very popular market in the heart of the East End's Bengali community.
>
> —London Anti-Fascist Action.

Ever since the days of Mosley, the East End of London has been a focus for the anti-fascist struggle, and no one place symbolizes this more than Brick Lane. In the post-war era, Beckman and the 43 Group were frequently involved in confrontations near the area, and during the 1970s the squads had seen 'active duty' there, around the time of ANL Carnival #2. The 1980s and 1990s were no different for AFA, which found itself regularly contesting what remained a violent and much-disputed political zone. Brick Lane has always been the site for migrants seeking sanctuary, from the French Huguenots to East European Jews fleeing religious oppression, to the recent intake of Bengalis and others. At the north end of Brick Lane are a pair of bagel bakeries, and all the way down are curry houses catering for all pockets and taste buds as well as pubs where fascists would hang out and where 'they seemed to receive a warm welcome...The Blade Bone, The Sun or The Weavers, all under the benevolent gaze of Bethnal Green police force'.[32] Perhaps the most symbolic building is the church built by the Huguenot Protestants that became a synagogue and is now a mosque.

The far right had traditionally held a regular weekend paper sale in Brick Lane where they could mobilize several dozen members from the varying groupuscules who would either drink themselves into oblivion or drive off in a van to distribute race-hate literature on the local estates. Collins paints a dismal picture:

Milo Books, 2001), 10.
32   Bullstreet, *Bash the Fash*, 11.

Nazis and cranks from across Britain would converge there on Sunday mornings to sell newspapers and abuse the Asian men and women who lived there. The NF and BNP would compare battle scars from the previous days' activities before heading off for the pub at midday together...[others] made do with knocking on doors just as the *Eastenders* omnibus was due.[33]

As the unreliable *Searchlight* mole Tim Hepple wrote of the time, 'The Brick Lane sale is the number one regular event for the BNP. It takes place, with written permission, from around 10 to 12 every Sunday morning and attendances vary from 15 to 60. Passersby just ignore the sales.'[34] This clearly presented an interesting and somewhat formidable challenge to AFA who rose to the occasion. In early October 1990, a group of AFA militants turned up to occupy the regular fascist spot on Brick Lane and distributed a leaflet announcing an AFA public meeting: 'At approximately 11.30 fascists who had been dispersed by the arrival of anti-fascists launched an attack. Four anti-fascists and three fascists were arrested...and charged with affray'.[35] As the far right had approached AFA, the police stood by watching until AFA attacked, quickly gaining the upperhand, causing the far-right mob to disperse yet again. The police made their move and the chief cop demanded that AFA 'fuck off', to which the chief steward responded by saying, 'You fuck off!' In 1991, London AFA wrote,

The Sunday we took over their paper sale was the day after the BNP national rally (which sadly had to be rearranged after the two original venues were informed as to the real identity of the Chesterton Society) and the London BNP activists looked mighty peeved when they were unable to remove anti-fascists

---

33   Matthew Collins, *Hate: My Life in the British Far Right* (London: Milo Books, 2011), 44.

34   Tim Hepple, *At War with Society: The Exclusive Story of a Searchlight Mole Inside Britain's Far Right* (London: Searchlight Magazine, 1993), 21.

35   London Anti-Fascist Action, *An Introduction to London AFA* (London: 1991), 12.

from their pitch—in front of their 'racial comrades' from up north.[36]

The following week, aware that AFA had seriously encroached on their 'territory', the BNP/NF turned up ready for a large confrontation. The AFA contingent, drawing on the squads' previous tactics at Chapel Market, opted to stay away, using the 'strategy of nerves' that had been so effective in Islington when the far right could never predict what opposition they might face that day. AFA continued to monitor the situation closely as the far right was becoming very aware of.

Six months later, AFA showed up again three-hundred-strong and occupied the BNP/NF pitch. Having previously announced this audacious move, the police were aware of AFA's moves and made arrangements to contain them. AFA increased the pressure by visiting pubs frequented by the far right, further limiting the physical space for fascist organization. London AFA reported,

> We called a demonstration against the fascist paper sale at Brick Lane and then successfully blockaded The Sun pub to prevent the BNP using their usual watering hole. The 250 anti-fascists easily outnumbered the 50-odd (very odd) fascists the BNP managed to mobilize, including people from as far away as Leicester.[37]

Six months later, AFA did the same again, this time coinciding with the BNP AGM where their leader, Tyndall, 'rose to foot-stomping, Sieg-Heiling and chants of "Leader", which became "Fuhrer" in a roar'.[38] It was a colourful day:

> A vicious brawl ensued. Bethnal Green Road came to a standstill as railings were flung and BNP members battered to the ground. The reds had stolen someone's Union Jack and began to burn it, which led to another charge into their ranks. The police had

---

36   Ibid., 14.
37   Ibid.
38   Collins, *Hate*, 268.

set up barricades on both sides of Bethnal Green Road so that both sides could shout abuse at each other. There were torn up newspapers and posters everywhere. That afternoon C18 was officially launched.[39]

After the rival groups had been dispersed, several fascists were apprehended and battered by AFA at King's Cross Station. To add to the fascists' misery, they were arrested shortly after for offensive weapons. Whilst working 'undercover' for Searchlight, Hepple recalls attending the court case with these hapless goons as part of the 'security team':

> The next moment…a quite different group of around 20 large characters turned up. I found this rather amusing to say the least, but I was also rather worried. I remember that none of these guys would know that I was really on their side. I don't know whether this was the feared Red Action, but I supposed that it was. This was the only time I saw the BNP thugs terrified. They all looked pale and worried and were muttering on about the need for reinforcements.[40]

As Collins has pointed out, the far right was often unnerved because many in RA (and by extension AFA) 'look just [like] us, talk like us', and they consequently had difficulty identifying friend from foe.[41] This was because many in AFA were from exactly the same places as the fascists, went to the same football matches as them, and wore the same casual or skinhead attire (though not all by any means—there was always a contingent of punks and dreadlocked members visible out on 'manoeuvres'). Following a 'static confrontation' between the BNP and ANL (that is, much abuse exchanged and too many cops) a group of men came marching round the corner singing 'Rule Britannia' to the relief of the fascists. The police ushered the new group over to the BNP who did not realise that this was, in

39   Ibid., 267.
40   Hepple, *At War with Society*, 30.
41   Collins, *Hate*, 241.

fact, a team of AFA/RA. In the cordon 'battle was enjoined' and the BNP was attacked and scattered, the ANL cheered and the police stood still. Yet again, the far right made the same mistake as before: they dismissed all anti-fascists as 'soft', 'students' or 'middle class', which led to their undoing.

It took several years of concerted efforts before AFA finally cleared Brick Lane of its fascist presence. As K. Bullstreet writes,

> Ironically the fascists were only finally knocked off their Brick Lane pitch after the BNP got a councillor, Derek Beackon, elected locally. The election was on a Thursday, and the following Sunday when the fascists were expected to be having a victory parade at Brick Lane a massive punch-up got rid of them.[42]

Not only did the far right underestimate the ability of AFA to 'out-violence' them, but they confused AFA with ANL in their discussions and analysis of events. One notorious 'revenge' incident in Brick Lane was the fascist attack on ANL/SWP members in February 1992. As the left-wing group set out to leaflet one of the estates nearby, a large gang of skinheads and Combat 18 thugs attacked them, assaulting them severely with bricks, bottles and metal implements. The attack was vicious and the left-wing group was unprotected, with neither the numbers nor the muscle to protect them against such an attack. With thirty thugs against fifteen men and women, the SWP should have known better than to go unprepared into what was, at the time, a violently contested area. It was a huge morale boost for the far right, in particular C18, which had begun to organize itself better in response to the BNP being turned over by AFA. The same thugs attacked an ANL bookstall in Brick Lane that summer whilst campaigning in a local election:

> Thirty C18 supporters had been mobilized the day before by phone. Taking up position in the Blade Bone pub in Brick Lane, they awaited their prey to arrive.... They stopped off in the

---

42   Bullstreet, *Bash the Fash*, 12.

market, arming themselves with an array of Lucozade and milk bottles, bricks and stones.[43]

The unprotected left-wingers were seriously assaulted. None of the attackers were arrested, despite *Searchlight* being able to name them all.

Marching in South East London: A Harsh Lesson

It is not the amount of teeth lost, heads cracked or numbers gathered that creates a victory but often the amount of propaganda that is generated over time. The National Black Caucus (NBC) march through Bermondsey in August 1991 to protest the racist murder of Rolan Adams was such an example of handing an easy physical and propaganda victory to the far right. The NBC march through a potentially volatile area was poorly stewarded and ill-advised: it presented a focus for the far right in the locality, an opportunity for mayhem by an assortment of fascist hooligans and football thugs and remains a classic example of how not to do things.

There had already been a similar march through Thamesmead in May 1991, which had attracted a large amount of fascist attention. The march was sponsored by an array of anti-racist groups, with AFA on hand in an advisory capacity—although the advice was not ultimately heeded. The BNP had organized their own march past the site where Rolan was murdered to pay their own sort of homage, which was briefly intercepted by AFA. Collins also reports that the BNP bussed in members from outside the area to inflate numbers, and they went on to opportunistically attack pubs and counter-demonstrators: 'The team was led by hardened BNP activists and joined by the south London British Movement'.[44] Collins also notes that the BNP had now eclipsed the NF in terms of support and was capitalising on its notoriety in the East End. Earlier in the day, AFA had arrived in the vicinity and immediately got embroiled in a 'robust political discussion' with some opponents in a pub near Abbey Wood station. Police had then forced AFA to relocate from the area,

43   Lowles, *White Riot*, 5.
44   Collins, *Hate*, 237.

apparently guiding them past a mob of fascists at another pub, a situation that proved tense but ultimately did not explode. Activists continued to clash with the far right throughout the day.

The August 1991 march by the National Black Caucus went through Bermondsey, attracting three hundred in comparison to the two thousand that marched through Thamesmead. This had all the signs of disaster, with Lowles referring to it as 'foolhardy' and to the area as 'hotly contested by the BNP and the NF'.[45] As the marchers gathered up, tensions increased as the BNP marshalled support from other far right groups and Milwall hooligans, with one declaring to Matthew Collins, 'There'll be no football until we've cleaned all the niggers out of the area'.[46] The police manoeuvred the march into a park and lost control as the outnumbered marchers were besieged by missile-throwing racists. Realising their error, the police then attempted to push the march back the way it came, and the racist mob began to run amok through the local estate, smashing shops, police motorbikes and other cars along the way. Birchall reports that this was 'one of only two occasions when the BNP could be said to have "controlled the streets"'.[47]

In a polemical article about the day, *Fighting Talk* reported that 'we should have no illusions about the events of 24th August. It was a major disaster. It has set back the work AFA is doing in South London appreciably'.[48] One Red Action scout reported rather more succinctly: 'We were lucky to get out alive—that was our only success.'[49] It became clear to AFA militants that the day had been compromised by ineffectual leadership. This meant a significant boost to the confidence of the far right after suffering many defeats over the last few years at the hands of AFA.

In 1992, a march was organized to commemorate another racist murder, this time of Rohip Duggal in Eltham (where Steven Lawrence was later murdered in a racist attack). C18 mingled with

---

45   Lowles, *White Riot*, 11.
46   Collins, *Hate*, 254.
47   Birchall, 246.
48   Anti-Fascist Action, *Fighting Talk* 2: 14.
49   Hepple, *At War with Society*, 20.

BNP and NF thugs ready to confront the march. The situation deteriorated and AFA stewards managed to successfully get most of the marchers out of the area before it turned too violent. Others did not heed the advice of people who had been heavily involved in militant anti-fascism for a decade and a half and instead wandered off to be attacked by fascists looking for easy pickings. AFA stewards knew that marching through dangerous areas was ultimately self-defeating and, more depressingly, these marches did little to inhibit the racist murders they protested.

Kensington Library

The Thamesmead march in May 1991 proved to be a contentious one, but the day was saved by a highly successful and audacious action that, despite being a victory, could have ended up with serious consequences. As the marchers dispersed from Thamesmead, AFA set off to West London where a League of St. George meeting was being held in Kensington Library. AFA activists infiltrated it with forged tickets, and others battered their way past the ineffectual security at the door and locked them in a room. Jeffrey Hamm was to address the meeting, as were other fascist luminaries, but AFA took control, the meeting was halted and the whole event was a rout and embarrassment for the far right. Lowles reports that 'in a scene reminiscent of a war zone, the street outside the venue, Kensington Library, was littered with the bodies of unconscious skinheads. It was to be the right's most comprehensive street defeat for years'.[50] Collins had arrived earlier with a friend but, luckily, nipped off for a quick pint, thus missing all the action. When he returned, it was to chaos. One half of the AFA group had taken over the door whilst the others secured the room as Gerry Gable, *Searchlight* editor, gave the assembled hard core national socialists a stern talking to. Meanwhile, some more skinheads had forced themselves through the door only to be hammered by militants who were about to leave the scene. The skins were caught between two highly charged groups of AFA with inevitable results. Eventually, point well made, AFA withdrew from the scene of carnage.

---

50   Lowles, *White Riot*, 10.

Collins recalls that Tony Lecomber, the jailed Nazi bomber who almost blew himself up, arrived well after the ruckus had ended to report that the BNP had not done as well as they thought in Thamesmead and that 'despite a good start, [they] had been turned over there too by the sheer weight of reds'.[51] According to Collins, Lecomber then tried to get people to finger Gable as the main antagonist and a case was brought against him and a leading RA/AFA activist, which fell to pieces through poor coordination of prosecution witnesses in court. There is also some confusion over the role of the League of St. George's Keith Thompson in the 'Kensington Library Massacre'. In his unreliable memoir, Hepple writes, with the help of *Searchlight*, that 'Thompson turned out to be one of Gerry Gable's key paid informants in the late 1970s and early 1980s'—which, given the guiding hand of Gable in the tract, we can take as either pretty reliable or misinformation.[52] Collins, then under the aegis of *Searchlight*, confirms that 'as Gable left the building Thompson thanked him for his restraint'.[53]

Meanwhile, it was business as usual for AFA when right-wing populist Jean-Marie Le Pen visited London in late 1991:

> The mood for the demonstrators was militantly confrontational and displayed a determination to impede the progress of the meeting.... The demonstration continued for some three hours, blockading The Strand and Trafalgar Square, forcing the French fascist to scuttle out of the back entrance.[54]

The BNP would soon try to emulate Le Pen's populist racism under Nick Griffin as it moved away from street-level confrontation and into more formal politics.

The Battle of Waterloo

One of the most successful mobilisations by AFA was the 'Battle of Waterloo' in September 1992 and 'was probably the biggest

51   Collins, *Hate*, 239.
52   Hepple, *At War with Society*, 18.
53   Collins, *Hate*, 239.
54   Anti-Fascist Action, *Fighting Talk* 2: 4–5.

anti-fascist battle since Lewisham (1977). It was even covered on national TV news, radio, tabloids, etc'.[55] Blood & Honour, a Nazi music venture, announced a large-scale event with 'White Noise' bands at an as-yet-undisclosed venue. The organizers instructed their hopeful followers to meet at Waterloo station where they would be redirected to the gig. Seeing as this was exactly the same tactic as the Hyde Park debacle in 1989 it was pretty much guaranteed that AFA would turn up to confront them. Which is exactly what happened. AFA called for a national mobilization and put out a leaflet calling on people to 'Unscrew Skrewdriver', the pro-Nazi band, which was widely distributed, especially at AFA's rain-sodden Unity Carnival in London the week before. Hann states that AFA contacted the various anti-fascist and anti-racist groups to present a broad show of strength but that 'no-one seemed interested…but then we never really expected anything else'.[56] This did not prevent the *Sunday Times* from claiming that the day was won by the ANL, who were not quick to deny responsibility.

Knowing that Blood & Honour could call on hundreds of violent fascist skinheads from all around Europe, K. Bullstreet recalls initial trepidation over the hundred-strong AFA group he was in being outnumbered and 'slaughtered', but events proved quite the contrary. On arriving at the station concourse, several militants started proceedings by attacking two skinheads in the buffet (who were later rumoured to be undercover police). As more and more fascist skinheads arrived, they were met, with dire consequences, by an ever-growing number of anti-fascists. The far right soon lost their contact point and dozens of clueless skinheads, many from mainland Europe, wandered around the area wondering what to do next. They were met by AFA activists and redirected well away from the station. Not only did AFA battle with the skinheads but also with police who were determined to clear the station so 'normal service could be resumed'. Whilst this took some time, it also meant that the battle spread out further round the area onto Waterloo Bridge and along the south Embankment. The

55   Bullstreet, *Bash the Fash*, 17.
56   Steve Tilzey and Dave Hann, *No Retreat: The Secret War Between Britain's Anti-Fascists and the Far Right* (London: Milo Books, 2003), 194.

skinheads continued to be dispersed and constantly attacked by anti-fascists, whose numbers had now increased to over a thousand. The police had by now completely lost control. To make matters worse, mobs of football hooligans began turning up, which caused further chaos and eventually affected central London. Reported Lowles and Silver somewhat mildly,

> At 5.00pm they decided to evacuate the station, signalling a victory for the anti-fascist movement as the nazis' meeting point was now closed. A group of nearly 100 skinheads, who were assembled outside the station waving swastika flags, came on the receiving end of a hail of missiles. A car containing skinheads was smashed up and nearly turned over.[57]

Charing Cross and other stations had also been closed down. Ex-fascist Collins recalls arriving into the chaos to be 'greeted by the sight of bloodied skinheads sat around dazed and confused.... The skinhead security had been given a pounding earlier in the day, and there was no one around to redirect the stragglers who had come from as far as France and Sweden'.[58] Members of Combat 18 had been behind the gig but were nowhere to be found. It turned out that the 'brigade of fearless storm-troopers' were hiding in a pub in Victoria several miles away, drinking and taking drugs and watching events unfold on TV whilst the very people they should have been protecting from 'the Reds' were being battered and chased out of London.[59] Collins claims, quite plausibly, that this was a deliberate rather than cowardly act (although it could have been both): 'It seemed incredible but it dawned on me, that C18 deliberately let the skinheads get done over at Waterloo so that they could run Blood & Honour themselves'.[60] If this is the case, it shows C18's ulterior

57   Nick Lowles and Steve Silver, *White Noise: Inside the International Nazi Skinhead Scene* (London: Searchlight, 1998), 27.
58   Collins, *Hate*, 284–85.
59   Angus Roxborough, *Preachers of Hate: The Rise of the Far Right* (London: Gibson Square Books, 2002), 244.
60   Collins, *Hate*, 287.

pursuit as money more than any ideological attachment to the far-right movement. Indeed, the schism between the C18 casuals and the Blood & Honour-inclined skins proved to be a fatal one in the collapse of support for C18.

Blood & Honour claimed that the eventual arrival at the gig of about four hundred war-torn skinheads was somehow a victory despite the fact that less than half had turned up and more anti-fascists had arrived outside. Eventually, after an hour or two of turgid din, the landlady of the pub pulled the plug, so the defeated Nazis headed off bruised to bed. One skinzine wrote despondently, 'What had we got in the end? A few cuts and bruises, a case of dented pride, the reds running round cock-a-hoop'.[61] The fallout from this embarrassment had long-reaching effect: AFA's by-now regular magazine *Fighting Talk* reported that they

> heard an interesting little tale about C18 and 'the brothers' from Germany after the Becontree/Bow/Waterloo fiasco on January 15th. Seems our short-haired friends from Germany weren't over impressed by C18's handling (ha!) of the gig that never happened and it all kicked off! No more brother wars eh?[62]

To make matters worse for Blood & Honour, principal cash cow Ian Stuart died along with several other Nazi musicians in a car crash in Derbyshire shortly after.

Copsey writes that whilst Waterloo was a major blow for Blood & Honour it did little to impede the progress of the BNP, and that instead of chasing Nazi skinheads out of Waterloo Station, AFA 'should have been concentrating efforts on Milwall', where the BNP had been organizing with considerable success.[63] In mitigation, AFA did mobilize against the BNP in Milwall, but given the nature of its anarchist and revolutionary socialist members, was not really in the business of standing candidates against them; it was most effective on the streets and as a propaganda outfit staging successful carnivals,

61   Lowles and Silver, *White Noise*, 27.
62   Anti-Fascist Action, *Fighting Talk* 7: 15.
63   Copsey, *Anti-Fascism in Britain*, 173.

gigs and marches to raise awareness of the political climate. However, the political picture was beginning to drastically alter, with the BNP gradually withdrawing from the streets, following a Euro-fascist line like the French National Front, which would also make AFA question future tactics.

The Battle of Welling, 1993

> A massive riot ensued, which didn't achieve anything but it's always a good laugh when everyone is chucking paving stones and other stuff at cops.
>
> —K. Bullstreet in *Bash the Fash*

With such militant activity, a high profile, and considerable public and political success, AFA was bound to be targeted by the state, which would prefer anti-fascism to be containable, moderate and, overall, legal. AFA was not inclined to follow this line and it was a riot in South London that confirmed AFA's suspicions about state manoeuvres against them. In October 1993, a march in Welling was organized by the ANL and others against the BNP headquarters/'bookshop', which was not far from Eltham where the racist murders of Rohip Duggal and Stephen Lawrence happened. The pro-parliamentarian Anti-Racist Alliance (ARA) held a simultaneous rally in Trafalgar Square, well out of the way. AFA had been calling for 'unity' with various anti-racist groups for some time, which had been rejected, and did not see how holding two separate marches was unifying anyone. *Fighting Talk* also queried the efficacy of the march: 'There have been six marches and 27 lobbies to remove the BNP HQ and none of them have worked'.[64] The march would do little to deal with increasing fascist influence in London's working-class areas.

As the march, numbering between forty- and sixty thousand, headed towards the bookshop, riot police formed a blockade across the street, backed by mounted officers, and as the march pressed forward the police blocked off the way back. The police baton charged

---

64   Anti-Fascist Action, *Fighting Talk* 6: 3.

the march, and a contingent of anti-fascists began fighting with police, and bricks, sticks and bottles started flying over the melee. Also involved were members of Militant's 'Away Team', a small 'squadist' group set up to protect their political activities. A red smoke bomb was sent over, which added televisual drama to the scene as the anti-fascists fought back against the police. Masked up or not, brick-flinging militants supplied the appropriate 'Shock! Horror!' requisite for news teams. Being pressured by police at the front, unable to move backwards, people tried to get out of the cordon as the fighting broke out. A cemetery wall was demolished and used as 'ammunition' as others left the scene through the gaps. There were multiple injuries and arrests. Kelly and Metcalf write about their suspicions of the riot being police inspired:

> Relatively few police officers stood at the front and took a bit of a hammering. Meanwhile hundreds of officers sat in their buses a few hundred yards away from the 'riot'. Information from inside the police confirmed that they never really feared that the demonstrators would break through.[65]

The riot, which had been started by the police, received coverage at peak time on national TV with the usual condemnation of 'left-wing troublemakers'—which AFA felt was the real reason for policing on the day: to discredit militant anti-fascism as much as fascism, and to lump fascist and anti-fascist militants together as one violent entity. Increased state interest had been suspected by AFA following incidents in Enfield and at Abbey Wood. Copsey reports that right-wing tabloid *The Sun* offered 'a £1,000 reward for anyone who could provide information on the rioters. As expected, even though it had not sponsored the march, Anti-Fascist Action/Red Action was suspected of being responsible for the violence'.[66] The *Evening Standard* reported that 'the information gathered by MI5 and police surveillance units on the march would soon result in the arrest of extremists

65   Jim Kelly and Mark Metcalf, *Anti-Nazi League: A Critical Examination* (London: Resistance, 1995).
66   Copsey, *Anti-Fascism in Britain*, 176.

from two organizations, one of which was Red Action'.[67] Although police fingers were pointed at AFA, for once, to paraphrase AFA's paraphrase, 'it was AFA that didn't do it,' and they had a pretty solid alibi. Their paper reported that 'at the time when Red Action were according to MI5 attacking the police, Red Action were in fact involved in a confrontation with C18 some distance away in Abbey Wood'.[68] The main body of AFA militants that day, in the form of a hundred-strong stewards group, had split off from the march before the riot started. They found C18 gathered in a beer garden nearby surrounded by a protective cordon of police, which enabled them to do little but shout abuse at the AFA group outside, a cordon that supplied RA/AFA with 'reliable' witnesses to their exact whereabouts.

Shortly after Welling, World in Action produced a condemnatory documentary on the various anti-fascist and anti-racist groups, clearly delineating between the good guys—ARA—and the bad—SWP, ANL and, despite their absence, AFA. Soundtracked by the usual gloomy music and unconvincing reconstructions, the programs featured relatives of the victims of racist murders speaking against organizations who were using them for their own purposes. There is a misconception, amongst the far right as well as others, that anti-fascists are fighting 'for' ethnic minorities in some misguided role of political social workers. This is mostly untrue. AFA was fighting against fascism as an ideology, not just 'for the victims of racism', which is only a part of that ideology. As an amusing coda to the whole Welling fiasco, Copsey notes that despite the attempt to frame and discredit AFA, 'the militant wing of the anti-fascist movement did not suffer for World In Action's treatment—AFA expanded to over 20 branches in 1994, rising to over 40 in 1995'.[69]

67   Ibid.
68   *Red Action* 67: 12. *Red Action* archive: www.redactionarchive.org.
69   Copsey, *Anti-Fascism in Britain*, 177.

Blood & Honour: Beware
Mancunians Bearing Lucozade Bottles

These Nazis are also involved in carrying out racist attacks. When 'Blood & Honour' started drinking around Kings Cross last year the number of racist attacks increased with a prominent anti-fascist's house petrol-bombed and Asians stabbed in Euston Square and Drummond Street. An anti-fascist campaign removed them from the area for about 9 months, but now they are back.

—London Anti-Fascist Action

In 1979, the National Front began to organize Rock Against Communism, a rather feeble and tiny response to Rock Against Racism. This developed into the White Noise Club, which became a profitable sideline, with the NF selling hard-to-get LPs, cassettes, T-shirts and other merchandise, although little money went to the bands. This underground movement spread across Europe and over to the States, and the bands organized themselves into Blood & Honour by 1987. At first the White Noise and Blood & Honour bands seemed to be a continuation of the Oi! music genre, without the commercial appeal or the backing of the music press. They specialised in unmelodious thrash, bad punk stripped to its basics with extreme, racist and fascist lyrics, and recordings festooned with neo-Nazi insignia. The music was aggressive and the bands and followers dressed in the fascist interpretation of skinhead gear—scruffy combat boots, army greens, and flight jackets—as opposed to the traditional skin wardrobe of Crombies, Fred Perrys, Levis, and Dr. Martens. White Noise and Blood & Honour gigs were always discretely publicised and held in obscure places in case anti-fascists located the venue and turned up to disrupt it or get it cancelled. It was the clandestine nature and the anti-social politics that were attractive to many. The right-wing bands started to make money for themselves, organized outside of the NF, and the sales of merchandise all over the world was considerable and threatened the NF's downfall. By 1993, C18 muscled in and saw how easy and profitable it was to produce, print, and distribute CDs, eventually taking over Blood & Honour, ostensibly to fund their useless terrorist organization.

Blood & Honour naturally attracted the attentions of Red Action and Anti-Fascist Action, and a concerted effort to drive them off the streets of London began. One of the first successes for AFA against Blood & Honour was a campaign against shops in Carnaby Street that specialised in far-right memorabilia and merchandise. Fascist skinheads had also been targeting gigs much like they had done in the late 1970s, trying to determine who could play in London. The shops were picketed, pubs used by Nazis were harassed, and the campaign gained considerable momentum with the 'respectable' wing of anti-fascism who offered support. The shops were eventually closed down, the pubs were forced to seek new clientele, and on the evening of one shop's timely demise, AFA held a Cable Street Beat gig in North London, which the far right chose to completely ignore.

A few years earlier, in 1989, Blood & Honour was subject to one of AFA's biggest and most successful mobilisations so far. Shortly after the campaign against the shops, Blood & Honour attempted to hold a 'secret' gig in London, confidently claiming that 'the Jews and reds are going to be trashed by our international efforts'.[1] Despite several setbacks, Blood & Honour organized the 'main event', which featured several prominent White Noise bands, and began to shift a considerable amount of tickets—which with the illicit tat and overpriced beer on sale at the gig would be extremely lucrative. But it was not to be. Blood & Honour had instructed the fascist skinheads to go to a redirection point at Hyde Park Corner then, when suitable numbers gathered, to relocate to the secret venue somewhere in London. AFA found out just in time that Blood & Honour had booked

---

1   Lowles and Silver, *White Noise*, 15.

Camden Town Hall as the venue and forced the council to cancel it. AFA also had foreknowledge of the skinheads' rendezvous point and mobilised accordingly:

> A minibus load of us came back to London for the day. It was another of those occasions when most of us were convinced we were going to be massacred! Everyone knew that Blood & Honour could muster several hundred or even a thousand bodies.... After we met Red Action and various other anti-fascists we headed down to Marble Arch about 100 strong, and considerably more confident. And what a success it turned out to be![2]

Dozens of fascist skinheads, or boneheads, arrived in London and headed towards Speaker's Corner to be met by a determined anti-fascist presence:

> A 20-strong gang of older skinheads, some armed with bottles, tried to clear the area of opposition. Young students saw off the first attack and as more anti-fascists, and fascists, arrived, fighting broke out on the fringes of the area. In numerous skirmishes skinheads were sent away licking their wounds. At one point a coach load of skinheads came round the corner and was attacked with every conceivable missile that was at hand. A metal dustbin went crashing through a side window in the melee.[3]

Scenes like this continued for several hours, and Blood & Honour and the skinheads were in complete disarray: 'If all the bones had been able to mob up, things might have been very different, but as it was, we had a field day.... There was no one to give them leadership.'[4] There was a much smaller police presence than usual because of an anti-*Satanic Verses* demo in town, so they were overstretched and could give the boneheads little succour. More and more skinheads arrived, some from the European mainland, and were met not with

2 Bullstreet, *Bash the Fash*, 14.
3 Lowles and Silver, *White Noise*, 16.
4 Tilzey and Hann, *No Retreat*, 188.

open arms but a large mob of anti-fascists determined to drive them out of the city. Individuals were apprehended and coaches and vans were attacked, some several times by roving gangs of militants who had eluded police escorts and popped up seemingly out of nowhere. Birchall reports that once police reinforcements arrived, the AFA stewards group disappeared into the tube and went on the hunt for roving fascists; 'there was an immediate clash with a group of foreign skinheads' before they broke into groups to reassemble on the outskirts of the city centre.[5] Blood & Honour had trumpeted this gig widely, intending to show the left and far right that they were in the ascendancy, but AFA got the drop on them, and Blood & Honour was utterly humiliated. The gig did go ahead but in a venue which only held three hundred, so many who eventually got there ended up standing around outside looking foolish. AFA reported that 'of the fascists who did get to Gravesend, half of them couldn't get in to the gig because it was too small. So all in all their plans (and many of *them*) were badly damaged'.[6] Many of the punters, and especially those who had travelled from afar, were furious at Blood & Honour's failure to manage the event properly, or to provide protection from anti-fascists. To make matters worse, that night

> a small group of anti-fascists attacked the Blood & Honour shop in Riding House street, smashing the windows and pouring bleach over the stock inside.... They lost a £900 deposit on Camden Town Hall and a lot more money was lost refunding bones who couldn't get in. They lost a lot of face for failing to confront AFA in Hyde Park, and lost a lot of respect from their comrades abroad who complained about the shambolic organization of the event.[7]

It was a significant blow for Blood & Honour and caused many fallouts. In October 1992, Blood & Honour decided to organize a gig in Folkestone, which forced a broad local and anti-fascist mobilization. The venue was identified and the gig cancelled. Six hundred

---

5   Birchall, *Beating the Fascists*, 159.
6   London Anti-Fascist Action, *An Introduction to London AFA*, 11.
7   Tilzey and Hann, *No Retreat*, 191.

people turned up to protest, and several boneheads were subject to 'a short but frank and to the point discussion', which resulted in the arrest of three anti-fascists. The demonstration then marched to the police station, forcing police to release the anti-fascists, whilst 'the other fascists were holed up in a run-down flat complete with police protection'.[8]

Ian Stuart Donaldson, or Ian Stuart, the singer from Skrewdriver, was a visible presence on the Blood & Honour scene and was often surrounded by acolytes who were attracted to his 'mystique'. They were subsequently disillusioned by continuous attacks round Kings Cross Station where Stuart lived. Red Action particularly took an interest in harassing Stuart and his cronies whenever they crossed paths, which was frequently. Stuart 'went out early one morning to buy a newspaper and a pint of milk and was hit across the head by a large Mancunian wielding a Lucozade bottle'.[9] Birchall writes that

> on returning from an early evening jog, Stuart was spotted at his front door by a passing RA member and coshed. Even more disquieting must have been the ambush of a group of visiting foreign skinheads, who were beaten and left lying unconscious, literally toe to toe, on the doorstep of his hotel.[10]

A skinhead fanzine once referred to Red Action as Pink Action, for which Stuart took the brunt yet again: 'On his way home with a take-away meal one evening, [Stuart] was set about and left lying on the ground. Having several enemies he cried, "Who are you?" "Pink Action" came the reply'.[11]

Stuart's 'racial comrades' did equally badly on the streets and were often attacked by Red Action. In one incident RA members apprehended a small group of fascists in a restaurant who were CS gassed and battered with one fascist getting a fork stuck in his arse whilst escaping through a serving hatch. Two other fascists were served

8   Anti-Fascist Action, *Fighting Talk* 4: 13.
9   Tilzey and Hann, *No Retreat*, 191.
10   Birchall, *Beating the Fascists*, 162.
11   Lowles and Silver, *White Noise*, 17.

similar fare after taking liberties in an Indian restaurant where three RA members were eating. Such was the intensity of the campaign against him that Stuart eventually fled London and attempted to sever his links with the various far-right organizations who were clearly using him. One of Stuart's acquaintances recalled,

> Y'know 'e had his fingers fucked up by AFA [Anti-Fascist Action]? Yeah, with an 'ammer. He didn't want to go through that kind of thing anymore.... 'E wanted to leave, y'know. Get out, while he still had a chance.... But it was all the others who wouldn't let him go. People like Charlie [Sargent] and that.[12]

Stuart died in a car crash in 1993, and his ghost has been milked dry ever since by fanatics. There is no doubt that Stuart received brutal treatment at the hands and boots of anti-fascists. This was in response to the brutal, racist lyrics and attitudes that he and his followers propagated. He was a violent fascist skinhead with a blindly loyal following who helped instigate an increase in racist attacks and tensions in London. Skrewdriver was a propaganda outfit for the far right and as the leading figure, Stuart was targeted and 'martyred' accordingly.

12   Nick Ryan, *Homeland: Into a World of Hate* (London: Mainstream Publishing, 2003), 86–87.

AFA and Ireland: 'Short, Sharp and Painful'

It must be acknowledged that AFA was about much more than violent street confrontations with fascists. Initially they operated in a reactive manner but then increasingly took the initiative and branched out into other activities. Propaganda was always an important part of anti-fascism, so thousands of leaflets, stickers, pamphlets, football fanzines, magazines and papers were produced; a prisoners welfare fund was set up to aid anti-fascists in jail for 'active duty'; Cable Street Beat, an anti-fascist music organization, was set up in 1988; and gigs, marches and carnivals were successfully organized. AFA members were also involved in many other political campaigns independently, one of them being the Irish Republican struggle. There has always been a crossover between the far right and the Northern Irish loyalist movement: paramilitary figures were often admired if not canonised by members of the NF and BNP, and members of the far right have been arrested gun-running for them. It is also well known that some loyalists distrust the mainland far right, seeing them as unreliable, fair-weather or 'state', and viewing them as handy foot-soldiers and valuable purchasers of propaganda. Aware of this often uneasy relationship, members of AFA and RA stewarded pro-Republican meetings and marches, fully aware of the rabid sentiments of the far right who would claim that all Irish or Republicans are 'IRA'.[1] It must be noted that, although RA had strong Republican sympathies, not all AFA members felt the same, but AFA did protect Republican marches, as roving gangs of fascists were often determined to break up the proceedings. Tilzey recalls the NF mounting an attack on a

---

1   O'Mahoney, *Hateland*, 76. O'Mahoney and Collins both had Irish
     fathers, and O'Mahoney points out that 'most members of our little
     group had at least one Irish parent'.

Troops Out Movement (TOM) meeting in Manchester in the late 1970s. NF and loyalist supporters had been harassing members over the phone, so the Manchester squad was prepared. Twenty-five fascists and loyalists approached the meeting and were met by the squad, one of whom fired a magnesium flare over the heads of the NF; it exploded, unnerving some of those in the forefront. Others from the meeting appeared and the NF was run off. The first serious confrontation between pro-loyalists and AFA occurred in Sheffield in 1987 when a gang of NF members tried to attack another TOM march only to be faced with a sixty-strong stewards group, who chased them off, with one unlucky fascist being battered to the ground. The large march was subject to haranguing and accidentally split in two. The police started to arrest AFA members who were busy repelling marauding fascists. After being halted for some time, the march finally reached its destination, there was a rally, and the marchers departed. AFA remained in the area waiting to collect those arrested earlier in the day and also to confront a group of NF members who were hanging around looking for stragglers.

O'Mahoney recalls being part of a right-wing mob attacking a Troops Out march circa 1984 (although factual accuracy is questionable throughout his book, it gives an idea of the fascist mindset): 'On the morning of the march, we met up in a local pub when it opened at eleven. By the time we headed for Lambeth North tube station, we were all drunk. As we made our way to meet the red hordes other people from pubs along our route joined us'. They attacked the march, but 'in a few seconds it was over', and they ran as police arrived.[2] They plotted up in another pub but were contained by the law.

One militant recalls the mixed emotions of such days:

> The pro-Republican marches could be very lively. We were in Manchester for either a Manchester Martyrs or Troops Out March, about the mid-1980s, which attracted the usual loyalist/ fascist eejits, and a brave few who tried to attack the march. I hated going on those things but we had a lot of handy republicans,

---

2   Ibid., 103–104.

Red Action and AFA stewards about and it was nice to see one gobby fash running into the march then being bounced back across the pavement. The cops were extremely nervous and the fash ended up much worse off. At one point we were marching under what was the Arndale Centre bridge (which the IRA blew up later) when the leading Republican band stopped and played with all its might, the sound echoing across the city. It was one of the most exciting and terrifying things I have ever heard. It must have freaked plod and the fash right out. It freaked me out, that's for sure!

In 1988, fascists attacked an anti-internment march but were successfully repulsed; police looked on and later arrested the stewards involved (although they were not necessarily AFA). After another march, AFA stewards gathered at Euston spotted a gang of fascists and loyalists in the area. They followed, and later ambushed them in a pub near Tavistock Square. The next year, fascists had been attacking people as they left the anti-internment march despite the large AFA presence. A van full of AFA activists located them and chased them into a tube station where they received a savage beating.

Despite the gravity of the issue and the very real threat of serious violence, the possibilities of humour, if not outright oddness, were not far away. Simon Davies from AFA recalls the following:

This was either a Troops Out or Bloody Sunday march (think probably the former as the weather was always fucking awful for Bloody Sunday marches and this was a warm sunny day) sometime in the late '80s. Rumours had been flying about that the fash were planning something and as the march passed Marble Arch and started up the Edgware Road we discovered that this was true—but not at all in the way we might have expected. At least one of this group of fash must have spent some time as a Maoist or WRPer, because their counter protest took the form of street theatre—the barbarity of the IRA being displayed by a couple of the fash done up in bloodied bandages, attended by 'doctors' in white coats and stethoscopes, and a couple of nurses in blue dresses and sensible shoes. The only trouble was the 'nurses' were actually blokes, complete with wigs and Les Dawson-style *Cissie and Ada* false knockers.

The militants still managed to harangue the fascists, despite considerable mirth, until the rest of their group arrived to discuss matters further.

As LiamO remembers,

On one Manchester Martyrs march the local plod (or Dibble, as the Mancs would have it) were somewhat hostile. Thus they would encourage loyalists and fash to get right in our faces, with the plod in between. They could pretty much do as they liked but any response from our side was often jumped on, thus we either wound them up or just had to ignore them. The free hand they were afforded often allowed the fash to whip themselves up into a demented, self-righteous frenzy. One Scouse fella was thus infected and had decided PC was to be the special focus of his ire. 'See you. Yer fuckin dead. DEAD d'ye hear me, SCUM? YER FUCKIN DEAD. I'm GONNA SLIT YOUR FUCKIN THROAT YOU FUCKIN SCUM. D'YOU HEAR ME, EH CUNT? SOON AS THIS MARCH IS OVER YOU FUCKIN SHIT CUNT TERRORIST BABY-KILLER SCUM.' etc. PC just gritted his teeth, kept his eyes front and ignored him. The alternative was probably a nicking. Yer man managed to keep this tirade up for a couple of minutes and even the old bill were beginning to get annoyed with his constant raving. Now he was facing into the March from the side, so to keep up with PC he had to keep sidestepping and jumping which added to his demented little pixie look and, combined with his ranting, drew quite an audience. All of which made it all the funnier when he took a giant sideways leap, straight into a concrete lamppost—and knocked himself completely unconscious, splitting his face like a peach in the process. The whole March was held up cos no-one could walk for laughing, especially when one copper—amongst the chorus of raucous catcalls—who had been encouraging him, gave him a sly boot and told him 'gerrup you daft cunt you're making a show of us.' This set us off again worse than ever and yer man suffered the ignominy of coming to, being laughed at by chorus of 150 of his arch-enemies, whilst his comrades just shuffled away in embarrassment, trying to pretend he was nowt to do with them. PC had to be half-carried for the next mile or so as he was rendered completely incapable of walking by hysterical laughter.

Collins recalls that in 1989 a 'derisory thirty of us' turned up to oppose a march by 'Irish Republicans' and were told that '[we] had to stick together and be careful of a group called Red Action who would be sending spotters out to try and ambush us before we got to the march.' When asked what Red Action looked like, 'I was told "like everyone here".'[3]

The NF decided to tactically withdraw into their usual drunken stupors. Another militant recalls the following:

> In the late 1980s I was staying with some SWP comrades in Brighton and we went down to this fringe meeting that Gerry Adams (Sinn Féin) was addressing at the Labour conference, which would have been about 1989. There was me (useless) and this big lad called Jez who had actually lost a kidney after a fascist assault, and some female comrades. We got to the meeting and there was a lot of pro-Republicans there (the SWP were supporting Sinn Féin 'critically') and we sat down apprehensively. There was a real tension in the air and I have never felt anything like it in a meeting. Then Adams got up to speak. All of a sudden this old bloke on the front row grabbed the water jug on the speakers table and tried to throw it at him and there were all these hecklers as well. Adams hadn't even started yet! I assume he was used to far worse than minor interruptions and a damp

---

3   Collins, *Hate*, 33.

blazer. Anyway, he did his thing—which I thought was pretty good despite his politics—and he was funny, which helped dispel the tension a wee bit. Then it was over. We left in a large group and hit the pub for a drink—and we needed one! On the streets were little gangs of agitated skinheads running about like eejits, which was a bit edgy and we knew there were some minor clashes between them, anti-fascists and plod. I now realise that there would have been plenty of handy Republicans knocking about as well as the Red Action lot and local anti-fascists but at the time it was intense. I remember that walk back up the hill feeling very relieved. I can't remember a single thing Adams said.

In 1989, *Searchlight* reported,

> A hundred Nazis tried to attack an Irish meeting at London's Conway Hall...the BNP reports that it was a cross party operation and was in fact led by Richard Edmonds (two lovely black eyes), John Morse (two lovely black eyes and a broken wrist) and Tony Wells, aka East and Lecomber. Wells, the barmy bomber, claims he was sprayed in the eyes with CS gas.[4]

Hann recalls the Stewards Group ambushing a group of loyalists and fascists as they approached the hall early on: 'The first thing we saw was virtually the entire leadership of the BNP walking brazenly into the meeting. A brawl broke out, and they were attacked with fists, boots, and a variety of weapons...the BNP were kicked all over the pavement'.[5]

The Irish organizers of the meeting were not best pleased about such violence but were ill-prepared for the hostilities it would create. The fascists and loyalists regrouped and, now numbering about a hundred, approached the meeting again: 'A strong AFA counter-attack led to clashes in the darkness of the square and the surrounding streets, with the right-wingers again forced to retreat'.[6]

---

4   Anti-Fascist Action. *Heroes or Villains*, 41.
5   Tilzey and Hann, *No Retreat*, 207.
6   Birchall, *Beating the Fascists*, 146.

Following this, AFA took over stewarding and escorted attendees back to the tube station. It was this successful and violent repulsing of loyalists and fascists that soured relations between AFA/RA and the Troops Out Movement. It was also one of several incidents that would cause relations between loyalists and the far right to degenerate after being caught short of nerves on the night.

On the Bloody Sunday march in January 1990, fascist 'face' Nicky Crane was apprehended by three anti-fascists and seriously assaulted; his head was slammed repeatedly in the door of the taxi he was trying to escape in. In August of the same year, a gang of fascists had travelled to North London to attack an Irish Freedom March and luckily lived to regret it. They were chased into Holloway tube and savagely beaten. Probably some small comfort for the three anti-fascists who were jailed for between three and four years each that September for the Crane incident. AFA organized fundraising activities to help the incarcerated militants.

In Kilburn in 1993, Combat 18, loyalist supporters and hooligans gathered to oppose a Bloody Sunday march, greatly outnumbering AFA, which was split between the march and a pub in Notting Hill. Unfortunately, the far right could not capitalise on their superior numbers; the police rounded up and mass arrested three hundred fascists and contained many others as the march got underway several hours late. *Fighting Talk* recognised that without the police, things would have been very different: 'The march organizers, through the efforts of the police, were able to march so the Bloody Sunday Commemoration didn't suffer a defeat either—but it certainly wasn't a victory against fascism.'[7]

Fighting Talk also wrote, 'At least one large group of fascists, when they were released without charge a few hours later, were encouraged to travel home "through Kilburn" (where the march ended). The fascists needed little encouragement and two Irishmen were stabbed.'[8] This raises the spectre of state interference against Republicans. (One issue of *Fighting Talk* also featured a 'special supplement' on AFA and the Police.)

7   Anti-Fascist Action, *Fighting Talk* 4: 2.
8   Ibid.

For O'Hara, the mass arrests were an intelligence-gathering exercise and that this was the 'first indication that the state was taking a close interest in C18…those arrested were detained by the police, questioned, and in some cases had their photographs taken—with virtually no charges being proffered'.[9] For Birchall, this was more sinister: 'This was the first time Loyalists had confidently operated with mainland fascists since the debacle of Conway Hall in November, 1989, and the potential in the partnership was visible for all to see'.[10]

Fighting Talk #11 reports one busy weekend in particular for AFA. On a Bloody Sunday march in Manchester, 'three AFA squads patrolled the route' and saw off several fascist incursions:

> One group of unfortunate BNP members, who had gathered outside a pub, were trapped in a classic pincer movement by two AFA stewards groups and suffered accordingly. Clown of the Day award goes to the idiot who, while stood next to several AFA stewards, started brandishing his St George's flag and boasting about doing the 'reds'. Predictably, the ensuing debate was short, sharp and painful.[11]

AFA gleefully printed photos of said 'Clown of the Day' in *Fighting Talk*, which proved so popular that it was also printed on an 'AFA's Greatest Hits' T-shirt. On the same day in Winchester, a small AFA squad apprehended several fascists in a pub waiting to attack an anti-fascist march:

> By convincing this group that they were sympathetic, the AFA members accompanied these fascists up the city centre high street with the intention of 'picking off lefty stragglers'. The fascists were, in fact, led directly into a contingent of militant anti-fascists where they were 'dealt with' in the appropriate manner.

---

9   Larry O'Hara, *Turning Up the Heat: MI5 After the Cold War* (London: Phoenix, 1994), 74.
10   Birchall, *Beating the Fascists*, 310.
11   Anti-Fascist Action, *Fighting Talk* 11: 3.

In 2000, they were still at it, according to Nick Ryan who attended a Bloody Sunday march: 'A small screaming band of crop-haired National Front supporters chanted, "No Surrender to the IRA!" and other insults.... To our left, a gang of 30 or 40 men peered silently, snarling in our direction. I recognised several people.... The group surged forward, but the cops were there first.'[12]

In more recent times, fascists who were once associated with the English Defence League tried to disrupt Republican events in Liverpool—which was less than successful. There is nothing quite like the Irish struggle to get the far right in a fury.

AFA in Ireland

Although AFA Ireland was formed in Dublin 1991 from a mix of politicos, punks and skinheads, some members had been involved in anti-fascist activity already. In 1984 a busload of anti-fascists and trade unionists went up to Coleraine to protest an NF march where the Ulster Defence Association had threatened to turn up, but failed to show—to the relief of many. Several AFA members had been in London with Red Action in the mid 1980s and one militant wrote,

> The first major thing I was involved with in London was one of the early AFA mobilizations against the NF on Remembrance Sunday. Harry decided to go over and chat to RA: 'I was in full skinhead gear with a tiny, yellow Free Nelson Mandela badge.... About five or six of them came at me straight away. I saw metal bars coming out of people's jackets but luckily one of them espied the badge and tensions dispersed.[13]

The Irish contingent were thrown in straight away: a fascist meeting was apparently taking place so they were sent in as scouts: 'The barmaid smiled at us...[and] this auld fella at the bar looked up from his pint and said, "If you were looking for Ian (Stuart) and the lads, they're

---

12 Ryan, *Homeland*, 101.
13 Bernardo O'Reilly, *Undertones: Anti-Fascism and the Far Right in Ireland, 1945–2012* (Dublin: Anti-Fascist Action Ireland, 2012), 38.

upstairs".'[14] Cue mayhem. In November 1988, Holocaust revisionist David Irving was scheduled to speak at University College Dublin, but on the night five hundred anti-fascists made sure it did not go ahead. AFA Ireland set up a branch in Dublin with Red Action members who had been living in London, inspired by the strategy of physical and ideological opposition. Gigs, meetings and propaganda were all organized as well as physical confrontations—most notably when Le Pen, the French National Front leader, visited in 1991: AFA militants attempted to sabotage the press meeting, which gained them publicity. As usual, AFA in Dublin was to be disappointed by the responses of cooperation with other anti-fascists and prepared for the long haul on their own. They faced up to anti-abortion group Youth Defence three times in quick succession. A socialist picket was attacked by a group of right-wingers; the following day there was a standoff between the two sides, and then a large Youth Defence demo ended up in a brawl. The court case following the inevitable arrests almost ended in a pitched battle in front of cops in a pub. The Dublin anti-fascists also had to face up to the usual bonehead provocations on the music scene and in pubs. The far right were again found lacking in '*espirit de corps*' during skirmishes with Blood & Honour and Celtic Dawn. Despite AFA Ireland being seen by the local left as 'some sort of small-time, drinking gang who beat up Nazis every now and again', they were making headway and they adopted the class analysis of AFA.[15]

During the Lansdowne Road football riot in 1995, AFA managed to accumulate some vital intelligence and made links with Manchester United's *Red Attitude*, Celtic's TAL fanzines, and later fans of St. Pauli, a team known for their anti-fascist stance. AFA Ireland linked up with hunt sabs and anti-drugs campaigns and was involved in several brouhahas with the Immigration Control Platform (ICP). AFA organized a meeting called 'From Blueshirts to Bigots', which featured a former International Brigader, and when Holocaust denier David Irving came to visit Cork in 1999, six hundred anti-fascists turned out to make sure that 'Irving never made it onto campus'.[16]

---

14   Ibid., 39.
15   Ibid., 56.
16   Ibid., 66.

The new millennium started with the bizarrely named 'National Socialists Are Us' facing a large Socialist Party picket that was augmented by Sinn Féin and AFA members. Thousands of anti-racist leaflets were distributed during the General Election of 2002 and graffiti campaigns initiated. Jörg Haider, the Austrian nationalist, came to visit in 2003 and did better than Irving when he actually managed to speak, although some AFA members 'caused a bit of disruption'.[17] AFA made contact with Eastern European anti-fascists and anarchists, and they joined in local campaigns against the Celtic Wolves who, in 2006, had their meeting broken up, after which they fled. In 2011, AFA was part of a protest against Nick Griffin and kept tabs on the far right's developments. As well as maintaining intelligence and organizing events, AFA Ireland also found time to produce *No Quarter* magazine and take part in the Anti-Racist World Cup in Belfast.

---

17   Ibid., 72.

Combat 18: The Nearly Men

> The British National Party had a brigade of fearless storm-
> troopers guarding its meetings and demonstrations. They
> called themselves Combat 18 after our leader Adolf Hit-
> ler. Now the BNP is led by an honest man of great integrity
> with more than a lifetime of nationalist activities behind him.
>
> —Hyperbole from Combat 18 website

It is rare to see militants agreeing with their fascist opponents, but in regards to Combat 18 (C18), anti-fascists and John Tyndall actually agreed on one thing: 'For all their bluster, C18 actually achieved very little', recorded Dave Hann,[1] which unintentionally corroborated Tyndall's earlier statement that 'Combat 18 just did nothing'.[2]

It is generally accepted by both sides that C18 was eventually compromised by the state and imploded into self-interest and murder, but perhaps more important is the fact that they failed to achieve their fundamental goal to 'defeat the reds'. The BNP and NF leadership had a tendency to underestimate AFA/RA, still thinking they were up against the less aggressive ANL, but they were proved wrong. C18 had the dumb insight to see that they were up against 'blokes that look just [like] us, talk like us' but not that they would be out-violenced.[3] In its brief history, C18 never had a single convincing success against the militant anti-fascists it had been set up to counter, and it could only claim a few cowardly attacks on individuals and

---

1   Tilzey and Hann, *No Retreat*, 203.
2   John Tyndall, 'On Harold Covington and Combat 18', *Spearhead Online*, http://noncounterproductive.blogspot.co.uk/p/john-tyndall-on-harold-covington-and.html (accessed October 26, 2012).
3   Collins, *Hate*, 241.

property, some late night phone calls, a misguided bomb plot, and occasionally excessive violence against soft targets like the ANL in Brick Lane. They were also keen on attacking other fascists.

Six Possible Narratives

There are at least six separate narratives about C18 which can be dealt with briefly here. The first 'anti-fascist narrative' is the one featured in *Searchlight* magazine, which was then expanded into the full-length investigation *White Riot* by Nick Lowles and subsequent documentaries, such as *World In Action*. Lowles's book claimed that C18 had orchestrated a 'campaign of terror...to start a racial war', although this has since been found to be a wee bit exaggerated. The second and more convincing 'anti-fascist narrative' is by Larry O'Hara in, amongst other things, *Turning Up the Heat: MI5 After the Cold War*, in which O'Hara makes the case that the first version of C18 was not created by the state but that it was subsequently manipulated by state forces of either MI5 and/or Special Branch. This is certainly qualified in part by revelations—following the C18 murder case—that members were operating as police informants. O'Hara also implies that both *Searchlight* and state agencies had deliberately inflated the threat of the Combat 18 'terror group' as part of a job-creation scheme.

The third narrative is that of John Tyndall, the leader of the BNP, who initially welcomed the protection of this 'elite crew'. After having many meetings and marches severely compromised by anti-fascist activists, as well as suffering repeated physical assaults, Tyndall needed better security than he was getting. Also, the inflation of his ego by what he wrongly perceived to be his own personal 'praetorian guard', was an added bonus. Tyndall was a poor judge of other people's characters and motivations and, in a later distancing exercise in 1995, he claimed that C18 had been compromised and that, anyway, he did not really know them, despite being photographed with C18 on several occasions. Tyndall also said he did not know David Copeland, the neo-Nazi 'nail bomber', with whom he was photographed after being attacked in Stratford in the early 1990s. Tyndall also documented the incompetence and infighting that characterises so many far-right groupuscules in his magazine, *Spearhead* (now on-line): he reported that a fellow BNP member 'was set upon on his own and beaten by a mob of these brave [C18] warriors outside a pub in London just before a BNP social was about to start.' The BNP member was then accused of being 'a red' and assaulted at a Nazi festival in Belgium where 'the heroes were supporters of Combat 18'. And not only that, but 'BNP officials Tony Lecomber and Eddie Butler were assaulted by personnel belonging to Combat 18'. (Lecomber was later to assault Butler at Loughton tube station, with Lecomber dressed as a 'ninja', in 2007.) Tyndall goes on to question why C18 leaders had not been prosecuted for various outrages, and warns of the BNP becoming associated with C18's illegal operations. He dismissed C18 as 'small-time gang leaders, class warriors with huge chips on their shoulders, ambitious to build their own little back-street empires' and with the tacit acknowledgement of the state. For Tyndall, the constitutional way was the only way! O'Hara quotes Tyndall from one BNP publication which said that 'there is grow-ing evidence to suggest that C18 has been heavily infiltrated, and probably taken over, by government agents who are acting as "agents provocateurs" in order to incite nationalists into criminal activities thereby making them vulnerable to arrest and imprisonment.'[4]

The fourth narrative comes from C18 itself. Nick Ryan, whose re-search was augmented by Lowles, quotes C18's Charlie Sargent as saying, 'The Reds were going around, beating the living daylights out of the right wing.... Red Action [an extreme left group] were abso-lutely battering the right.' Which was true, although his claim that 'we fuckin' battered 'em wherever we met' is not borne out by any evidence.[5] Subsequent events saw them battering each other more than AFA.

The fifth narrative is that, after its initial breakthrough, C18 split into two, with one faction following Sargent, who claimed that 'his' C18 were bona fide 'race warriors', and another group who claimed Sargent was 'state', 'a grass' and that he had helped create a 'honey trap' to monitor and hopefully convict fascist thugs, which seems to have hovered quite close to the truth.

4   O'Hara, *Turning Up the Heat*, 66.
5   Ryan, *Homeland*, 17.

The sixth, and for us the most important narrative, is AFA's, which implies that, although some members were individually dangerous, C18 was simply 'not all that' and completely failed to orchestrate AFA's demise. In fact, the appearance of these 'hard men' was followed by the BNP's complete withdrawal from the streets in the face of sustained physical opposition from AFA.

The Reality

The myth goes that after AFA had turned over the League of Saint George meeting in Kensington in 1992, a small group decided to 'take on the reds' and defeat them. Their strategy was characterised by the inky hate sheet *Redwatch*, which listed the names, addresses and phone numbers of left-wing activists, such as ANL organizers and trade union members. The cunning tactic was to ring them up late at night and threaten and abuse them. As far as political strategy can be rated, this was playground bullying of the most sinister kind and not pleasant to be subject to. The group gradually operated with some of the Chelsea FC hooligan gang, the Headhunters, and were muscling in on the skinhead music scene.

C18 formed to protect the BNP and other related interests but failed to do so. In 1992, whilst the Battle of Waterloo raged, the leaders of C18 had ensconced themselves at a very safe distance in a pub at Victoria as the various skinheads and hooligans were chased and beaten by anti-fascists. In 1992, C18 along with various hooligans and squaddies found a small group of AFA/RA in the Enkell Arms in North London, but despite outnumbering the anti-fascists they failed to 'take' the pub. This was a spontaneous incident but again C18 did not gain the initiative, and the anti-fascists had to defend themselves with pool balls, bottles, glasses and anything else that came to hand. The battle was nearly a victory for the fascists and a lucky one.

C18 also claimed a victory over Red Action at a confrontation in Old Street, but it was actually a small contingent of anti-fascists, which did not include them, although this fact did little to curtail their bragging. In October 1993, during the Battle of Welling, AFA/RA

COMBAT 18

activists kept their distance whilst C18 lurked in a pub awaiting easy targets who would be drifting from the demonstration later. AFA spotters located them and a hundred-strong contingent headed over to greet them. C18 members in the beer garden recognised the approaching anti-fascists and scurried back to the safety of the pub. To their obvious relief, the police arrived and stood between AFA and the pub, and 'apart from lobbing a few beer bottles over the wall, C18, for all their fearsome media reputation, made no attempt to come out'.[6]

> Indeed [C18s] potential to do damage to the social fabric was sometimes overstated by certain anti-fascist organizations, which had a perverse interest in exaggerating its importance.
> —Mark Hayes & Paul Aylward in 'Anti-Fascist Action: Radical Resistance or Rent-A-Mob?'

In January 1994, C18 was in the Little Driver pub in Bow, East London, plotting up to steward a Blood & Honour gig, when AFA located and attacked them. The C18 members who were drinking outside hurried back to safety as a flare shot overhead. One leading C18 bravely sought refuge in the back of a police car as the riot squad blockaded the pub. AFA had come very close to routing them. The police moved the disappointed AFA mob away from the area in a Lenin-esque 'sealed train' (though to Earl's Court rather than Petrograd), but the day was not over. According to *Fighting Talk*, the Battle of Waterloo #2 was staged, although this time with the riot police understudying AFA. The fascists relocated to a pub near Waterloo station, hoping to attend their Blood & Honour gig. *Fighting Talk* relays the bizarre scene:

> News of the arrival of over one hundred AFA militants in the immediate vicinity caused C18 at the Wellington [pub] to internally combust. Initially the fascists wanted to get out, seconds later the riot police smashed their way in. Badly beaten fascists, covered in blood, were dragged faced down from the pub and laid on the pavement. The pub smashed, the gig was cancelled. Fascists

6 Birchall, *Beating the Fascists*, 322.

attempting to flee the Wellington met a similar fate at the hands of AFA militants…. It was AFA's intelligence gathering capacity which revealed the redirection points and the planned venues. On the day we controlled the play, were ahead of the game and made all the decisive moves.[7]

This really wasn't C18's lucky day: rumbled and ran by AFA, protected by riot police, then attacked by both. The latter point on the value of 'inside information', as much as the ability to quickly mobilise in changing circumstances, proved decisive. The 'inside information' in question was gained by female undercover AFA operatives at the Little Driver pub, showing that AFA was well prepared. As one member of C18 later admitted somewhat ruefully, 'We always lagged behind in things like intelligence. The Reds were always better at that sort of thing. More to the point, no-one wanted out of the pub.'[8]

Fighting Talk reported that a loyalist march in Bolton 1996 was stopped by police 'after AFA members clashed with C18 stewards and police officers. This coincided with the arrival of a group of local Asian youths in the area, and meant the police could not guarantee public order'.[9] Matt gives the following account:

There was about a dozen or so of us, who'd travelled up to Manchester then got a lift with Bolton people who took us the rest of the way. We'd waited in a pub for what seemed like bloody ages. Finally someone came in and gave the word to move, and I remember being directed across a large car park. Not far away was a street leading up a hill to where we could see lines of cops, and the Fash plus Loyalist bandsmen (the latter playing music and forming up). We all moved forwards and I remember some guys on the left-hand side walking towards us. One was wearing a Totenkopf/C18 T-shirt. I remember his face, he had short brown hair with a fringe and he was smiling at us. He quickly stopped as everyone went at them and they were sort of pushed up against

7   Anti-Fascist Action, *Fighting Talk* 7: 3.
8   Lowles, *White Riot*, 17.
9   Anti-Fascist Action, *Fighting Talk* 11: 3.

264

a wall taking a kicking. The funniest thing at this moment was seeing N, one of the Birmingham lads run across the street to aim a high kick at one of them, and splitting his jeans straight along the crotch. The madness was added to as I looked up the road and the cops (along with several mounted police) came rushing at us. By this point some of the AFA people had got closer to the march and were being hemmed in next to a church which had a wall and fence overlooking a drop into another car park on the side. As the cops were pushing into them I saw a number of people climb and lower themselves over the fence and drop down. Impressive because it was a fair way down. Forward of me in the street, by about three steps, was P. I watched as a police dog handler's Alsatian (with its fur almost standing up on end) grab P by the arm, and he just dropped to the floor. It was pretty fucking horrible. I later was told he'd been arrested, charged, and was finally given a prison sentence. By the time of the mauling by the mutt, people were streaming back down towards me with the cops giving chase. We left the area after meeting up again, laughing about the Brummie's split jeans, and being told that the march had been cancelled—although P's arrest, and hearing that he'd been injured, sobered the mood somewhat.

In 1996, C18 was meant to be protecting a Loyalist gathering in London but again came unstuck as AFA attacked, and many of the fascists and bandsmen received a beating.

Fighting Talk piles on the shame for C18's failing overtures to the Loyalists:

> Two weeks after the Bolton fiasco the Loyalists had a second march in Central London. Once again the information was that C18 would be in attendance. AFA mobilised over 100 stewards to confront the fascists/Loyalists and despite a heavy police operation from early in the morning, a full blooded assault was successfully made on one of their pubs.... What was significant was for the second time in two weeks C18 had been unable to

protect the march. The march itself saw a much smaller C18 contingent than last year (possibly related to fall-out from Bolton?).[10]

Despite the relentless attentions of AFA, as is often the case with home-grown fascists, C18 proved to be their own worst enemies. The split was both acrimonious and violent, which disillusioned many on the far right, and their connections to loyalist paramilitaries and football hooligans only helped the activities of the police and other state agencies. C18 succumbed to fallouts over money, egos and strategy. It ended acrimoniously with two members murdering a 'racial comrade'. A sordid end to a sordid history.

By this time the state agencies had begun to clamp down and there were several arrests and jailings for a variety of offences that initiated their decline. C18 continued as a name on a website, ostensibly 'to strike terror' into the opposition, but in reality they did not do the job they had set out to do, apart from achieving some hysterical media coverage: C18 split into two bitterly opposed factions; it failed to initiate the 'race war' it had promised; it failed to protect the BNP; it failed to combat AFA or even dent anti-fascist morale; it caused long-term divisions in the far right; it unwittingly led loyalists into danger from state agencies; and the BNP had to distance themselves from C18 as they were surplus to the electoral respectability and the new cheap suit strategy. It is tempting to speculate that, perhaps, this was the point.

Combat 18 had a confrontation with the EDL who had started to organize in central London in October 2009, when the ageing neo-Nazis were overpowered by younger and fitter hooligans. After a brief scuffle, C18 ran off, leaving one of its members—who had been battered with a fire extinguisher—in the middle of the road. Fallouts publicly ensued.

---

10   Anti-Fascist Action, *Fighting Talk* 14: 3.

AFA Grows: *Fighting Talk*

As the 1990s went on, AFA vigorously pursued the 'No Platform' strategy against the far right: 'no rallies, no marches, no meetings, no paper sales, no leaflets, no stickers, no shops selling their badges, records and pamphlets. We say that "no platform" must be changed from a rhetorical slogan into a practical policy.'[1] AFA had consolidated itself and grew in strength: groups started up in Scotland, the Midlands, the North East and North West, and Ireland, amongst other places. The sectarianism and 'professional anti-fascism' that had frustrated RA/AFA#1 continued: rival groups pursuing non-physical strategies refused to present a broad front against the BNP and included Anti-Racist Alliance (ARA), who had come into existence as the SWP revitalised the ANL, and Militant, who set-up Youth Against Racism in Europe (YRE). Militant members had also organized the 'Away Team', which was prepared to confront the fascists physically and were also accused of being instrumental in the Welling Riot. They remained small compared to a nationally thriving organization like AFA. *Fighting Talk* did report that, in Scotland, Militant members 'have been prepared to confront the fascists where necessary but seem reluctant to involve themselves in a broader, non-sectarian anti-fascist organization like AFA'.[2]

Fighting Talk covered not only confrontations with the far right, but it had many articles on international anti-fascism, music and football, as well as special issues on the Spanish Civil War, which saw AFA as continuing the legacy of the anti-fascist volunteers. *Fighting Talk* was supplemented by regional fanzines as well as football related journals, such as Manchester United's *Attitude*. The online

1   Anti-Fascist Action, *Fighting Talk* 2: 2.
2   Anti-Fascist Action, *Fighting Talk* 1: 6.

Fighting Talk archive, like the online Red Action one, is essential documentation of militant anti-fascism as it happened (and from which much of this chapter is mainly drawn). *Fighting Talk* continued to report the growth and success of militant activity as being self-critical, identifying the weaknesses of the anti-fascist movement and the changes in BNP policies. *Fighting Talk* reported an attack on a meeting by the NBC, which was addressed by Reverend Al Sharpton: 'The fascists got away scot free after the assault, in which they used tear-gas and coshes.... Two coppers were [seen] helping away an innocent bystander who was hurt in the fracas. Not so innocent, as it happened—he was a well-known member of the BNP who was hurt as he fled into the road away from those trying to defend the meeting.'[3]

The second issue of *Fighting Talk* could confidently report that AFA was setting the rules of engagement in the anti-fascist struggle and that, according to one author, 'our Unity Carnival in Hackney attracted 10,000 people to a day of music and protest. A month later, in October, some 300 attended our picket of the fascist paper sale in Brick Lane.... Our national march against racist attacks brought 3,500 militant anti-fascist on to the streets'.[4]

This was a considerable achievement for AFA and it was hardly surprising that other left groups saw anti-fascism as a recruiting opportunity. The Unity carnival was a huge success and continued for several years. Despite what other anti-fascist and anti-racists claim, organizing things like the Unity Carnival meant that AFA was not solely about violence. As *Fighting Talk* stated, 'Remember, though we've said it before, a physical commitment by us doesn't require every individual in the organization to be a super fit street-fighter, what we do want is people who agree with our policy, and who will work together towards its implementation in the capacity best suited to them.'[5]

Hemel Hempstead

As the new branches set up around the country, *Fighting Talk*

3   Anti-Fascist Action, *Fighting Talk* 1: 3.
4   Anti-Fascist Action, *Fighting Talk* 2: 2.
5   Anti-Fascist Action, *Fighting Talk* 7: 5.

reported on progress: this early report from Hertfordshire in 1991 gives a fairly typical picture of AFA activities—although local militants had been involved in the forefront of anti-fascism since the 1970s:

> Following a highly successful mobilisation against a National Front local election meeting in the Hertfordshire area as a result of which the fascists were forced into a precipitate and humiliating retreat, Red Action members in Hatfield decided it was high time that anti-fascist activity in the region was co-ordinated.... In addition to unattached individuals, representatives from the SWP, Militant, Direct Action Movement, and a hitherto little recognised local organization AGM (Asian Gang Movement) plus a healthy number of Red Action members already linked with London AFA participated.[6]

The AFA group set up a defence campaign following a number of arrests of militants on 'active duty' against the NF election campaigners. The group, like those elsewhere, organized meetings, gigs and responses to racist attacks in the area to prevent fascists from acting with impunity. *Fighting Talk* #1 reported that 'one Asian man had been attacked twice by the same people.... Action was taken that hopefully will have ensured that the problem, at least with these individuals, does not recur.'[7] In 1993, the NF decided to hold a march in Hemel Hempstead to promote their candidates. AFA members intercepted the march but they were held off by riot police with dogs. They then headed to the school where the march was to finish and gained entry:

> Front leader Ian Anderson looked on in horror as anti-fascists filed in one by one into the hall.... After the shortest speech of his life, Anderson attempted to rouse his edgy troops in a chorus of the National Anthem. It was cut short by a volley of chairs

---

6   Anti-Fascist Action, *Fighting Talk* 1: 4–5.
7   Ibid., 5.

from the back of the hall as scuffles broke out.[8]

The police forced AFA out of the hall, but they then surrounded the school. After several hours, the police had to transport the NF away in their vans.

No North West Nazis!

Since the 1970s, continuous militant pressure in Manchester against the NF and BNP ensured they had difficulty in organizing centrally, but the far right did find some scant success in the smaller towns around Lancashire and the North West. One attempt to rally in Blackburn attracted little interest and was cancelled, although AFA members were on hand and 'the few unwitting fascists who did turn up found themselves unwillingly involved in some impromptu "street theatre" and had to be escorted out of town by the local constabulary'.[9] Another meeting ended in disarray with Tyndall addressing his few followers 'on a patch of waste ground behind a railway station. Unfortunately for the dedicated few, some of the waste land landed on them!'[10] A typical AFA tactic was to make sure venue managers were made aware of the pseudonymous group bookings, so they cancelled them to avoid bother. One NF meeting in Manchester was forced to cancel and as other anti-fascist groups held their own marches, 'a 30–40 strong AFA stewards group [moved] around the city centre free from the attentions of the police. The stewards group was able to deter several fascists from attending the meeting when they took over the redirection point at Victoria Station'.[11]

The Lancashire town of Rochdale was targeted by the BNP, which tried to increase local tensions between the white working-class communities and the large Asian community: AFA responded on several occasions. In February 1992, the ANL and AFA mobilised six hundred supporters to confront BNP electioneering, despite the inevitable differences over physical opposition. Mass leafleting and

---

8   Anti-Fascist Action, *Fighting Talk* 5: 3.
9   Anti-Fascist Action, *Fighting Talk* 1: 5.
10   Ibid.
11   Anti-Fascist Action, *Fighting Talk* 1: 6.

a public meeting were organized, and AFA occupied several pubs where the fascists were thought to be gathering. Apart from a small group who fled on seeing the size of the opposition, the BNP failed to show up. The BNP decided to make yet another attempt to rally in Rochdale in March 1992, but AFA arrived two-hundred-strong to oppose them with even the ANL joining up with AFA at the BNP redirection point. BNP supporters arrived but were seen off by the anti-fascists. The BNP had subsequently relocated to another pub, as did AFA who reported it in their usual manner:

> Once AFA arrived at this pub we made our presence felt and after a vigorous encounter in the pub with the master race's goon squad we left them cowering inside awaiting police protection. When the bulk of the counter-demonstrators arrived we simply surrounded the pub, withstood police attempts to clear us off and kept the fascists pinned down for three hours.[12]

Not content with this, AFA returned for a rematch in April 1992. A hundred and twenty anti-fascists arrived to contain a BNP leafleting team in a pub whilst their minibus was wrecked. The BNP managed to hold a small rally a week later on the townhall steps, surrounded by police who were surrounded by AFA, thus ensuring few people could hear their message. The evening before the demo, police had raided the houses of militant AFA members and held them in custody until the whole thing was over. Despite this, an on-the-spot reporter for local anarchist tabloid *The Bolton Evening Noose* wrote gleefully that one BNP organizer 'was caught by anti-fascists and given a sound thrashing and his head was formally introduced to a wheel brace' and that several BNP members 'spent several hours cowering under tables while police and anti-fascists clashed outside'. At the later BNP rally, 'anti-fascists trapped 9 nazi maggots in a pub...[and we] heard from a reliable source that the scum inside the pub didn't exactly act in a manner befitting such proud examples of Aryan manhood. Two of them started crying when asked to leave by the landlord and one of

---

12   Anti-Fascist Action, *Fighting Talk* 2: 7.

these actually shit himself when he saw us waiting outside.'[13]

The BNP again came under serious pressure from AFA when they met up in Todmorden to attend a rally in nearby Colne. As the ANL handed out leaflets in the town, AFA militants were able 'to move freely around the area without arousing suspicion of the local police. This enabled AFA to avoid police lines and occupy the hall, which by 1.50pm was surrounded by anti-fascists. Early arrivals were given a stern talking to, and sent packing'. The police mistook AFA for the BNP and moved them over to join their 'racial comrades'who scattered and hid behind the police, demanding that they clear the hall for the rally—which the police failed to do. A passing carload of fascists was attacked by AFA 'while the fascists in the park were forced to watch their mates take a pasting'. Eventually, the BNP gave it up and left town 'for their own safety'. The ANL later stated, 'We have the same aims as AFA, but don't necessarily approve of their more direct methods.'[14]

Later, in nearby Burnley, the BNP again faced concerted opposition from AFA 'when prior to a mass leafleting of the estate, the BNP were ambushed at their redirection point (again in Todmorden) by "anti-fascist militants"'.[15] In August, 150 AFA activists arrived in Burnley but were quickly checked by police. Members of the local football firm who had been 'wound up' by local BNP members attempted to attack the AFA group. AFA then met up with their leaders, who expressed annoyance over transgressions on their 'turf'. Lowles reports that during racial riots in Burnley in 2001, 'a significant proportion of the white offenders were known football hooligans'. Burnley hooligans also tried to link up with Chelsea and Stoke a year later to attack Asians. One thug was elected as a BNP councillor though lasted less than four months when he was jailed for glassing the Leeds BNP organizer at the 'Red, White and Blue festival'.[16]

---

13   *The Bolton Evening Noose* 5 (1991–92): 4.
14   Anti-Fascist Action, *Fighting Talk* 5: 18.
15   Anti-Fascist Action, *Fighting Talk* 6: 2.
16   Nick Lowles and Andy Nicholls, *Hooligans: Vol.1, The A-L of British Football Gangs* (London: Milo Books, 2005), 185.

It was the intention of the BNP to use Burnley fans against AFA, then the plan backfired because the police refused to allow the BNP to leave their redirection point, due to 'serious public disorder' in Burnley. This sparked a furious row between local activists and party leader John Tyndall, who meekly complied with police orders.[17]

Several BNP members were attacked by angry Burnley fans, whilst other fascists contented themselves by attacking each other. One of the BNP candidates withdrew in disgust whilst another received nine votes.

The Midlands

In the East Midlands, AFA organized against a previously confident opponent. One gig was threatened by Blood & Honour, who 'at the sight of the stewarding team AFA put on the door...promptly resigned their subscription to Valhalla and ran'.[18] AFA increased its local activities and worked alongside other anti-fascist groups. The ANL was also active in the area, but some of their more militantly minded left to join AFA. Matt gives an account of how he became involved with AFA. After a disappointing anarchist meeting,

> just before I was about to leave, a crowd of other people turned up. This was a much more rough and ready bunch. As the speaker mentioned attending an upcoming CND march in London, one of the new comers dressed in a flight jacket with a shaved head covered in a jigsaw puzzle of scars, said ironically, 'Aye, fuck, I bet it'll kick off.' To which the rest of them laughed. Discussion was then re-directed for the afternoon with talk of 'kicking fuck out of the fash' and how 'two BNP brothers who looked like the Proclaimers, and a rat-faced bastard called GT' had been done for attacking an SWP paper sale. Seemingly, the general consensus amongst the new comrades was that the judge's hammer was probably best replaced with the sort you could buy

17   Anti-Fascist Action, *Fighting Talk* 6: 2.
18   Anti-Fascist Action, *Fighting Talk* 5: 17.

from a Wilkos hardware store.... I agreed to meet up with them in Nottingham over the following days, and that's pretty much how I came to be involved in Anti-Fascist Action for the next several years.

There were fascist 'hotspots' in the county, 'places like Heanor, Ilkeston, Mansfield, Sutton, etc. [that] had seen surges in Fascist activity in previous years. Especially when [Ian Stuart] Donaldson had relocated there after being booted out of London. There were still Blood & Honour gigs and other activities, which had kept up his legacy after his demise'.

Mushroom Books, a long established radical bookshop in Nottingham, was attacked when

> a bus load of fascists descended on the city many of them shouting abuse at people, Sieg Heiling, and so forth. On reaching the target many of them steamed in and started assaulting members of staff and customers, whilst trashing the place. Computers were wrecked and a fire extinguisher was thrown through the front window. Due to the ad-hoc nature of the attack around 39 arrests were made as they tried to make an escape.

Only nine of the attackers were bought to trial, so AFA kept an eye on things both inside and outside the courtroom. Matt recalls, 'We had people sat in a pub round the corner, a couple in the public gallery, and two of us doing circuits around the nearby streets. One of the first things to do was immobilise their vehicle, so three of us in a scout car pulled up into the parking lot next to their van.' AFA put spotters out and plotted up in a nearby pub recalls Matt:

> I could tell people were getting restless plus there was the typical eye of suspicion from the pub landlord at having to serve 30 people halves of coke for two hours. But as I came out the bar and walked down the street towards the court I saw one of our female members who'd been sat inside come running up

'they're coming out!' So I turned and ran like fuck, to stick my head round the door and notify everyone that it was all on. We'd briefed people the day before about not rushing straight in front of the courthouse (due to CCTV and obvious Press cameras) so we took a back route behind the court and up a side street into the car park. On entering it we saw just two guys next to the van, and their jaws just fucking dropped. We didn't know it but the other several members had been sent down and they had no back-up with them—these were the only ones left. With no other main exit from the car park I saw one of them, who was dressed in a Crombie, run and launch himself at the top of a wall. It must have been the adrenaline because he caught the top and managed to scramble over onto the canal walkway as three guys were trying to grab his legs.... A bunch of us approached what was probably at that point 'the loneliest man in the world'. He began by saying in a terrified voice, 'I'm not a Nazi!.... I just give lifts to boneheads!' (It always amazes me how the fucking master race are quick to deny their ideology under pressure. I don't think if I was cornered in the same way I'd be screaming, 'Don't hit me! I'm not a Socialist!'). Anyway, immediately afterwards I remember a few of us hoofing him around the car park whilst he desperately grabbed onto wing mirrors and bumpers to steady himself.... As we walked back out, the parking attendant, who throughout all the commotion carried on sweeping the ramp and puffing on a fag, just said, 'C'mon now lads, he's had enough.'

One AFA member was arrested near the site whilst another hid under a car:

Later that day local TV news showed the Fascists defiantly walking into court, with the hapless individual coming up the rear smirking and giving a finger to the cameras not knowing what would befall him. The voiceover pointed out 'this man was later hospitalized by political opponents'.

AFA was accused by various other anti-fascist groups of being male, macho and overtly violent—'as bad as the fascists!'—and one misconception was the role of women, but as Matt writes,

> I can assure you that the role of women in AFA wasn't limited to intelligence gathering. There were two women in particular involved in our local group and they definitely put themselves at the physical end on a number of occasions. I can remember watching one of them break a glass Lucozade bottle over a fascist's head when we ran up against them in Mansfield one day. Regarding their abilities for garnering information, the fash more often than not were blinded by their adherence to an ideology that saw women as 'the lesser sex' and (in particular) those on the left to be hairy, dreadlocked aberrations. Therefore by wandering into pubs, dressed up for a night out and chatting to lads at the bar, it meant they could access intelligence in places where male activists couldn't (or wouldn't) go.

Although Matt, like many in the AFA ranks, had come from the anarchist/punk scene, it soon became essential to not stand out:

> I always assumed the concept of camouflage was 'to hide in plain sight'. Which is why the majority of AFA and Red Action people weren't your usual crusty looking Black Bloc types (aside from not emerging from that background anyway). Stepping off a train platform to go scouting around some town centre looking like that, immediately exposed you as a member of the political opposition. Even though there were some very good activists of the hippy type, many of them began to change their appearance out of sheer operational necessity. One of the advantages of AFA at the time was that the Fash just didn't know where they could be hit from. It meant psychologically they were on the back foot all the time. They could walk into a bar or cafe and not realise that the table full of people sat across from them were political opponents until they felt the chairs crashing over their heads. As

an example, one of my first times out around Leeds as an AFA member, I remember being sat in a pub and two middle aged businessmen came walking in (newspapers, briefcases, suit and ties) and my colleague excused himself to go and talk to them. When he came back I asked, 'Who the hell are those guys?' and he replied, 'Oh don't worry, they're our scouts.' I thought to myself, 'Fuck me, these lot don't mess about.'

Leeds

Of all the Northern cities and towns, Leeds was to prove problematic for AFA as it had a strong far-right element, some of which can be traced back to the terraces of Elland Road. In the 1970s, the 'golden age' of football hooliganism, the battle for top firm was played out in the back pages of *Bulldog*, the NF's paper, and Leeds was a strong contender for number one in the 'League of Louts'. NF paper sales were a regular occurrence at the ground, and various members of the Leeds Service Crew (LSC) openly aligned themselves with fascist groups. One call to arms, prior to visiting Chelsea, was signed 'Dave, Leeds United Service Crew, National Front'.[19] Unfortunately, their Yorkshire braggadocio did not prevent Chelsea from battering them as they 'ripped into the Leeds, even chasing some of them off the end of the Tube platforms and into the dark tunnels.'[20] The argument that Leeds was free of racism was hardly helped when, in 2000, two of their players were caught up in a brawl that the victims claimed was racially motivated. After the controversial court case, the Leeds players ended up with community service orders.

> Leeds United would develop a reputation for racism, but by no means all of them subscribed to it.
>
> —Caroline Gall in *Service Crew*

One LSC hooligan stood for the NF in a local election, so two fellow supporters, who were also members of the Socialist Party, got hold of his nomination form and posted round the names of those who nominated him. These same two had boarded a bus only to bump

19   Lowles and Nicholls, *Hooligans: Vol.1*, 457.
20   Ibid.

into 'two biggish NF lads'; one of them made a racist remark, so they were battered and warned never to come into Leeds again by the two socialists. However, Caroline Gall concedes that 'Sieg Heiling was a Leeds trademark adopted by the masses in the heyday of football violence'[21] and that 'several pubs had become known as NF haunts, and some lads attended their marches'.[22] One unlucky lad attended a march 'in Halifax in the early 1980s. He was bombarded by missiles by the Anti-Nazi League and halfway through thought, fuck this, and switched sides'.[23] Not everyone had such a Damascene revelation, so they stuck with fascist politics. One LSC member says the following in mitigation:

> Some of the Leeds lads around in the seventies were into racist things and a lot of the younger lads took that on their shoulders and made it look ten times worse than it actually was. Ten years later there were hardly any racists, apart from the staunch ones, but it always looked like the main Leeds firm was racist. It was fashionable to be racist then—the lads did all the Sieg Heiling and all that—and it stuck over the years, even though it wasn't really the case.[24]

A fanzine for Leeds supporters called *Marching Altogether* was set up by Leeds Fans Against Racism and Fascism (LFARAF) in 1987, responding to the NF encroachment at Elland Road and to the club denying there was a problem with racism or fascists. C, a local militant anti-fascist, said, 'I think the most important thing to come out of Leeds was the football campaign and the fanzine.' Racist politics were hardly exclusive to the ground and were prevalent within certain pubs and streets. One LSC firm member referred to the 'Years of the Race War' when there would be pitched battles between black and white youth. All of this contributed to the political climate that

---

21 Caroline Gall, *Service Crew: The Inside Story of Leeds United's Hooligan Gangs* (London: Milo Books, 2007), 115.
22 Ibid., 116.
23 Ibid.
24 Ibid., 182.

Leeds AFA found themselves in, but they still managed to produced their own local bulletin, *Attitude*, and the spring 1994 issue detailed a 'Catalogue of Nazi Violence'. Hit lists of left-wing activists were circulated by Nazis, socialist paper sales were harassed, alternative record shop windows were smashed and the *Northern Star* alternative paper was under siege from regular fascist attacks.[25] The Leeds streets were becoming seriously contested. *Attitude* claimed that much of these activities were being carried out by Combat 18, but other sources, such as Larry O'Hara and the 'Leeds Nationalist Council' themselves, think this was exaggerated and was in fact a police set-up to ensnare right-wingers. However, some of the names being passed around then were still aligned with other fascist groupuscules as late as 2014.

> Everyone's memories are hazy after two minutes of adrenaline and flying Lucozade.
>
> —Leeds Anti-Fascist Action

Leeds AFA monitored and confronted the various fascist groups that continued to emerge and disappear and, one night, at a pub near Leeds University in the 1990s, a group of well-known fascists dropped in for a drink, as C writes:

> Two AFA lads who were having a quiet pint stepped back and scanned the room as they could see some of the Punks in the back room scatter out the back door. As usual there was gonna be no back up from that lot so they were on there own. Three lads and two lasses waltzed through the pub in full Bonehead gear, snarling at students and obviously enjoying themselves. N goes 'Fucking yes' as he realises it's X and proceeds to flick a lit cigarette at his face. X crumbles as he realises the pub's not full of students they can bully and they all do an about turn and head straight back out of the pub followed by N and D. As they head out of the door one of the fash says, 'I'm gonna do that little cunt.' Now D had a fair few run ins with the local fash and wasn't shy

25   Leeds Anti-Fascist Action, *Attitude* (1994): 1.

at coming forward so walks up to him, taps him in the chest and asks who he's talking about? Before he gets a chance to reply D pulls out a can of pepper foam he's just bought in the States and empties it all over his head and face, the fash starts screaming and D asks X if he'd like a go as well? X ends up looking like an extra from *Tiswas* with half his head covered in what looks like red shaving foam. It came out of the can so fast it bounced back and got D in the face as well as one of the fash women. D can testify it burns like it said on the tin so was well worth the money. One of the fash who appears with a large knife gets a pint glass in the face and they run off leaving one of the women screaming abuse. D and N apologise for the mess they've caused, flag a taxi, and drive off. Big bad Combat 18 came back that night to smash a window and bravely leave a message on the pub answer phone threatening revenge.

It was a revenge that, like so many C18 boasts, never happened, although replays elsewhere did happen. Leeds AFA had an informer on the inside of the BNP, which was to prove a very mixed blessing as he was also trading information to the BNP and the police. This informant gave LAFA information that a regional BNP meeting was being held:

With very short notice we put the info out to all the Trot groups who turned up in good numbers on a Thursday evening. We planned on using them for cover and went sniping around the city centre looking for targets. While the police were watching the ANL/YRE outside one pub a few of the Bradford lot spotted four fascists and gave chase, cornering them in a pub doorway. X said, 'Leave it out lads' and tried to get inside but the landlord was having none of it and barred the doors leaving them trapped outside as AFA proceeded to steam in to them with the usual bottles of Lucozade, fists, and boots. A late arrival to the fight smashed a full bottle of red wine over X's head, which really nailed the 'covered in Claret' saying. At one point in the scrap there was about ten AFA trying to land a punch or a kick but doing no real damage due to them huddling in the doorway, then someone shouted, 'Cops!' and as they stepped back from the doorway, D, who'd been biding his time, stepped in quickly and splattered X's nose with a Lucozade bottle. The local BNP now realised they had an informer and used the leaking of the meeting to flush out their main suspect, T.

An interesting and, for once vaguely literate pamphlet, *White Lies*, written by the rather grandiosely titled Leeds Nationalist Council in 1995, is quite revelatory about this informant: although the writers claim they knew exactly who he was, they took a long time doing anything about it, and despite 'ignoring him', he was still around in 2013. The pamphlet also details the marginalised social milieu in which fascists operate and the all-day drinking sessions that heightened the sense of self-importance of far-right cranks. On one page of this political screed there are five references to drinking, and Leeds fascists at the time seemed to have operated in a perpetual drunken fog of violent racism. The pamphlet states that Leeds BNP had withdrawn from 'paper sales and set-piece activities that can be used by anti-racists for their own ends'.[26] It details far-right attacks on SWP paper sellers and the escalation of violence whilst denying that C18 had any real presence in Leeds at the time.

AFA continued with their activities, at one point happening across a gang of fascists hiding in a pub: 'A bar fight then broke out, with tables, chairs and bottles flying around the room'.[27] The far right came off considerably worse and retaliated by firing a crossbow bolt through an AFA member's window whilst an ANL member's windows were trashed. On the day of an anti-racist march, 'Leeds nationalists wanted to make a date of it with Red Action', but they conveniently had 'an out-of-town leafleting activity planned for that day' and when 'police had warned several known nationalists to stay away from the city centre or face arrest', they meekly complied.[28]

26 Leeds Nationalist Council, *White Lies* (Leeds: 1995), 6.
27 Ibid., 24.
28 Ibid., 34.

Needless to say, the three thousand anti-fascists who turned up were negatively viewed by the LNC and the day was dismally compared to BNP events that could attract scarcely a couple of hundred nationally. The claims that when 'AFA had had the chance of a confrontation with the "nazis" in the past, they had run away' bears little relation to reality.[29]

Dover

> The anti-fascists numbered about 300...the direct action road protesters who look like Swampy and could have done with a bath, the Class War anarchists who probably think Kropotkin is a class A drug and the Anti-Fascist Action (AFA), a bunch of crew-cutted hardnuts who believe that fascist violence should be met with anti-fascist violence.[30]

Dover is one of the main ports for traffic between the UK and mainland Europe, and it was also the scene of several skirmishes between anti-fascists and the far right, who were protesting against immigration. In November 1997, the NF re-emerged from hibernation to demonstrate against Romanies who were seeking sanctuary from attacks by neo-Nazi gangs in Slovakia and the Czech Republic. The far right could only manage a meagre sixty, amongst whom were the usual C18 and BNP members, whilst other anti-fascist groups who had organized on the day were 'both in the wrong place', according to *Fighting Talk:*

> As the NF moved off AFA stewards managed to block the road and confront the march. Police reinforcements were rapidly called up and dogs set on the anti-fascists, but the imaginative use of firecrackers caused considerable confusion to the extent that the dogs ended up attacking the NF.[31]

29   Ibid., 35.
30   John Sweeney, *Observer*, 16 November 1997.
31   Anti-Fascist Action, *Fighting Talk* 18: 3.

Despite this, AFA managed to slow the march down and the situation soon got out of hand. The police called up the NF bus and escorted them away from the scene. According to AFA, 'it took the NF one hour to walk less than 500 yards'. Shortly after, John Tyndall addressed the BNP in East London: 'It seems that all the anti-fascist groups were informed of this and there was a general air of expectancy that "something would happen".' This indeed was the case, and Tyndall got turned over by ANL supporters outside the pub where the meeting was.' This incident is perhaps more renowned for the photograph that was widely published which showed a bloodied Tyndall speaking to police whilst standing nearby is a small man in a baseball cap. This man turned out to be David Copeland, a fascist and fantasist who planted three bombs in London, which killed three people. It is interesting that Copeland and Tyndall's days were numbered.[32]

The far right returned to Dover in the new year and anti-fascists mobilized accordingly. In the (non-)event, only thirty NF members turned up, whilst the anti-fascists outnumbered them five to one. This time a large-scale police operation harassed the anti-fascists with stop and searches and set about busily filming them. The police penned the anti-fascists away from the tiny NF march and, as *Fighting Talk* reported, 'the scale of the police operation meant any meaningful activity was hopeless'.[33] This was an indication of the increased criminalisation of militant anti-fascism, in particular AFA and a fading far-right street presence.

---

32   Ibid.
33   Anti-Fascist Action, *Fighting Talk* 9: 4.

AFA in Scotland: 'We Don't Talk to Fascists'

In Scotland, militant anti-fascists not only faced the problem of fascism, but also the sectarianism that ran through local politics, social life and football. The BNP amplified their commitment to the loyalist cause to gather much needed support, although AFA militants still mobilized successfully against them: *Fighting Talk* mentions that 'in Edinburgh, Dundee and Glasgow, they have had their activities severely disrupted by violent demonstrations against them'.[1] Glasgow AFA could count on Red Action, Class War, Direct Action Movement, Workers Party Scotland, Scottish Anti-Racist Movement and the Republican Bands Alliance as allies, although *Fighting Talk* noted that sectarianism 'only plays into the hands of the enemy'.[2] Red Action Scotland ran the heading 'BNP Battered!!!' and reported with grizzly relish that

> Some BNP members out on a sticker run came unstuck yesterday. The members of the master race were followed around the city…. Two of the fascists were immediately confronted. One of them, a bonehead with a swastika tattoo on his cheek, was clearly seen head-butting iron bars and hammers…. To add insult to injury, Swastika-face was then pursued to a BNP watering hole where, as he emerged from the bog still licking his wounds, he was set upon again.[3]

Glasgow AFA was busy to say the least, and in late November 1992 they clashed with the BNP who ended up somewhat embarrassed:

1   Anti-Fascist Action, *Fighting Talk* 1: 6.
2   Ibid.
3   Red Action Scotland, *Red Action* 2 (1992): 1.

The BNP leadership were holed up in their 'secret' meeting place, the Gallery Bar on Argyle Street. For several hours the BNP and their 'Fuhrer' John Tyndall cowered behind the pub doors and their police guardians, in fear of the 200 strong group of anti-fascists who had surrounded the pub. While Tyndall and the other racist rats inside the pub escaped through the sewers under Central Station, many of his other brain-dead followers were being physically confronted on the streets.[4]

The toxic link up between loyalists and fascists caused AFA several headaches. In Edinburgh in 1993, an Orange group marched with the BNP, who then enthusiastically 'Sieg Heiled' their way through the streets as police surrounded the AFA group: 'However, not all the anti-fascists were penned in and a militant contingent were able to "join" the march at one point, which resulted in the march being held up for 40 minutes, the police having a hard time restoring (Orange) order'.[5]

In 1993, there was a large anti-racism march and rally in Glasgow featuring a strong AFA presence, which was 'once again interrupted by Sieg Heiling fascists.... Several fascists were eating the pavement before the day was over. We understand that their snarling Cumbernauld organizer was reduced to a blubbering wreck'.[6] Although a success, several anti-fascists were arrested, but, in the usual AFA style, benefits and fundraisers were organized and an appeal set up in support. AFA groups also issued their own local bulletins with one issue of *Fighting Talk* Edinburgh featuring the headline 'C.18—Are You Terrified Yet?' next to a report on the BNP's election win.[7] In 1995 at a James Connolly Commemoration in Edinburgh, a group of AFA stewards had mobilised to prevent fascist assault but were attacked by a group who turned out to be plain clothes policemen. And the police came off worse. *Fighting Talk* reported it thusly:

4   Anti-Fascist Action, *Fighting Talk* 2: 3.
5   Anti-Fascist Action, *Fighting Talk* 5: 8.
6   Ibid., 12.
7   Edinburgh Anti-Fascist Action, *Fighting Talk Edinburgh* 4 (1993): 1.

As the AFA contingent was making its way towards the march they were attacked by a dozen men. By the casual nature of their dress and their aggressive attitude it was instantly assumed they were fascists. The anti-fascists defended themselves against this attack. It was only when their attackers appeared to be taking second prize that they apparently decided to 'break cover' and identified themselves as police officers. According to press reports four police officers were hospitalised as a result of this incident. Ten anti-fascists were arrested and charged with 'Police Assault', 'Resisting Arrest' and 'Breach of the Peace'.[8]

At the trial, most charges were dropped and eventually four anti-fascists received community service orders. *Fighting Talk* reported one cop saying to a defendant, 'You lot gave us a terrible hiding today.' Small compensation for the months of expense, hassle and worry that the defendants had to go through. *Red Action* #76 reported an attack in Glasgow by loyalists, fascist skins and casuals on Celtic fans 'connected to AFA', which escalated with AFA seeking revenge and ambushing one of the leading fascists in a pub. When his mates stepped in to help they were likewise battered. Another bar was raided by an AFA squad with predictable consequences.[9] In Glasgow 1997, there were several confrontations between AFA and the BNP in a rambunctious general election campaign, not all of them successful. As Steve L writes,

We had a serious confrontation with the BNP in an area of the Govan constituency called Penilee that they regarded as a bit of a stronghold. I was calling the shots that morning and made a serious error of judgement in splitting our troops into two groups, complacently believing that it was a 'no show' from the fash and that our 'leafletters' were safe to split into groups of ten to get the leaflet job done quicker. Five minutes later, my group turn a corner and get hit with everything from a well tooled up gang of about fifteen fascists and casuals. I think it was the first-time

8   Anti-Fascist Action, *Fighting Talk* 12: 3.
9   *Red Action* 73 (1996): 3.

experience of having flares fired at them that caused most of the boys to run, leaving me and an RA member from Edinburgh to stand up to them on our own. I got fucked on the head with an iron bar during that one, but was swinging a dog chain and gassing their front line at the same time. The Edinburgh lad was a kickboxer and he decked one of their main men straight away and they stood off, the silly bastards.... Our 'runners' recovered their composure and started to come back down the road, but the fash had made their point and headed back into a safer part of the scheme for them. It was a defeat for us though, they got a boost out of it because we were hearing stuff within hours from Celtic casuals who'd been phoned up by crowing Rangers lads about the BNP chasing AFA out of Penilee, which wasn't strictly true, but we'd have probably claimed a victory ourselves had we been in their position.... We went back two weeks later with forty AFA and leafleted the whole area to no response from them, even though they came by in a couple of cars but they obviously didn't fancy it.

At the election count in 1997 in Glasgow, recalls Steve L, there was a frank discussion with the BNP local organizer who

tried to approach me twice to discuss how they were 'no longer a violent organization'. This was only a couple of weeks after the Penilee clash. First time he came towards us was as we entered the count, I was at the front with one of the top lads from the Celtic casuals. He came towards us and said, 'What are you lot doing here? We're not into violence any more...' To which the Celtic lad immediately quipped, 'You're fucked then, cos we are!' Second time was when AFA made a move towards them and he came towards me again with hands out saying, 'Look, we don't want this, we're political now' and was immediately punched in the mouth by one of the boys and told, 'We don't talk to fascists.' He went immediately to the cops and tried to get me and the other lad arrested, but the cops didn't want to know, they'd been surprised by the AFA 'infiltration' and were still weighing up which side would be easiest to get out of there.

The confrontation between AFA and the BNP made the BBC *Newsnight* programme, causing Scottish presenter Kirsty Wark to state, 'And there you can see some of the real citizens of Glasgow showing the BNP just exactly what they think of them.' As the BNP de-escalated their street campaign in their bid for respectability, anti-fascists responded as and when necessary, as our Steve L recalls:

> Post-1997, Edinburgh AFA with support from Glasgow were still mobilising squads off the James Connolly Commemoration and I'm sure they had run-ins with the fash in 1998 and beyond that.... Regarding whether AFA did or did not 'leave the scene of the crime' in Scotland, no one stood down or was told to stand down. It was a natural drift. The organizations wound down because the fash had moved on to try to assert themselves in the political mainstream.

By the end of the 1990s, the BNP had withdrawn from the streets, so AFA had to reappraise their tactics in light of this. The BNP was now quite different; AFA had kicked the NF off the streets; they had confronted C18 who were dismissed as a minor threat (though not, obviously, individual members); and the focus on physical confrontation was no longer a primary political necessity. This was not to say that AFA as an organization was simply ended. *Fighting Talk* was published until 2001 and anti-fascists responded appropriately, as and when, to their local situations, which obviously differed around the country.

But what of the BNP?

The BNP: Reach for the Gutter!

The BNP in April 1994 made a conscious effort to eschew the politics of street confrontation in favour of a Euro-Nationalist strategy which prioritises success via the ballot box.
—Mark Hayes and Paul Aylward in *Soundings* journal

In 1994, the BNP under John Tyndall was still following the traditional fascist line that the route to political power lay in controlling the streets, although AFA had successfully confronted them on many occasions, and the BNP found increasing difficulties in organizing and maintaining an effective public presence. Not only that, but the situation in mainland Europe was changing with the rise of Le Pen in France, and later, of Jörg Haider's Freedom Party in Austria. Euro-fascism increasingly looked towards a more respectable image or 'suits not boots', so as the 1990s progressed, 'modernisers' within the BNP started to move away from the ideas of the ageing and unpopular Tyndall in favour of the newer model. The skinhead and hooligan fraternity, which included C18, was ostracised in favour of the white working-class voters who had been ignored by Labour. The BNP stated that 'confrontational street politics…hindered our political progress and was the only thing holding our opponents together.… not that such brawls were the party's making, but the party inevitably got the blame.'[1] In other words, the BNP had finally admitted that they came off worse in street clashes; that their violent image kept them politically marginalised; and that there were to be 'no more marches, meetings, punch-ups'. The BNP had also recognised a fundamental weakness in the anti-fascist movement: although they

1   Mark Hayes and Paul Aylward, 'Anti-Fascist Action: Radical Resistance or Rent-A-Mob?' *Soundings* 14 (Spring 2000): 59.

could organize an effective physical street presence, the diverse array of anti-fascists had little to offer at the ballot box.

The BNP's move towards 'respectable' politics had been indicated as early as September 1993 by the election of Derek Beackon, their first councillor, who had taken the seat, despite extensive campaigning by the various anti-fascist organizations. To say that this was a shock to the left is an understatement, although it did temporarily regenerate anti-fascist energies in campaigning against the new challenge to some extent. Like so many BNP councillors after him, Beackon lost the seat in 1994—although, unlike them, his actual vote count had increased. After Beackon was deselected, the ANL, ARA and YRE began to wind down, and AFA had to reconsider its tactics.[2]

Nick Griffin proved to be divisive in more ways than one: he led one of the three factions that splintered the NF post-1979; he divided opinion, on both the left and right, as to his political efficacy and ulterior motives; and for many on the far right, Griffin was viewed as both incompetent and a shady 'state asset'. When Griffin ousted the media unfriendly Tyndall in 1999, he dropped the rhetoric of 'well directed boots and fists' in favour of Euro-nationalism. Over the next decade, the BNP's demand for compulsory repatriation, reversal of multiculturalism and 'whites only' membership policies was either legislated against or proved politically unrealistic as, despite much dissension in the ranks, Griffin took the BNP successfully into the twenty-first century.

Although Griffin was on record as a 'holocaust denier'—which came back to haunt him several times—the BNP dropped its overt anti-Semitism (though maintained it covertly) and its public declamations against ZOG, the Zionist Occupation Government conspiracy nonsense that even some of their ardent followers found irrelevant, obscure or even occultist. Instead the BNP played on the resentment felt in some white working-class communities against 'Muslim' communities, particularly Pakistanis and Bangladeshis, who were accused of receiving the usual preferential treatment over benefits, housing and other local services. They were also criticised for

---

2   Copsey, *Anti-Fascism in Britain*, 181.

failing to assimilate into the local community, their traditional culture and religious observances were seen as 'foreign,' and they were easily differentiated on the streets by the colour of their skin and their clothing. There was also the opportunistic use by the BNP of panic over 'asylum seekers' from the former Yugoslavia or elsewhere, or Romanies fleeing oppression.

Griffin was to become the most successful leader of any far right party in the UK: by 2010 the BNP under Griffin had two MEPs, a seat on the Greater London Authority and council seats all round England. But despite this, and following his disastrous appearance on the BBC's *Question Time* programme, the fact that the BNP website went down just before the General Election, the BNP's fortunes rapidly declined with a resurgence of infighting, expulsions and accusations that all but wrecked the party.

In 1995, members of London AFA/Red Action (RA) issued a programme entitled 'Filling the Vacuum', which suggested organizing political activity in working-class communities as an alternative to the BNP, who had effectively withdrawn from the streets under pressure from AFA. RA was fully aware that whilst AFA had been successful in defeating the Nazi threat on the cobbles, it was hardly going to offer what the other 'mainstream' anti-fascist groups were advocating—vote anyone but BNP. In places like the East End of London, Labour councils had exacerbated social problems so militant AFA supporters were unlikely to support them. For some in RA/AFA, it was therefore a logical step to formulate a community or electoral challenge to the BNP in order to continue to ideologically oppose them. This initiative eventually resulted in the Independent Working Class Association (IWCA).

For some of the anarchists in AFA, the situation was problematic in two ways: whilst RA, other socialists, non-aligned individuals and anarchists had been unified in their physical opposition to the far right, obviously, being anarchists, they could not follow an electoral strategy. Secondly, whilst for London AFA/RA the physical challenge had been very successful in their principal strongholds of London, Manchester, Glasgow and elsewhere, other AFA groups like in

Liverpool or Bolton, who were predominantly anarchist, felt that the fascist threat was still extant to some degree locally so surely, 'instead of being wound up, it was more pragmatic to wind [AFA] down to a level appropriate to the nature of the challenge now being offered by the Far Right'. Although AFA had been organized in a national structure, they also operated on a regional level (i.e., the Northern Network), and on a local level, with each of these levels requiring different assessments and responses. This was to cause a schism between the anarchists and RA and its supporters. However, as one Scottish militant writes,

> The thing is no one really stopped doing anti-fascist work. To this day, there are still people in Scotland who were involved with AFA and RA doing monitoring and surveillance around the fash. Older heads have also acted in an advisory role to a new generation of younger militants. I spoke as a former AFA organizer to an eighty-strong meeting of Celtic Ultras in 2009 along with two IWCA representatives and the son of a recently deceased Spanish Civil War veteran. Two years ago at the twentieth anniversary party of the TAL Celtic fanzine we also had a number of young lads who had formed themselves into a militant group and were doing martial arts training for the possibility of clashes with a violent fascist minority in the SDL. They looked to AFA as their inspiration, so all us old men and 'retirees' couldn't have been doing so badly still to be sought out and asked for advice.

Smaller fascist gangs, including less controllable elements of the BNP, were still active in some areas, although not on the same scale as the BNP had been, and despite the larger national picture, many anti-fascists wanted to finish off the far right in their locales. Although the fascists may be fewer in number, many anti-fascists instinctively follow the aphorism that 'if you cannot destroy them when they are weak, how can you hope to destroy them when they are strong?' and there were still confrontations with the same old faces well into the new millennium. After 1996, when C18 had been turned over at Holborn[3] any remaining fascist street presence receded in London, although AFA continued publishing *Fighting Talk* until the final edition in 2001. If anything, the scale had changed as the battle moved elsewhere, but this did not mean there were no more fascists. The neo-Nazi skinhead and hooligan element, which the BNP depended on for muscle, membership and money, was elbowed out of the 'New BNP', and they gravitated towards more extremist groups like the NF, C18 and their National Socialist Alliance, and Blood & Honour.

In 1999, eight-five NF members held a march in Margate and nearly four hundred anti-fascists turned up to oppose them. One ex-AFA member went along with a very mixed group as 'there was no organized anti-fascist group...we didn't know what to expect'. The police were on hand in numbers, but the anti-fascists managed to stop the march despite the attentions of over-enthusiastic and under-fed police dogs. The anti-fascists returned the following year and ended up confronting the riot police as well as a breakaway group of NF.

No Platform (NP) was formed around the start of the millennium and was a post-AFA group consisting of anarchists and Socialist Party members from London, Leeds, Essex, Brighton, Nottingham, Bristol and Bradford; 'tactics were more on a small scale due to numbers, and a more hit and run policy was used but always on intelligence information'. These anti-fascists were responding to particular local and regional circumstances to prevent the far right from becoming over-confident. Compared to AFA's national reach, NP was small with around sixty members: taking their cue from AFA's 'multi-media anti-fascism', Hann records one militant saying that they 'put out a fair bit of propaganda with leaflets and stickers and put on various fundraising benefits. We did security work for some large squat parties and donations from that went into the pot'.[4] No Platform also pre-empted an NF demo at a Republican meeting near Euston station, which was only a partial success. Although one group made 'contact' with the NF, there were several arrests.

3   Birchall, *Beating the Fascists*, 348–352.
4   Dave Hann, *Physical Resistance: A Hundred Years of Anti-Fascism* (London: Zero Books, 2013), 360-361

In the Midlands, No Platform planned an attack on an NF march and sent out a car-load of spotters. They followed a suspicious looking vehicle that turned out to be ex-members of Nottingham AFA who were monitoring *them*. The anti-fascists eventually located the NF on the motorway and followed them until the police, assuming they were NF, forced them to join the convoy where they were quickly hemmed in by the mobile fascists and forced onto the hard shoulder. The NF members tried to attack the car but were batoned back by police and then sent on their way to the collective relief of the anti-fascists.

No Platform mobilised in Halifax at an election count only to be almost dragged into a battle with a minibus full of Asian youth until they recognised each other. The BNP candidate and three comrades attacked the NP group, which numbered fifteen. A police car drew up, sprayed the combatants with pepper spray, and drove off again. As the anti-fascists headed back to their vehicles, riot police turned up but failed to make any arrests.

In August 2001, the NF attempted to organize in Pudsey outside Leeds with disastrous results. On the day, anti-fascists gathered on the opposite side of the road whilst the NF numbers increased, with local youth and football fans gravitating towards them. Although tense, the day did not end in violence, and the NF reported it as a resounding success. The NF's hopes of building on this started to backfire: the following week a group of twenty ex-AFA and younger recruits organized, hoping to ambush NF members on their way to their pitch, or if not, occupy the pitch peacefully. One NF spotter was apprehended on his scooter and pummelled. As the anti-fascists approached the NF, the riot police in attendance assumed they were fascists and let them through their lines. C recalls the following:

All plans for peacefully blocking the NF went out of the window as X cracked one NF over the head with a pint Grolsch bottle and all hell broke loose as they were attacked with bottles, boots, and fists. K as usual was the first to go down and received a very nasty head wound and ran into a bank, whilst another was punched once and ran for his life. Their biggest lad, a local bouncer with a big reputation, was done over by two of the younger lot and can be seen on the photos with his T-shirt covered in blood. TW's dad tried to intervene to save his son and had his nose broken.

The enthusiastic locals from the week before proved less confident on the day and kept a very safe distance. The police were outmanoeuvred but five anti-fascists ended up with nine months in prison after NF members made statements to the police, despite the fact they 'never grass'. The NF subsequently fell out over who ran away, as their 'racial comrades' took a savage beating. TW, the NF member, was later jailed for distributing racially inflammatory material to school kids.

No Platform went to Leicester to prevent a proposed fascist attack on a gay pride march, and as one Bolton member recalls, 'We were able to score some hits on the fascists around the train station and get out without any incident.... There was a network but a very loose network.'[5] This 'loose network' evolved into Antifa, which was predominantly anarchist and took their cue from militant groups in Europe, especially those in Germany who developed the 'black bloc' approach. Antifa emerged around 2004 with members of the Anarchist Federation, Class War Federation and No Platform. Their mission statement said, 'We believe in the "no platform" philosophy and the tradition of fighting fascism/racism stretching back to Cable Street, Red Lion Square, Lewisham and Waterloo. We are a network of various organizations and individuals who see anti-fascism as part of the class struggle.'[6]

With widespread use of the Internet, anti-fascists could reach more people, but in keeping with AFA's strategy they also operated on the music and football scenes. Antifa turned out in numbers to greet Holocaust revisionist David Irving who was speaking in Sussex, and they successfully stopped the meeting: 'They tried to reschedule the meeting to go ahead in a pub, the meeting was invaded, broken

5   Ibid., 363.
6   *Antifa* website, http://www.antifa.org.uk/About%20us.html (Accessed March 13, 2013).

up and loads of David Irving's books ended up in the river. There was a scuffle. Two of ours were arrested and then were released.[7]

In July 2005, the minuscule Nationalist Alliance was to hold a meeting in Brighton, but anti-fascists discovered the venue and it was cancelled so they had to meet at a small train station in the suburbs. A hundred anti-fascists assembled at the Unemployed Centre nearby and, as the police tried to block them in, they gradually escaped out of the back door to the station, where 'the fascists soon panicked and moved their few supporters, mostly from outside Brighton, to another prearranged venue where we had an infiltrator present'.[8] Brighton is the 'gay capital' of England and the annual Pride march is one of the biggest celebrations in Europe, with thousands descending on the town for a weekend-long party. So in 2007 the NF and tiny BPP decided to protest it with negligible results. When they started their picket, 'they were the target of various objects and they left the area battered'.[9] Their report stated,

> We were attacked [but] fought back...until it had got so out of hand that the police ordered us to leave. Hit by a plastic bottle of soft drink that had not been opened, I was sporting a black eye and broken glasses. Others received cuts and bruises and if they think we won't be back next year, they'd best think again.[10]

The BPP was just another tiny far-right group, existing on the edge of the periphery, but there were still local clashes. West York-shire anti-fascists were blamed for assaulting two members of the BPP in January 2006. Two members were attacked with bottles and kicked to the floor by anti-fascists. Antifa added that 'as well as be-ing battered that day...[one] was relieved of his briefcase, which had some very interesting Intel.'[11] One of the BPP was badly affected by this and withdrew for a long period of R and R, although he later

---

7   Hann, *Physical Resistance*, 365.
8   Greenstein, *The Fight Against Fascism in Brighton*, 65.
9   Ibid.
10   Ibid., 66.
11   Hann, *Physical Resistance*, 367.

reappeared trying to wrest control of the NF from its ageing and shaky leadership and incurring the wrath of BNP members. The fascist website blamed

> members of Antifa, the network of Left–Anarchist groups who have declared themselves committed to opposing British White Nationalists with violence. More specifically, we believe that the attackers belong to the West Yorkshire–based 635 Group.... The 635 Group has also been boasting about how it forced a private company hosting a central Leeds BPP mailbox to close that mailbox.[12]

The BPP claimed that 'unlike the website of the 635 Group, [we don't] advocate or publicly incite others to commit acts of political violence', whilst conveniently forgetting about the *Redwatch* website—which was run by a BPP member—that had long published photos of left-wingers in the hope of inciting violence against them. The BPP attempted to hold a meeting in London, which was again rumbled and their members were attacked and fled:

> They were turned over one day, near Victoria Station. They were trying to have their national meeting. Antifa counter mobilised and the whole thing ended up in a punch up that the fascists lost. No arrests.... It was a good example of a small group being successfully pushed out of existence by the use of physical force. Job done. Physical force anti-fascism worked there.[13]

In 2007, the BNP hosted Jean-Marie Le Pen, the leader of the French National Front in London, which led to chaotic scenes as hundreds of anti-fascists surrounded the building. Le Pen and Griffin were hurried to a car protected by inadequate security guards as anti-fascists pelted them with rotten fruit and tried to turn the car over. They only just got away, but the car was less than roadworthy. As

12   Quotes from *Redwatch* website, http://www.redwatch.co.uk (Accessed March 13, 2013).
13   Hann, *Physical Resistance*, 367–368.

usual the BNP held their Red, White and Blue festival that year in order to rally the troops with bands, beer and lectures, which disrupted the local village besieged by anti-fascists. In 2008 during protests at the BNP's Red, White and Blue festival, thirty-three anti-fascists were arrested but only one person was charged.

On 18th October 2008, the BPP attempted to hold a demonstration in Leeds 'against racist hip-hop' by picketing the local record shop. Because of their size they had to call on a couple of other tiny fascist groups who failed to show on the day, and the BPP were outnumbered by the opposition. An anti-fascist on Indymedia wrote: 'When anti-fascists got wind of it we spoiled the party. Several hundred anti-fascists turned up, having been organized by Workers Power, Revolution, Unite Against Fascism, Antifa and some other left activists. There were two demonstrations, one marching from the university and the other congregating in the city centre.'[14] The anti-fascist demonstration split in two, effectively sealing off the record shop, whilst the BPP cowered in a pub until the fifteen members were taken to a pen protected by two hundred police. As K. Bullstreet reported on Indymedia,

> For weeks beforehand the BPP had been crowing about 'taking back the streets' from the 'filthy reds', but as everyone who was there saw, their 'demo' (such as it was), began more than 2 hours late, while they hid (unwelcome) in the back room of a closed pub, under police guard. Then eventually, after the cops had finally managed to clear a space for them, about 11 fascists shuffled out to a sheep-pen, protected by more than 200 cops. Here, they stood, completely isolated, being jeered and laughed at, for 45 minutes, before running away to be driven out of Leeds by Asian taxi drivers.[15]

The police, outnumbered by anti-fascists, were heavy handed and made several arrests, as well as attempting to tear off face coverings, but the day was a victory for anti-fascism.

14   *Indymedia*, www.indymedia.org (Accessed March 13, 2013).
15   Ibid.

Militant anti-fascism suffered a serious setback in March 2009 when 'the core of Antifa...had been immobilised by a large conspiracy trial to do with a confrontation with Blood & Honour skinheads'.[16] Twenty anti-fascists were put on trial, charged with conspiracy to commit public disorder in a protracted case which ended with six people jailed and one person deported. One of the defendants wrote in *Freedom*, the anarchist newspaper, that at Welling Station there was

> an altercation between two neo-nazis and three or four anti-fascists. One neo-nazi was briefly knocked unconscious but was so badly injured that he discharged himself from hospital. The violence was spontaneous and did not involve the majority of anti-fascists at the station or in the vicinity. The Battle of Cable Street this was not.[17]

The police launched 'one of the largest policing operations of 2009...[which] involved hundreds of police officers simultaneously raiding properties all across the country. Dozens of people were arrested and 23 eventually charged'. It was a concerted police effort against antifascists and the group 'Antifa' in particular, and an attempt to criminalise militant activity.[18] During the court case, the prosecution attempted to use the tactics that were used against the Welling rioters in 1993 by claiming fascists and anti-fascists were all 'extremists'. The case had a serious effect on Antifa operations, with many militants under the heavy manners.

By 2010, the BNP was facing increasing difficulties: their Summer School was a disappointment by all accounts, and what few pictures were published showed a handful of dispirited looking types in a mainly empty field. The Summer School and the Red, White and Blue festival (RWB) were money-spinners for the BNP, but in 2010 only about two hundred attended their 'Indigenous Family Weekend' and this annual do was eventually stopped through lack of interest.

16   Hann, *Physical Resistance*, 384.
17   *Freedom* vol. 12, no. 12 (2009): 6.
18   Ibid.

Griffin was embroiled in a court case over discriminatory elements in the BNP's membership criteria, and the party was rumoured to be close to bankrupt with allegedly a half-million-pound debt, amongst other legal hassles. Griffin's disastrous appearance on the BBC's *Question Time* contributed to the BNP's general misfortunes, as did the BNP's website disappearing the night before the 2010 General Election. Their only member of the Greater London Assembly resigned the BNP whip, two membership lists were leaked and a considerable number of local councillors disappeared rapidly as once-strong areas fell apart and members left, staff resigned or were sacked, and fallouts and recriminations abounded. A BNP Westminster press conference trumpeting their two new MEPs had to be abandoned when anti-fascists turned up to protest and the scene degenerated.

At the BNP Annual Conference in Leicester in 2010, Griffin proposed a new phase of militancy, attempting to capitalise on the EDL's success on the streets, forgetting that the BNP had started off as an aggressive street force that had been kicked off the cobbles by AFA. The BNP continued to stumble over its own incompetence through organizational inadequacy, nepotism and a loss of membership. Despite the BNP's political impotency, Griffin's public appearances continued to be faced with fervid opposition, and in July 2012, a far from flattering photo was circulated of Griffin with a panicked look on his face as his 'bodyguards' failed to repel an anti-fascist apparently armed with a roll-up and lighter. Although the anti-fascist in question was arrested, he luckily received a non-custodial sentence. In Westminster in June 2013, anti-fascists clashed with BNP members who were trying to capitalise on the Lee Rigby murder. This may well have resulted in some dramatic photographs of the far right under siege by the black bloc and others but also ended with the mass arrest of fifty-eight anti-fascists. They were bussed out of town and served bail conditions that forbade them to demonstrate in London. By chance, the next anti-fascist mobilization was in Bradford, so the conditions were fairly irrelevant and it was clear that the police were not keeping an extensive diary on far-right demonstrations.

In 2014, Griffin lost his seat in the European parliament and stepped down as leader to take up a swiftly inaugurated presidential position. The BNP was in a terrible state and it was clear that the UK Independence Party (UKIP) was going to absorb a significant percentage of their votes by selling a slightly less toxic and stigmatised form of exclusionism. UKIP lacked the embarrassing Nazi/holocaust denial history but was not exempt from being tripped up by its members' careless comments, dodgy backgrounds and mainstream media exposures. It was also clear that UKIP required very different strategies for anti-fascists.

The EDL: 'Neither Racist Nor Violent, but Both'

The English Defence League (EDL) had its seeds in the 24th May 2009 demonstration when the 'United People of Luton' counter-demonstrated against 'Islamic radicals' who were protesting the homecoming parade of the Royal Anglian Regiment. Anti-fascists were not slow to recognize members of the BNP, BPP, NF and other far-right groupuscules amongst them, and although the EDL claimed to be 'neither racist nor violent' and 'peacefully protesting against Islamic extremists', this façade quickly evaporated as continuous racist abuse blighted their demonstrations. Their next significant event was in Birmingham on 8th August 2009, which was a shambles: many EDL supporters bemoaned the size of the turnout and the thirty-five arrests. EDL demos in the Midlands were continually characterized by violent outbursts, like their follow-up demo in September, which saw ninety arrests, and later in 2012 when their mob violence in Walsall saw dozens jailed. The EDL's next appearance in Manchester created a model that was oft repeated: massive police presence, a large policing bill, forty-four arrests and much negative publicity, something that hampered the EDL throughout their turbulent career.

The continued presence of well-known fascists was to prove problematic for the EDL. As they had started chants such as 'Black and White Unite' (which reflected the more benign relationships between contemporary black and white football firms), news footage of Hitler-saluting thugs kicking off with the police severely undermined such a claim and made anti-fascists realise that these were just the same old fascist faces, plus hooligans, that they had been up against for some time. The allegations that the EDL were a racist and far-right organization proved difficult to refute with so many incriminating photographs circulating on the Internet. The EDL standard rebuttal, that these were either 'Photoshopped' or anti-fascist 'plants', was unconvincing to say the least. The EDL claimed to be neither far right nor aligned to the BNP until *Searchlight* exposed several BNP members amongst them. Then the BNP proscribed the EDL, not wanting their 'respectable' image soured by violent racist thugs.

Anti-fascists were surprised by the rapid growth of the EDL, and what became increasingly obvious was that they were unlike other tiny fascist groupuscules, who pop up and vanish on a regular basis, given the numbers they could gather. What was also clear was that this was a trend that caught on with football casuals; that neo-Nazis quickly jumped on the bandwagon and successfully infiltrated it; and that BNP members or sympathisers were right behind it. The problem for the left was that there was no significant anti-fascist 'movement', AFA having dissolved, ANL having folded and the No Platform and Antifa groups being relatively small. It was the SWP-led Unite Against Fascism (UAF) that was the most consistent and best organized group that also had a national reach.

The EDL's 2009 Nottingham demo saw a concerted reaction by anti-fascists who were now taking these unwanted incursions into their towns seriously, and is best remembered for the photograph of EDL members urinating on the old castle behind thick police lines. For such avowed 'patriots' to be seen doing this on a national monument seemed incongruous but highlighted their negative image. More importantly, local youth, anti-fascists and anarchists had mobilized for the occasion with the UAF for a large counter-demonstration.

The final demo of 2009 in Stoke exposed the 'real' EDL when they started fighting with the police, breaking out of their cordon and rampaging through an Asian area in a booze-fuelled frenzy. The police had kettled them into a cheap pub where two rival football firms started fighting amongst themselves. Five hundred EDL members broke out, smashing windows, damaging cars and battling police. At the time Stoke had a strong BNP group on the council, and the EDL made a concerted effort to get there in numbers, knowing there would definitely be local support. Fallouts between moderates, extremists and the hooligan faction over drinking, violence, Sieg-Heiling and ideology increased noticeably and began to threaten the initial cohesion of the EDL.

2010

March 2010 saw the EDL cause a major disruption in Bolton with about two thousand in attendance: this was a serious number, although successive demos rarely increased beyond this. What was noticeable was the large counter-demonstration of local anti-fascists and that community groups were subject to arbitrary police attacks and arrests.

Like most far-right groups, the EDL relied on quantity not quality, which meant that all manner of uncontrollable hooligans had tagged along, many simply for the chance of a bit of drunken aggro with police, local Asians, anti-fascists or themselves now that they could not fight at football. The shady past of some of the leadership figures was also exposed: a photograph of emerging leader Tommy Robinson at a BNP meeting was released, causing him to 'hand over' the leadership to someone else—which was to prove very temporary. The EDL demo in Newcastle saw about six hundred EDL members confronted by many more anti-fascists, who were now a constant presence whose numbers fluctuated.

The EDL's political naivety was also shown up by the fact that they only saw the opposition as either 'UAF' or 'Muslims', as opposed to local people objecting to gangs of drunken racists coming into their communities to cause trouble. Their standard thinking followed the syllogistic fallacy of 'I hate Muslim extremists; anti-fascists hate me; ergo anti-fascists support Muslim extremists'. They also claimed to be a working-class organization when, in fact, they had no support from working-class organizations, unions, local community groups or political figures of any repute.

Aware of falling numbers, the EDL called for 'ten thousand' to turn up for 'the Big One' in Bradford (with some supporters calling it a potential 'bloodbath'), but the Home Secretary banned all political marches in the area so the EDL was forced to hold a static protest in a specially constructed steel pen. 'The Big One' turned out to be 'the little one,' with only seven hundred of the much-trumpeted 'ten thousand' showing up. The EDL was throwing projectiles and fighting amongst themselves before breaking out of their pen. After a brief run-around and a confrontation with local anti-fascists and Asian youth, they were escorted back to the demo site.

A day or so after 'the little one' in Bradford came a demonstration that would continue to infuriate the far right for several years hence. The tiny and ambitiously named English Nationalist Alliance (ENA) called for a provocative march through Brighton, which ultimately showed that the far right was spreading its resources too thinly. As the EDL trend spread, splinter groups attracted by the status, merchandise sales and potential for a drunken brawl began to proliferate. The ENA hoped to surf on the back of the expected Bradford success, but on the day thirty ageing football hooligans, some with children, turned up and were surrounded by police at the train station. A large UAF demo stood opposite whilst many other anti-fascists were outside the police lines to avoid kettling. Anti-fascists easily outnumbered the ENA ten to one. No sooner had the ENA march set off than it ground to a halt as militant anti-fascists blocked the route, struggling with police for some time. Eventually the police cleared a way through and guided the small march to their RV point. The UAF had been penned so Asian youths reacted angrily by tearing down the metal fences. The ENA held a few speeches surrounded by hostile anti-fascists until the police decided to march them back. It was a dismal turnout made worse by the large amount of local opposition and the fact that the police had to protect them on the way back to the station. It was an embarrassment that the far right failed to revenge.

After Brighton, several things became clear: the EDL was fragmenting and its numbers were dropping; their ranks were full of racists despite what the leadership may say; there was little political unity from top to bottom; the media had characterised the average EDL member as a violent yob, which many supporters played up to; and anti-fascists had finally gotten themselves together in opposition and, at times, could outnumber and contain them.

The EDL held another provocative demo in Leicester, where there were skirmishes when local youth turned out. The EDL attacked a restaurant; this was filmed on a mobile phone and the footage widely circulated on the Internet, exposing the violent racism inherent within the EDL, despite the leadership's feeble protestations otherwise.

As was becoming a regular feature, the EDL made big claims that they could no longer carry out, and Robinson announced that the EDL was going over to Holland to support Euro-racist Geert Wilders. A few dozen EDL managed to get to Amsterdam, but it was not the jolly they had been hoping for: they were attacked by Ajax fans; one EDL member had his leg broken; anti-fascists smashed EDL's minibus; Wilders rejected them out of hand; and the demo was moved out of town. Much worse was the footage that showed Robinson having his flag snatched off him by anti-fascists before the EDL turned tail. This embarrassing incident was again widely distributed around the Internet and did little for Robinson's prestige.

2011

The EDL demo in Blackburn in 2011 was a damaging turning point for the EDL: the already fragile alliance between firms broke down as brawling factions attacked each other near the coaches. Not only did this look bad for unity but it also precipitated a serious North/South divide. There were also accusations that the EDL leadership were siphoning off funds as well as profiting from the sales of EDL merchandise. The EDL began to look like a one-trick pony heading for the glue factory.

The ENA and March for England (MfE) were still smarting over the previous year in Brighton and called for a repeat performance. The police were visibly nervous and heavy handed with the large and vocal counter-demonstration. The MfE were again heavily outnumbered and surrounded by police who quick-marched them to the meet and back again. To make matters worse for the MfE on this hot day, the pub that they were supposed to be ending up in had closed its doors to them.

The EDL wanted to stage a provocative march into Tower Hamlets in London but the Metropolitan police kept them under heavy supervision from the start. The numbers of anti-fascists had increased on the streets, and the RMT union refused to liaise with the police and transport the EDL, who are an anti-trade-union organization. Robinson, on bail for a previous offence, was warned to stay away from demo or risk being jailed, but he had foolishly talked up Tower Hamlets so was forced into a face-saving farce: If he didn't turn up, he would never live it down, and if he did, he would be arrested and taken straight to prison for several months. He turned up and was jailed shortly after. The main body of the EDL now lacked any leadership or co-ordination, their spokesman was in jail, they were blighted by diminished numbers and internal fallouts, and there was a visible opposition on most of their demos.

2012

Apart from an initial setback in February, 2012 ended as a successful one for anti-fascism. The year presented a welcome surprise with the conviction of Dobson and Norris for the racist murder of Stephen Lawrence. The EDL held a weak demonstration in Barking, then fifteen members headed off to Whitechapel and got drunk, a ruckus ensued, and one EDL member was hospitalised.

In Liverpool in February 2012, a mob from various far-right groups disrupted an Irish Republican march, referring to it as an 'IRA march' in order to whip up sectarian hatred in the city. The police diverted the Republican march whilst Liverpool anti-fascists came into conflict with others from the far right in the city centre. The day was a rare 'victory' for the far right as they claimed they had stopped the march. However, the day unified Republicans, socialists, anarchists, and un-aligned anti-fascists as they realized they were all against a common enemy, and a march celebrating the trade unionist James Larkin was better prepared. Another march, celebrating the International Brigades in October, turned out five hundred, as the far right kept their distance.

> We called for people to line the streets. That was a strategy for avoiding a kettle, not to gather at a fixed point, but it was also, and this is

THE EDL

important, a way to give people a chance to have their say. Stand on
your own streets and say your piece. And then the day came around...
—Brighton Anti-Fascists

Meanwhile, back in Brighton, anti-fascists were preparing for yet
another rerun by the March for England, which had been making
threatening noises about revenge. The seventy-odd MfE was outnumbered at least ten to one by anti-fascist protesters and, as usual,
completely surrounded by police. The march was to set off at 12.00pm
but was delayed as anti-fascists spontaneously lined the streets to
avoid kettling and then forced the march to a stop. Barricades and
confrontations with police forced it to be rerouted as bottles and missiles rained down on the fascists, and large groups suddenly appeared
out of nowhere to block the march, which was seriously delayed at
least twice through militant action. When the MfE got to their rendezvous point, anti-fascists had occupied it and were treated to the
sight of police escorting individual 'patriots' to the portaloos and be-
reft of their previous hubris.

At first we just watched this silent group of sullen fascists trudge past.
Their silence was indication of their defeat. We decided to enjoy their
silence, just watch their retreat.
—Brighton Anti-Fascists

Although anti-fascists could outnumber the EDL on major demonstrations, 'regional' demos often saw little opposition. For their trip
to Walthamstow, the EDL met near Kings Cross station to get to
the demo site, but RMT (National Union of Rail, Maritime and
Transport) workers threatened action so police had to redirect
the drunken mob to Euston instead. Anti-fascists had completely
blocked the route and rallying point as the isolated leadership stood
arguing furiously amongst themselves. The numbers of anti-fascists
increased by the hour and blocked all roads around the area. After
several hours the police finally managed to move the EDL out of
the area and transport them back to the centre of town, by which
time anti-fascists were in full celebratory mode. The EDL had been
outnumbered and abandoned by their leadership who had fled, and

311

some militants got through police lines to attack the EDL with missiles in a fit of pique; the EDL declared they would return as 'revenge,' which failed miserably.

The EDL called a demo in Bristol, which was met with a similarly large anti-fascist mobilisation. The police shepherded the EDL into a pen as anti-fascists were either in mobile groups or lining the streets so the police could not contain them. The tactic of swamping was again successful and drowned out the EDL march. The police could not control the hundreds of anti-fascists, and when they started moving the EDL back to the train station, anti-fascists blocked the route. As one recalls: 'A long green banner was used to create a line of defence and those big plastic bins were pushed out behind and some rubbish set alight.... Police raised their truncheons. I got hit on the head. A warning shot rather than a big swipe. Others fare far worse.... The horse charge came next.'[1]

After the main body had been dispersed, a small group of EDL members were drinking in the Old Markets area and started harassing an anti-fascist who

> ran over to provide support. A fight started. A full-blown street fight.... The fascists now in a big group gathered outside the pub where they had been drinking, lobbed over a paving slab. It smashed in front of the line of anti-fascists. A figure that could have walked out of a piece of Banksy graffiti, except that this figure was female, picked up the pieces and threw it back.[2]

By now the EDL as an organization was in complete disarray as it had no formal membership, no accounts and appalling representation in the media, and its divisional meetings descended into infighting and drunken rivalry. EDL's demo in Walsall was a calamity with them fighting riot police and holding broken and bloody heads. Later, many members were given serious jail sentences.

The 'revenge' trip to Walthamstow was a washout: the police had

1   Brighton Anti-Fascists, *A Year on the Streets* (Brighton: Anti-Fascist Network, 2013), 17.
2   Ibid., 18.

banned them from going back so they staged a small demonstration in Parliament Square as hundreds of anti-fascists celebrated on Walthamstow's streets. Their demo in Norwich saw 150 disappointed supporters surrounded by two thousand anti-fascists, which served to illustrate the EDL's decline.

Following Robinson's incarceration, the EDL called a demo outside Wandsworth prison. A couple of stalwart anti-fascists turned up to monitor the small demo, but there was little else to do. The EDL demonstration in Southend was probably the worst as only six turned up to stand about in the train station car park before calling it a day. The year ended with the EDL leader in prison, many members leaving, multiple arrests and prison sentences, and the group having to face some of the biggest anti-fascist opposition in the UK for years at Walthamstow, Bristol and Brighton.

The Scottish Defence League (SDL) was set up in late 2009 and its successes were minimal. Its first demo in Glasgow attracted paltry numbers whilst a large counter-demonstration called by Scotland United numbered well over 1,500. After several clashes with militants, SDL members were hurriedly bussed out of the area. The SDL had difficulties in mobilizing numbers and were exposed as having links with the BNP, the NF and loyalist groups. Relationships, however, remained fractious: in November 2011, the SDL met with ex-EDL and a tiny contingent from the National Front in Newcastle, a meeting which descended into a drunken brawl. They also attacked members of Newcastle's Occupy protest. The SDL expressed annoyance about foreign workers in Scotland, conveniently forgetting the thousands of Scots who had emigrated all over the world to work. By now anti-fascists were well organized, and many from anarchist groups, student groups, trade unions, local community groups and other left-wing political organizations were coming together to confront the SDL. When they mobilised in Glasgow, anti-fascists turned out in force with spotters monitoring the situation. As Glasgow anarchists put it, 'Within a few minutes a beautiful site [sic] appeared as 50–70 anti-fascists confidently and loudly marched up Buchanan St., masked up, black flags waving.

The streets were ours to demonstrate on today, and the fascists were reduced to scurrying around.'[3]

A demo in May had one SDL member declaring, 'That was a shambles of a turnout', and they were again outnumbered by anti-fascists. When the SDL gathered to commemorate a murder victim (whose family had told them to stay away) over two hundred anti-fascists mobilised, at one point breaking through to confront them, but the police managed to contain the trouble. The SDL mobilizations were not impressive, but the long and successful history of Scottish anti-fascism was continued by all those who stood against them, and SDL collapsed into infighting, apathy and failure.

Digital Fascism

The Internet and digital technology played a key role in the growth and spread of the EDL, with groups organizing through Facebook pages and forums, through events publicised on websites, and through co-ordination on the day using mobile phones. This technology was also used by anti-fascists, and the forums and Facebook pages were infiltrated by anti-fascists causing mischief. Along with the footage of Robinson having his flag snatched in Holland, there were other clips that went viral on the Net and damaged the EDL's credibility. The first was of a sizable Asian youth planting an EDL member into some bushes with an incredible punch; this was posted all over the Net. The second was the 'Muslamic Rayguns' video which featured a clearly intoxicated EDL member slurring allegations about 'Muslamic Rape Camps', 'Halal Pork' and 'Iraqi Law', which was later edited and put to music. Film of their demo in Cambridge showed twenty supporters staggering around a muddy field, incoherent with substances whilst five hundred anti-fascists marched by.

2013

In 2013, the EDL rally in Manchester started badly as two contingents arrived at Victoria Station and started fighting each other, continued it in the pub where they were kettled, and then attacked police.

3   https://glasgowanarchists.wordpress.com.

At Piccadilly Gardens, a few hundred counter-demonstrators—including trade-union representatives, community groups, local politicians and anti-fascists with flags—gathered and then marched to Albert Square, numbering 350, which was a small turnout. The usually visible UAF was having a conference on the day, but some critics felt that discussing what to do about fascists on the streets when several hundred fascists were on the streets seemed a wee bit absurd. The counter-demo rallied when a large group of anarchists and anti-fascists were shepherded into the square, swelling numbers; minor clashes in town with a breakaway group of EDL were reported, with one anti-fascist photographer getting into a scrape.

The MfE's return to Brighton saw a handful assembled at the front surrounded by hundreds of anti-fascists—locals, UAF, black bloc anarchists, trade unionists and a large group of punks from the Punx Picnic that was taking place that weekend. Fights were taking place as the police failed to contain the increasing number of counter-protesters, and several MfE stragglers were chased into a betting shop and splattered with black gunk. A large mob of anti-fascists then came across an unfortunate group of right-wing 'faces' who were bricked, chased and attacked before the police could protect them. As militants regrouped, several more MfE stragglers were caught and battered on the seafront. As the police escorted the MfE back to the station, the amassed anti-fascists marched through the town chanting, 'Whose Streets? Our Streets!' Suffused with hubris, the MfE threatened to come back to 'Smash Antifa' in November but predictably failed to show.

In May 2013, the EDL's fortunes were temporarily boosted by the murder of soldier Lee Rigby in Greenwich and they capitalised on fears of Muslim extremism. The EDL had decided to lay a wreath at the nearby army base to capitalise on tensions in the area. Small groups of anti-fascists mobilised to monitor proceedings, but the EDL was kettled into a pub whilst anti-fascists withdrew from the scene.

This temporary aberration from the EDL's downward slide was fading fast, but the biggest setback for the EDL in 2013 was

315

Robinson's abrupt resignation. He was facing charges over mortgage fraud at the time, so commentators from both left and right suspected that this was a move to invite a more lenient sentence. Critics felt this was confirmed by Robinson's statement that 'this is a complete stitch up'.[4] He got eighteen months and effectively left the EDL to numbly stagger on in decreasing numbers.

From two thousand in Bolton in 2010 to only twenty at Cambridge in 2013 was an appalling downward trajectory for the EDL and was caused by several things: many were bored after spending a lot of money for minimal returns; they were continuously shown as a bunch of drunken hooligans; all the media coverage had been mainly hostile; members got little support when they were arrested; others were given bail restrictions which prevented them from attending future demos; and there was suspicion of misappropriation of funds. There was also the fact that anti-fascists had mobilised in large numbers to drown them out, taken over their rendezvous points, swamped their march routes, and exposed them as racists, fascists and bigots.

By 2014, the annual March for England had become a show of strength for anti-fascists and, despite the MfE promising to return in numbers, they only managed to gather around a hundred. A small group had plotted up in a pub whilst a growing anti-fascist crowd blocked them in until police forced a way through to their RV point. By this time hundreds of anti-fascists had lined the route along the seafront and the customary insults were traded. The MfE assembled in the rain for a few brief speeches before being marched back towards the station. As the MfE headed back to the station, anarchists threw up a barricade to block their retreat as militants attacked the depressed-looking fascists from the side. There had already been a row outside a pub where furniture and beer glasses were exchanged, but by this time hundreds of anti-fascists had gathered around the station to wave the MfE goodbye.

4   *Guardian* (UK), January 23, 2014.

Conclusion

As we have seen, the complexion of fascism changes frequently, and its success is dependent on many factors: political opposition, state collusion, criminality and violence.

Fascist groups can flare up and seize the initiative in times of crisis—the Golden Dawn Movement in Greece capitalising on economic instability is an example. Each fascist group is different; each fascist group is the same. They can go to great lengths to disguise their real agenda or express previously taboo thoughts, which can rapidly become acceptable.

There is no ambiguity about the dangerous attraction of fascism to millions of people facing social and economic crisis: fascism offers simple solutions to complex problems.

On a local scale, there is always the initial attraction of violence and the chance to intimidate political opponents. Fascists blame minorities and others for their poor quality of life and play on the resentment that others are getting preferential treatment in housing, money, jobs and opportunities. Fascism can motivate the disenfranchised in the face of diversity and give a sense of unity with a large group of people who share similar sentiments. And in minor cases, like with the EDL, there is the desperation of attention-seeking fuelled by the chance of getting in the local newspaper or even on television.

On a larger scale, fascism shifts the blame from capitalism onto others, when in fact there are larger forces at work oppressing the working class. It appears to address the concerns of the bourgeoisie, the lower middle class and the working class, despite its opportunistic collaboration with the industrial class, the state and the church.

The ideological fickleness of fascism can give the illusion of radicalism despite being innately conservative.

On an organisational scale, the danger of fascism lies in the ability to gain support from the working class when the radical left has failed to influence or address their concerns.

The left can be as side-tracked by factionalism and petty disputes as much as the far right, and it is up to us to offer real solutions to attacks on living standards—such as the recent austerity measures that further alienate the working class—as well as alternatives to capitalism.

Anti-fascism needs to respond to the changing face of fascism because, despite our successes, fascists fade but never really disappear. Anti-fascism has evolved over time throughout Europe, and has operated in radically different political contexts, from print workers battling ultra-nationalists in Austria, to the anti-Franco militants in Spain and the youthful Schlurfs and Edelweiss Pirates elsewhere. In the UK we have seen mass mobilisations against Mosley and the NF, the initiatives of the 43 Group and the Squads, the physical and multi-media opposition of AFA, and the swamping techniques of contemporary anti-fascists: all these show that fascism can and must be beaten by whatever strategies we deem appropriate.

The rise in digital media and the Internet as a means to spread information (and disinformation) is now an essential part of the anti-fascist struggle, as is the propagation of information in mainstream media. But we always need to be there, on the streets, organised and ready.

Whilst writing this book (and the 'Malatesta' blog and the articles for *Freedom* newspaper) we have seen that intelligence, organisation, solidarity and strength of conviction are necessary tools. Anti-fascism can be tedious, unpleasant, violent, time consuming and depressing, but this is infinitely preferable to fascism. Finally, one of the reasons why we started to write this book was because of this quote from *Beating the Fascists* by Sean Birchall: 'We hope this book will encourage other histories, open the debate and ultimately strengthen the fight against fascism.'

It is a sentiment that M. Testa would like to repeat wholeheartedly. TODOS LOS ANTI-FASCISTAS AL LA CALLES!

"The Squad Erupts from Johnny's Cafe," by John Penney. Dedicated to Roy McNeil, revolutionary socialist and anti-fascist hero, 1956–2013.

APPENDIX
ANTI-FASCIST RECOLLECTIONS: 1971 to 1977,
by John Penney[1]

Background

I was a young (middle-class) student just up to Manchester University in late 1971, fired by the still very active wave of post-1968 revolutionary radicalism that had swept the entire West on the back of the protests against the war in Vietnam. I soon joined the small but fast-growing neo-Trotskyist grouplet, the International Socialists (IS, forerunner of the Socialist Workers Party, or the SWP). Student politics, as always, was very sectarian and barren at Manchester University, whereas the IS at that time had its main focus in working-class communities and factories. A refreshing difference to the incestuous political scene at the university.

The early 1970s were notable politically for two divergent trends on respectively Far Right and Far Left. As already mentioned, there was still a definite radical 'buzz' amongst students and major sections of (mainly middle-class) youth, fired up by the 1968 French student uprising, and the ongoing, often violent anti-Vietnam war demos in London and across Europe. Also, organised labour was confident and combative, gaining wage increases easily on the back of a large, often unofficial, strike wave right across industry—up against the Conservative government of Ted Heath—which served

---

1   Whilst writing this book we were lucky to be able to draw on the experiences of other militant anti-fascists from various generations, and the following is a description of anti-fascism in the North West of England in the 1970s, which we felt should be published in full. With many thanks to JP. —M. Testa

to unite all sections of the Left to a certain extent against the common Tory enemy.

In this lively political environment, the Revolutionary Left and Marxist ideas were on the up, growing from pitifully small numbers, to groups like IS, the Socialist Labour League, the International Marxist Group (IMG), and of course Militant, which were still deeply submerged in the Labour Party; they numbered in the thousands, which was still pitifully small, but they were growing fast, and starting to have some tiny roots in the organised working class.

At the same time, the Far Right—mainly the National Front—was riding a very different growth wave. Formed in 1967, membership rocketed into the thousands after the infamous 'Rivers of Blood' speech by Enoch Powell in 1968, which denounced the late '50s and ongoing 1960s mass immigration of Asian and black workers needed to fuel Britain's then-booming economy. Britain then, even more than now, was a country still in the ideological thrall of all the old Imperialist ideology of white racial superiority, which had powered the winning and maintenance of the British Empire, and the collaboration of most of the population of the white imperial heartland in the imperial project. Suddenly white Britons were confronted in the '60s with major influxes of non-white people into or alongside their communities. For many this was a major ideological shock. So, just as many Britons had shamefully opposed earlier waves of immigration to Britain—the Irish, the Jews—the new black and Asian influx provided the NF, under its hard-line Nazi leadership, the opportunity to campaign, through provocative marches, up and down the country, against this new immigration wave. The appeal of this strategy was illustrated of course by the spontaneous support marches held by sections of organised labour—dockers and others who were for Enoch Powell's racist views in 1968—and anti-immigrant hysteria was very widely felt across UK society.

Early Anti-Fascist Experiences

I quickly realised, by Christmas 1971, that I had made a mistake in choosing to do Town Planning at university, so I swapped over to do

Economics and Politics. This required me to leave and do a gap year until the following new academic year near the end of 1972. Having started to build a new IS branch in Stockport, and having gotten into 'revolutionary' politics, I decided to stay on the dole (much easier to do that in those days) in Stockport and work full-time for IS until my university course restarted at the end of 1972. It has to be said that despite the busy programme of provocative marches that the NF held at that time, opposing the marches wasn't a major priority for the Left. It would be the task usually of local university or polytechnic groups and local anti-fascist groups to oppose these marches when they arose. I can't recall going on a single anti-fascist event during my first few months as a political activist in 1971, and generally my political work was around leafleting factories, selling the paper (*Socialist Worker*), organising and running the Stockport Branch, and working around the unemployed—leafleting and selling the paper outside Unemployment Offices.

In Greater Manchester/Lancashire, the main area for growth for the National Front was in the old, run down mill towns like Blackburn and Bradford—also Preston, Dewsbury, Accrington, and Dewsbury. In these towns there had been a significant 1960s wave of mainly Asian immigration to provide cheap labour for the by-then fast declining mills. Thus, economic decline was matched by a new immigrant group competing in a declining job market amongst generally declining living conditions. Blackburn in particular was a NF growth hotspot—and indeed had been a hotbed of British Union of Fascists (BUF) activity in the pre-war and immediate post-war periods, too—and some of the old BUFers or their family members were still there to provide a base of support (for reasons which are not easy to work out exactly, given that the previous wave of then-hotly contested immigration into Blackburn had been the Irish, in the nineteenth and early-twentieth centuries).

Early in 1972, the NF called a national anti-immigration march in Blackburn, on the back of a lot of provocative propaganda the local NF had been putting out locally. Most of the surrounding universities and polytechnics committed to sending people to oppose the march, as did the Communist Party, Labour Party, local churches, Trades Council, and so on. Of course, the 'respectable' anti-racists organised a counter demo to take place miles away from the NF route on the day, leaving the counter-demo actually alongside the NF to the students and a few general anti-fascists. As it happened, there were many hundreds of students and a few others who opposed the NF that day. The NF march itself probably had no more than five hundred people on it—but at that time Tyndall and Webster had the brilliant strategy of getting NF members to bring along their entire families, including children. This meant that the NF march looked like 'Joe Public' and his normal British family (with a few boneheads of course at the front of the march as the 'Honour Guard') protesting against immigration—opposed by a right bunch of long-haired Leftie trouble-making, privileged students. It was a *very* successful propaganda strategy for the NF.

The tactics of the anti-fascists left a lot to be desired in those days; we really had no idea how to combat these marches, and being in the main, middle-class students, we tended to hurl vicious sarcasm and pointed *bon mots* rather than bricks or bottles! As it happens, this being my first anti-fascist do, it was actually a bit rougher than would be the case for years to come in that we had goodly numbers to oppose the march, and not enough police had been deployed to keep order. So we kept fruitlessly trying to interrupt the NF march, trying to break through the police lines, dodging police horses and snatch squads. Unfortunately, at that time the Left was still besotted with the organisational tactic so popularised by the French students in 1968 and the London anti-Vietnam War demos, namely the 'linked arm charge'. The IMG in particular used to rush around constantly exhorting everyone to 'link arms, comrades.' So that day we spent a lot of time farcically linking arms. This, though it might have worked well on anti-Vietnam demos charging against police lines, was in Blackburn that day completely stupid—tying us down in linked-arm bunched 'sausages', easily being corralled by the police, reducing our mobility and ability to seize opportunities to get at the NF. Even worse, as I discovered, it reduced one's ability to defend oneself, too. Hence I had opportunistically linked arms in yet another daft sausage chain of people with a particularly pretty fellow student I vaguely knew—an opportunity for a bit of chatting up as well as politics—perfect! My linked group were facing the NF march to its side with police in between when, bugger me, a horrible little ferrety NFer lunged through the police line and punched the pretty girl I was chatting up in the stomach, and then lurched back into the NF march. Of course, being linked, none of us could defend ourselves or respond. I think the pretty student forever more bore me a grudge for my abject failure to protect her. Then a bit later, to compound this tactical failure, the NF (anticipating the Left's eventual favourite tactic by many years) sent a hail of bricks they'd found on wasteground beside their march into our ranks. Now, when the bricks are coming over one doesn't want to be trapped, immobile in a linked-arm chain, believe me. By good luck I didn't head a brick that day.

A few months later, still in 1972, I participated in a broadly based anti-racism march in Blackburn, which was still bedevilled by NF activity and the aftermath of harassment of the Asian community arising from the earlier NF march. This event, attended by the usual church, Trades Council, community relations, Labour and Liberal Party, and sundry Leftie attendees, and a few prominent Asians (but no Asian Youth)—about two thousand in number—was quite a chilling experience. The white shoppers were often clearly deeply hostile to the march, gesticulating and scowling at us as we paraded past. Community relations were obviously not good. A depressing experience.

Marching and Counter-Marching 1973–1974

For the next couple of years, the NF continued their successful 'family outing' March and Build strategy all over flashpoint areas in Britain. The anti-fascists would turn out, too, of course—though the results, with the police trying to keep order, were always inconclusive. The NF also tried to establish paper sales in areas like Blackburn, Dewsbury, Bradford, Preston, Hyde, and the odd small public meeting in pubs and town halls. We opposed them all. For most of us though this wasn't a major part of our political activity. I was certainly more involved in routine paper sales and the excitement of supporting the 1973 Greater Manchester engineering factory occupations than in intensive anti-fascist work. Still, the attempts to disrupt small meetings and NF paper sales did increasingly lead to regular minor fisticuffs with the NF. These experiences taught us some hard lessons—mainly that most of the (mainly middle-class) Left was, to coin a 'Mickey Fennism' (a *very* tough revolutionary socialist London docker of the time), 'useless on the pavement'. Now for whatever reason, despite not being a burly bloke, I'm OK 'on the pavement' in a fracas or originally 'in the school playground', as was my formative fighting experience (possibly significantly aided by my perennial inclination to have a steel bar concealed up my sleeve—a great equaliser!). One wonders what the typical Leftie was doing at school—hiding behind the bike sheds? Whatever—most on the Left simply couldn't, or wouldn't, back up their searing verbal attacks on the NF with physical force when it came to the crunch.

The 'school of hard knocks' of regular minor fracas with the NF all over the North West, and the occasional demo in the Midlands or London, slowly established who the fighters were on the Left, and in Manchester we tended to increasingly go on events together. This was also boosted by the fact that in Stockport and Manchester generally we were starting to make contact with young unemployed or casually employed young workers through our political work, who were often quite 'up' for the odd barney with the NF. Indeed the excitement of touring away on demos or fighting NF paper sellers in the mill towns often kept these young men attached to the International Socialists, when the regular paper sale or branch meeting wouldn't have.

I had no idea that me and my chums' periodic outings to places like Blackburn had been noticed at all until sometime in 1974 when I was at an anti-racist meeting in Blackburn, really just because I'd given a lift up there to the meeting's speaker, Manchester organiser and ex-busworker, LK. Apparently at the start of the meeting, one of the local IS folk had whispered nervously to LK, 'What have you brought *him* up for?' pointing to myself quietly supping a beer on the side. 'What do you mean?' asked LK. 'The *beast*', the IS comrade whispered. 'There isn't going to be trouble is there?' LK was much amused, as was I. It obviously didn't take much 'pavement action' to be considered a fearsome madman on the Left in those days.

Most political work for me particularly, and the Left generally, during 1974 (despite the important anti-NF Red Lion Square London demo, at which anti-fascist Kevin Gately was killed by the police) wasn't about anti-fascism, but the ever-rising tide of industrial disputes, with the crowning achievement of the victory of the miners over the Heath Government. (This lead to barmy little plots amongst the ruling class and amongst the military for a coup, when Heath lost to Wilson in that year's General Election. In that case both the maverick ruling elite coup plotters and the Revolutionary Left alike were very mistaken in seeing the Wilson Government as any threat to the status quo.) Very quickly the Wilson Government, via its bogus 'Social Contract' con trick, and TUC class Quislings demobilised the rising tide of industrial and political struggle—though this was not at all obvious to us as keen young revolutionaries at the time.

By the end of 1974, the larger NF 'March and Build' family NF outing parades were running into trouble. Their very success initially was now leaving behind such a racist backlash for local ethnic minority communities that when they now marched again in Birmingham, the East End of London, Leicester, and so on, black and Asian Youth *did* at last feel that it *was* their problem, too—and they were starting to turn up in some numbers to oppose the NF alongside the white Left. Then the bricks and bottles started to be hurled into the NF family groups on the fascist marches. So the NF was starting to find their members much less willing to take the family on the marches, and NF marches started to look much more like a bunch of Nazi boneheads marching to stir up trouble, rather than 'real British families voicing a grievance'. Quite often on these marches, upon being confronted by jeering anti-fascists trying to break through the police lines, the 'bonehead' component on the fascist marches were wont to whip out blocks of soap from their pockets, then point at the crowd and then the soap. This was of course a gleeful reference to the rendering down of murdered

Jews in the Nazi death factories in slow ovens, to make soap out of the fat. So much for Holocaust Denial.

1975: The NF Adopts New Tactics and Priorities

The year 1975 was an important, negative milestone for the NF. It was riven by deep internal disputes between the (supposedly non-Nazi) 'populists' around John Kingsley Read and the 'old Nazis' around John Tyndall, Read taking over as NF Chairman in 1975. NF conferences at that time witnessed the amusing and bizarre spectacle of the 'populist' NFers chanting 'Nazis Out' at the opposing Tyndallite Old Guard Nazis. Amongst the internal disarray, however, the NF had also built good links with Loyalist groups in Northern Ireland and the UK, and they were gaining 'Loyalist' members fast through branching out from their single-issue anti-immigrant stance. These Protestant Loyalists were often an aggressive bunch, keen to get to grips with the 'Republican sympathisers' of the Left. And of course the NF was increasingly seeing its 'family outing' March and growth strategy diminishing as the increasingly violent response to NF marches put off family groups from attending.

The NF now made what was to turn out to be a catastrophic analytical and tactical mistake. The NF judged that their street-fighting activists could wipe the floor with what, after years of scuffles with Lefties, they judged to be an undifferentiated mass of long-haired middle-class tossers. So they decided, on the back of an 'anti-IRA meetings' campaign, to take on the Left physically, smash them off the streets, and disrupt or break up their meetings—particularly on Ireland. The start of this tactical turn wasn't always very dramatic—meetings in Ireland were often disrupted by NFers, women as often as men, simply sitting in the audience and then standing up mid-meeting and denouncing the meeting as 'anti-British' until removed by rather embarrassed and often incompetent stewards (if there were any, which there often weren't). Left-wing paper sales were also getting harassment, often quite trivial, sometimes serious, from NFers all over the country, too—often leading to scuffles and an undignified retreat by the Left. Quite why the NF, riven as it was by internal feuding, lurched into this militarist tactic at that precise time is unclear—possibly it was *because* of the chaotic leadership situation that it landed itself with—as it eventually turned out—such a foolish strategy.

We didn't at first clearly see the pattern of their new tactic. Then late in 1975, the new tactic did become clearer in Manchester. The NCCL held a meeting, with pacifist Pat Arrowsmith speaking, at UMIST in Manchester, on 'Ireland and civil liberties'. It was a big meeting, with a couple of hundred in attendance, of no interest to most of us really—bit worthy and dull. Local anti-fascist activist Graeme Atkinson and a few other Lefties turned up out of general interest. A large team, thirty or so, of NF and Loyalists attacked the unstewarded meeting, picking out known people on the Left for a beating. Graeme Atkinson had a glass smashed into his face. The rest of the audience apparently looked on passively, in horror, as the selective attacks took place. The meeting destroyed, the attackers literally *goosestepped* (yep, really) off down Aytoun Street. A foolish escape tactic, really, as many were picked up by the cops as they triumphantly marched away, and a number were subsequently put in prison for their crimes. So an initial tactical triumph for the fascists there then—but with a poor withdrawal strategy.

The next week I was part of a very large stewarding force, drawn widely from the Left, which ensured that a repeat of the NCCL meeting took place unhindered. But the damage was done, the gauntlet had been thrown down. What would the Left do next? Very little in the short term, is the simple answer. There was some high-flown, militant, 'now we go on the offensive' rhetoric at the following week's 'Manchester Anti-Fascist Committee' meeting of all the local groups (I was the IS area delegate). But as to what to do—not easy—we simply didn't have the intelligence info on the local fascists to set up reprisals or the people to carry them out, so for the next few months a group of us on the Left—mainly the IS—built up a loose, ad hoc stewarding team, which from then on spent huge amounts of our time providing security to any Left meeting or march, particularly on Ireland, likely to be attacked, right across the North West.

We drew members from the IS, from other Left groups, and also, *very* importantly, from the large social circle of 'mates' of our young working-class members and contacts, built up over the previous years of hard political work.

As the months (and years) passed we got more organised, particularly in the systematic collection of data on the fascists, where they lived, and their photos, gaining details when they were standing in local elections. At first, as the NF meeting disruption strategy continued, our heavy meeting stewarding was pretty passive—we simply wouldn't physically let them into meetings, whatever the law or police might demand. But of course the defence of meetings did lead increasingly to violent confrontations with the NF—they gave up sending little old ladies along and tried to just go in mob-handed. And here is where the NF had made their huge miscalculation—because they had in general got the pulse or character of the Left as a bunch of non-violent middle-class tossers quite right. But the preceding years of political work in the working class had, in Manchester and nationwide, equipped the Left with just enough hard and mainly working-class fighters to not only defend the rest of the Left against the NF attacks, but to then go on the offensive and eventually smash them off the streets.

1975: Left on the Offensive

In Greater Manchester, based heavily on resources built up in manpower in Stockport, from 1975 onwards a hard core of anti-fascist fighters on call pretty much 24/7 was slowly created, and intelligence on the NF was massively improved. This information was widely distributed to the loose but wide periphery of anti-fascist Left with whom we were friendly, from all the groups on the Left, from the Labour Party leftwards. A 'culture of attack' was built up, whereby people often just went off with the info and 'did their own thing'. So I'd hear from a leading Stockport Labour Party activist (later a very senior Stockport Councillor) one week that he'd put in the windows of the local NF election agent *again*, or from some vague contact that he'd put in the windows of the local NF organiser's Skoda car dealership ('Communist' Skoda car dealership—go figure!); other people seemed to voluntarily specialise in sending NF members special bargain/cash on delivery deals from Exchange and Mart—often of a very embarrassing kind. Others seemed keen to ring up local fascists, often late at night, for a pointed chat.

Our rather casually organised but regular roving teams of fighters now started to be much more assertive, with many NF paper sellers attacked when spotted and sometimes even individual NFers ruthlessly beaten up when sighted on the streets. So what did the NF do in retaliation? Well, actually very little. To their credit though they did keep on trying to catch us on the hop by organising to attack undefended soft Left meetings. But I'm pleased to say, despite some very close calls, throughout the next few years, at least in the North West, we were always ready for them. Many a likely meeting was visited by NF scouts who then had to sneak out again hurriedly to the main force in a local pub, to report that a group of heavy blokes with crash helmets were stewarding the meeting. Remember this level of organisation was still pretty haphazard and pretty ad hoc, long before the more formal establishment of the IS/SWP Central Committee ordered Manchester 'SQUAD' in 1977.

Why didn't the NF local heavies exact retribution on individual Lefties in return for all the harassment they were getting? A couple of reasons: Firstly, they were simply terrified of us—we simply *were* tougher than them. Although we actually drew *our* fighters largely from exactly the same (mainly unorganised, poorer working-class) social grouping as them, it was simply the case that their 'heavies' were mostly Nazi wannabe posers, uniform fetishists and perverts, simply cowards and bullies—whereas our comrades were real street fighters. I caution though that this shouldn't be taken as a blanket rule at all times as the experience of Italy in the 1920s and Germany in the late 1920s and early '30s clearly shows that, in a real major social crisis, plenty of genuinely able fighters *can* be attracted to fascism. But this simply wasn't the case in the 1970s.

Other reasons for the North West fascists' failure to take us on individually were (a) they had poor intelligence on who we were (our use of crash helmets in many street battles and whilst stewarding was a hindrance to identification) and (b) an event occurred in 1976 which seems to have permanently put the wind up the fascists in the North West. I was rung up one day by a *Searchlight* contact in Manchester advising me to 'leave home immediately as I was about to be "hit" by an NF team.' Now I always had doubts about *Searchlight*'s 'solid inside dope', having had a few bits of duff gen from that source over the years. I wasn't about to go into hiding either, whether it was true or not. So over the next three days, two separate teams of our heavies using our address lists paid 'home visits' to about twenty or so of the NF members on those lists. I established an alibi elsewhere. Each NFer had his door shoved open on answering the bell and was then pinned by the throat to the wall to be told graphically by the *very big* comrades selected for the task exactly what would happen if anything happened to me. Whether there ever was such a plot, who knows? But no one ever had any similar 'home visits' from the NF in all the years we were in operation—though we were notorious for our 'home visits' thereafter. The NF was simply too scared to respond like for like.

Why were we so ruthless? Partly because of the tough nature of the lads we recruited, working-class fighters completely used to heavy violence. For those of us at the core of these activities, the political militants, we were at that time (in Manchester at least) ideologically committed to what turned out to be a *completely mistaken* but actually psychologically useful future political perspective—which drove us to act in a completely ruthless way, unconcerned with possible consequences. Namely, we, the core political members of what would from 1977 become the Manchester 'Squad', had grown up in the early 1970s, a period of unprecedented (post-war) industrial and political militancy and radical rebirth. Especially during the battles with the Heath government up to the 1974 victory of the miners, the revolutionary Left was experiencing its greatest upsurge in members and influence since the 1930s. By 1974 the IS had nearly forty factory-based industrial branches and new area branches were forming all the time. That the new 1974 Labour government and its

Trades Union bureaucrat allies would be able so quickly demobilize the rising political and industrial struggle was inconceivable to us. The collapse of the working class's interest in revolutionary politics was, in hindsight, spectacular—by the end of 1975 the IS had only a handful of industrial branches. The working class decided to 'Leave it to Labour'—*again*.

We, however, fully expected the struggle to pick up again... soon—buoyed up by the ever-present over-optimistic propaganda of the looming 'capitalist crisis' from our own revolutionary press. Given our completely mistaken belief that the pre-1974 political wave of militancy would continue to rise up again in the near future, we saw the current level of struggle with the fascists as merely an opening, a relatively soft phase of a much longer, harder struggle—which would end up eventually in the armed struggle of revolution. Hard to credit now, after a generation of political stagnation—following on from the historic class defeat of the miners in the 1984 miners strike, and the subsequent destruction of activist mass trades unionism in the Thatcherite and Blairite/Thatcherite neoliberal economic period since. But at the time we couldn't/didn't see that future, so for us there really were no limits on our aggressive response to the fascist threat. Looking back, our mistaken historical expectation actually served as a useful 'motivating revolutionary myth', hardening our hearts and giving us the necessary ruthlessness to take on and beat the physical force aspect of the multi-pronged fascist threat.

1976: The NF Splits

The vicious internal battles in the NF between the factions around Tyndall and Kingsley Read reached breaking point in 1976, and Read went off with part of the membership to form the more 'populist racist' National Party. This left the NF smaller but pretty much as it had been before with the well-known national 'brand', and therefore the mass voting potential. The National Party at first did quite well, with the potential to make Far-Right politics less identifiable with Nazism. The NP won two council seats in Blackburn and built itself up in that area, but nationally it soon lost out to the NF and faded away. (Kingsley Read eventually became a mental healthcare nurse and then killed himself by drinking Paraquat.) For anti-fascists this split made little difference really—we still had to make trips to Blackburn and the odd places where the NP was operating—but in the main it was as before, the NF who held the provocative marches and tried to attack Left-wing meetings.

Also in 1976 I managed to get myself arrested, amazingly for the first time, at a quite boisterous anti-fascist counter action to a provocative NF march through the East End of London. About fifty anti-fascists were arrested that day—so the local police station cells were a tad crowded. I was held, with about fifteen others in some sort of big general holding room until bailed out by the IS solicitor later that day. At one point a cop stuck his head into our room and shouted 'Arnold Smith?' At this someone stood up and said, 'I am Arnold Smith', but then person after person also stood up and also said, 'I am Arnold Smith.' To his credit the copper had also seen *Spartacus* so chuckles all round. You see we may have been trying to overthrow the state but we still had a smile on our lips and a song in our hearts…touching! After being released, my coach to Manchester having gone, I was summoned to join a contingent of stewards defending the IS headquarters/printshop at Cottons Gardens nearby from an expected night-time NF attack. I spent most of that night with a large steward team on the windy parapet to the roof of the building, armed with a massive array of bricks, bottles, and clubs. Unfortunately the NF never showed. Probably yet another *Searchlight*-sourced piece of intelligence.

The level of activity on the anti-fascist front during 1976 was pretty hectic, alongside of course ordinary general political work—including for me, still a student, the regular routines of student politics, too. Later that year I would actually have to get a job, but fortunately that reality had not yet arrived.

Throughout '76, the ad hoc meeting stewarding force I led was constantly called out, often at *very* short notice to protect meetings that were, or much more annoyingly thought they were, in danger of fascist attack. It's a testament to the spirit of the anti-fascists involved that they were prepared to spend so much time lurking outside meetings in dingy pubs all over the North West—with only the very rare actual 'contact' with the NF heavies—who always backed off once they realised we were present. They kept trying though.

Postscript: 1977 Onwards—Lewisham, ANL, and the Formation of the Squads

My career as an active, physical-force anti-fascist carried on hectically for a further ten years, interspersed by periodic arrests and a prison term, until late 1987 (when I moved to Scotland for work reasons and retired from active politics—mainly for 'personal political burnout' reasons). However, the frenetic anti-fascist activity period from 1977 onwards with the Manchester Squad is already well covered in other books, like Steve Tilzey and Dave Hann's *No Retreat*, and as part of the bigger picture, like in Sean Birchall's *Beating the Fascists*. The narrative in *No Retreat* essentially begins where this account ends, with 'the Battle of Lewisham' and our pre-emptive attack on the NF coach in Manchester the morning of that nationally important demo—the decision by the IS Central Committee to instruct areas under particular pressure from NF attack to form local 'combat groups' to fight the menace—and the consequent formalisation of the hitherto pretty irregular stewarding force in Greater Manchester into a more structured combat group, the 'Squad'.

The term 'Squadism' has since become a well-recognised term of, usually, political abuse, to mean in its pejorative usage 'adventurist, semi terrorist, small elite group violence, isolated from mass action'. It is appropriate to reiterate that the 'squads', although indeed partly clandestinely run for obvious security reasons, were always intrinsically a part of a much wider political struggle, whether just enabling the broad Left to hold meetings in safety, or as the physical stewarding part of the national mass movement of the Anti-Nazi League and Rock Against Racism. For instance, I was also on the North West Steering Committee of the ANL from 1977 to 1979, as an indication of the very close interconnection of mass anti-fascist popular front work and the harder end physical action dimension.

A footnote about the name itself: 'the Squad' name didn't arise from a deep historical back reference to the very similar Italian anti-fascist 'People's Squads' of the early 1920s, as has sometimes been suggested. I have to admit that I hadn't heard of them at the time. It was simply a name made up during a long night 'lurking' yet again as meeting stewards in yet another pub somewhere like Accrington, as we responded to the IS Central Committee order to set up a Defence/Combat Group and started to formalise things. We thought of many names: 'the 77 Group', 'Red Fist" and so on. A bit like a new rock band trying to think of a good, catchy name. Anyway, 'Wayne Fontana and the Mindbenders' was already taken so when I eventually suggested 'the Squad' everybody present thought it sounded 'just right'—punchy and menacing. No doubt the earlier Italian Comrades thought the same thing. And so a new name, and eventually a term of long-term political abuse, was born. So whereas in *No Retreat*, the then–young Steve Tilzey suggests the Squad was set up in 1977, he's correct in formal terms, but really it had been going in a more informal, ad hoc form, unbeknownst to him, for years.

—John Penney

Index

Authors' Biographies

In 2009, M. Testa started writing as anti-fascist blogger 'Malatesta,' reporting on the various fortunes of the far right in Britain. The articles were linked to or copied and widely posted on various anarchist and anti-fascist websites, and it was from the research for these articles that this book developed. M Testa has written for the anarchist magazine *Freedom* and is a member of the Anti-Fascist Network.

John Penney has been a radical socialist and trades union activist for over forty years. He played a leading role in the anti-fascist struggle in the Northwest of England in particular, in the 1970s and 1980s, including leading roles in the militant direct-action anti-fascist form of struggle known as 'Squadism', and in the more populist Anti-Nazi League. He was a founder member of Anti-Fascist Action and was on its National Steering Committee in the mid-1980s. He is currently an active member of the new radical Left party, Left Unity.

Support **AK Press!**

AK Press is one of the world's largest and most productive anarchist publishing houses. We're entirely worker-run & democratically managed. We operate without a corporate structure—no boss, no managers, no bullshit. We publish close to twenty books every year, and distribute thousands of other titles published by other like-minded independent presses and projects from around the globe.

The Friends of AK program is a way that you can directly contribute to the continued existence of AK Press, and ensure that we're able to keep publishing great books just like this one! Friends pay $25 a month directly into our publishing account ($30 for Canada, $35 for international), and receive a copy of every book AK Press publishes for the duration of their membership! Friends also receive a discount on anything they order from our website or buy at a table: 50% on AK titles, and 20% on everything else. We've also added a new Friends of AK ebook program: $15 a month gets you an electronic copy of every book we publish for the duration of your membership. Combine it with a print subscription, too!

There's great stuff in the works—so sign up now to become a Friend of AK Press, and let the presses roll!

Won't you be our friend? Email friendsofak@akpress.org for more info, or visit the Friends of AK Press website: www.akpress.org/programs/friendsofak